What Do Philosophers of Education Do?

D1565423

What Do Philosophers of Education Do?

(And How Do They Do It?)

Edited by

Claudia Ruitenberg

⊛WILEY-BLACKWELL

A John Wiley & Sons, Ltd., Publication

This edition first published 2010

Originally published as Volume 43, Issue 3 of *The Journal of Philosophy of Education*

Chapters © 2010 The Authors

Editorial organization © 2010 Philosophy of Education Society of Great Britain

Blackwell Publishing was acquired by John Wiley & Sons in February 2007. Blackwell's publishing program has been merged with Wiley's global Scientific, Technical, and Medical business to form Wiley-Blackwell.

Registered Office

John Wiley & Sons Ltd, The Atrium, Southern Gate, Chichester, West Sussex, PO19 8SQ, United Kingdom

Editorial Offices

350 Main Street, Malden, MA 02148-5020, USA

9600 Garsington Road, Oxford, OX4 2DQ, UK

The Atrium, Southern Gate, Chichester, West Sussex, PO19 8SQ, UK

For details of our global editorial offices, for customer services, and for information about how to apply for permission to reuse the copyright material in this book please see our website at www.wiley.com/wiley-blackwell.

The right of Claudia Ruitenberg to be identified as the author of the editorial material in this work has been asserted in accordance with the Copyright, Designs and Patents Act 1988.

Wiley also publishes its books in a variety of electronic formats. Some content that appears in print may not be available in electronic books.

Designations used by companies to distinguish their products are often claimed as trademarks. All brand names and product names used in this book are trade names, service marks, trademarks or registered trademarks of their respective owners. The publisher is not associated with any product or vendor mentioned in this book. This publication is designed to provide accurate and authoritative information in regard to the subject matter covered. It is sold on the understanding that the publisher is not engaged in rendering professional services. If professional advice or other expert assistance is required, the services of a competent professional should be sought.

Library of Congress Cataloging-in-Publication Data

What do philosophers of education do? : (and how do they do it?) / edited by Claudia Ruitenberg.
     p. cm.
"Originally published as volume 43, issue 3 of The Journal of Philosophy of Education"—T.p. verso.
Includes bibliographical references and index.
ISBN 978-1-4443-3297-1 (pbk. : alk. paper)
1. Education—Philosophy. 2. Education—Research. I. Ruitenberg, Claudia.
LB14.7.W5 2010
370.1–dc22   2010000775

A catalogue record for this book is available from the British Library.

Set in 9 on 11pt Times by Macmillan India Ltd.
Printed and bound in Malaysia by Vivar Printing Sdn Bhd

01   2010

LB
14.7
.W5
2010

Contents

Notes on Contributors   vii

Foreword   ix
Paul Standish

1   Introduction: The Question of Method in Philosophy of Education
Claudia Ruitenberg   1

2   The Strict Analysis and the Open Discussion
Katariina Holma   10

3   'Anything You Can Do I Can Do Better': Dialectical Argument in
Philosophy of Education
Daniel Vokey   24

4   Education and Selfhood: A Phenomenological Investigation
Michael Bonnett   41

5   Examples as Method? My Attempts to Understand Assessment and Fairness
(in the Spirit of the Later Wittgenstein)
Andrew Davis   54

6   Witnessing Deconstruction in Education: Why Quasi-Transcendentalism
Matters
Gert Biesta   73

7   Under the Name of Method: On Jacques Rancière's Presumptive Tautology
Charles Bingham   87

8   Distance and Defamiliarisation: Translation as Philosophical Method
Claudia Ruitenberg   103

9   Between the Lines: Philosophy, Text and Conversation
Richard Smith   118

10   Method, Philosophy of Education and the Sphere of the Practico-Inert
Marianna Papastephanou   131

Index   150

Notes on Contributors

Gert Biesta is Professor of Education at the Stirling Institute of Education, University of Stirling, UK and Visiting Professor for Education and Democratic Citizenship at Mälardalen University, Sweden. He conducts theoretical and empirical research and is particularly interested in the relationships between education, democracy and democratization. He takes inspiration from pragmatism and Continental philosophy and educational theory. His publications include: *Derrida & Education* (co-edited with Denise Egéa-Kuehne; Routledge, 2001); *Pragmatism and Educational Research* (with Nicholas C. Burbules; Rowman & Littlefield, 2003); *Beyond Learning: Democratic Education for a Human Future* (Paradigm Publishers, 2006); *Democracy, Education and the Moral Life* (co-edited with Michael Katz and Susan Verducci; Springer, 2008); *Derrida, Deconstruction and the Politics of Pedagogy* (with Michael A. Peters; Peter Lang, 2008); *Good Education in an Age of Measurement: Ethics, Politics, Democracy* (Paradigm Publishers, 2010); and *Jacques Rancière: Education, Truth, Emancipation* (with Charles Bingham; Continuum 2010). In addition, he is Editor-in-Chief of *Studies in Philosophy and Education*.

Charles Bingham is Associate Professor in the Faculty of Education at Simon Fraser University, Canada. His research focuses on such themes as recognition, authority and self-fashioning as these themes become meaningful in curricular and educational interactions. In addition, his research addresses critical multicultural practices, philosophies of language and literary renditions of school experience. He is the author of *Schools of Recognition: Identity Politics and Classroom Practices* (Rowman & Littlefield, 2001) and *Authority is Relational: Rethinking Educational Empowerment* (SUNY Press, 2008), co-author of *Jacques Rancière: Education, Truth, Emancipation* (with Gert Biesta; Continuum, 2010), and co-editor of *No Education without Relations* (with Alexander Sidorkin; Peter Lang, 2004).

Michael Bonnett is currently Senior Research Fellow at the Institute of Education at the University of London, UK. Prior that that he was Senior Lecturer in the Philosophy of Education in the University of Cambridge and Reader in Philosophy of Education at the University of Bath. He has written numerous papers on education published in academic journals and edited books, and he is the author of the books *Children's Thinking: Promoting Understanding in the Primary School* (Cassell, 1994) and *Retrieving Nature: Education for a Post-Humanist Age* (Wiley-Blackwell, 2004). His current interests are in the philosophical exploration of issues arising from environmental concern, holistic education and the constitution of subjective identities in education.

Andrew Davis is Research Fellow in the School of Education at Durham University, UK. Prior to that he taught in primary schools for eight years and at Cambridge University for six years. He has worked for the Quality Assurance Agency as a Subject Specialist Reviewer and directed Argument Matters, a strand of the National Academy for Gifted and Talented Youth Durham summer school for four years. His publications include *The Limits of Educational Assessment* (Blackwell, 1998), *Educational Assessment and Accountability: A Critique of Current Policy* (Philosophy of Education Society of Great Britain, 2008), the best-selling *Mathematical Knowledge for Primary Teachers* (co-authored with Jennifer Suggate and Maria Goulding; David Fulton, 4th edn February 2010), and *New Philosophies of Learning* (co-edited with Ruth Cigman; Wiley-Blackwell, 2009). He is particularly interested in applying the methods of analytical philosophy to educational policy issues.

Katariina Holma is a Postdoctoral Researcher in the Department of Education, at the University of Helsinki, Finland. She teaches courses on philosophy of education and philosophy of science in educational research and has published articles in (a.o.) *Philosophy of Education* Yearbooks, *Journal of Philosophy of Education* and *Educational Theory*, in addition to numerous publications in Finnish. Her research interests include Israel Scheffler's philosophy of education, the intersections of epistemology and education, and research methodologies of theoretical research in education.

Marianna Papastephanou is Associate Professor in the Department of Education at the University of Cyprus. She studied philosophy in Cardiff, UK, and Berlin, Germany. She is the editor of *Karl-Otto Apel: From a Transcendental–Semiotic Point of View* (Manchester University Press, 1997) and the author of *Educated Fear and Educated Hope* (Sense Publishers, 2009). In addition, she has authored numerous articles on various philosophical and educational–philosophical topics.

Claudia Ruitenberg is Assistant Professor in the Department of Educational Studies at the University of British Columbia, Canada. She teaches courses in educational theory, critical social theory and philosophical research methods, and has published articles in (a.o.) the *Philosophy of Education* Yearbooks, the *Journal of Philosophy of Education*, *Studies in Philosophy and Education* and *Educational Philosophy and Theory*. Her current research interests include philosophical research methods; discursive performativity and its relation to freedom of speech, hate speech and censorship in education; agonistic political theory and the implications for political education; and epistemological diversity in educational research and practice.

Richard Smith is Professor of Education at the Durham University, UK, where he was for many years Director of the Combined Degrees in Arts and Social Sciences. He is Editor of the journal *Ethics and Education* and Associate Editor of the *Journal of Philosophy of Education*. His most recent authored book is (with Paul Smeyers and Paul Standish) *The Therapy of Education* (Palgrave Macmillan, 2006). His principal research interests are in the philosophy of education and the philosophy of social science.

Daniel Vokey is Associate Professor in the Department of Educational Studies at the University of British Columbia, Canada. Drawing upon his academic background in religious studies and in the philosophy of education, his professional experience facilitating wilderness-based experiential education programs, and his ongoing training in Tibetan Buddhism, he investigates the theory and practice of teaching professional ethics for educators, the contributions of philosophy to educational research, and the relevance of teachings and practices from the world's wisdom traditions for transformative initiatives in higher education. He is author of *Moral Discourse in a Pluralistic World* (University of Notre Dame Press, 2001) and of numerous other articles in (a.o.) *Educational Theory*, the *Journal of Philosophy of Education* and the *Journal of Moral Education*. He currently serves as the President of the Canadian Philosophy of Education Society and as Chair of the Association for Moral Education's Dissertation Grants Committee.

Foreword

The question of method in philosophy is a vexed one, and for good reason. Empirical research into education constructs its research questions and then determines the best means to find answers to them; and sometimes the methods that are available, or those in which the researcher is adept, determine the kinds of questions that can be asked. In philosophy too there can be this fit, and sometimes philosophy is none the worse for this. But one does not go far in philosophy without realising that one has embarked on an on-going engagement with the literature, and the consequences of this are multiple: the presuppositions one brings to the enquiry are challenged, the questions with which one starts change their shape, and whatever one might have thought of as one's method becomes caught up in the substance of one's research interest. Sometimes content and method are one. This is found most obviously to be the case when we examine the words we use, for surely language is the very stuff of the philosopher's work, messily entangled, as it is, with the conceptual clarity, perspicuity or theoretical alignments we seek to achieve, and inseparable, as we can scarcely deny, from the practical purchase the enquiry yields. Philosophers, then, are rightly wary of being too quick to explicate their methods.

Yet this is something philosophers are now commonly asked to do. This is most plainly the case in the context of applications for funding, where a box asking for a stipulation of 'the research methods to be used' remains to be filled. But it is there also in a more pervasive way where the politics of educational organisations requires the case for a subject's importance to be made in terms not so much of its realm of enquiry, the distinct modes of its understanding, but of its particular methodological expertise. Philosophers can easily feel that they are caught in a game they do not wish to play.

By contrast, however, a different response is possible: it is not as if there is nothing to be said about what philosophers do. Nor is it erroneous to talk of the different methods they employ. And for anyone new to philosophical enquiry—for anyone, for example, on a research methods course in Education or social science—there is much that can be said about the different ways one might go about philosophical research into education. Experienced philosophers too should be sensitised to the benefit that reflection on such matters can bring. Insight into this variety of approaches is not only practically useful: it also opens possibilities of thought that otherwise escape the agenda of research. And in the end these release the kinds of enquiry into education that answer to the demands of practice in unparalleled ways. Hence, there is every reason to attempt some kind of examination of what philosophers of education do and how they do it.

The collection of essays that follows was the brainchild of Claudia Ruitenberg, and she is to be congratulated for her perception of the need that the above paragraphs identify and for her creativity in imagining the kinds of account that might answer to that need. In the introduction that follows, she explains more fully, and in a more personal vein, the thinking and the context that brought the child to life, as well as offering an indication of the substance of the chapters that ensue. Her conscientious and skilful editing has contributed greatly to the coherence and focus of this volume. Claudia Ruitenberg and her contributors have made a multi-faceted and practical contribution to the philosophical study of education. Given the complex and in some ways controversial nature of the task, this is no mean feat.

Paul Standish

1

Introduction: The Question of Method in Philosophy of Education

CLAUDIA RUITENBERG

> It is possible to raise and solve philosophical problems with no very clear idea of what philosophy is, what it is trying to do, and how it can best do it; but no great progress can be made until these questions have been asked and some answer to them given.
>
> (Collingwood, 2005, p. 1)

In a graduate seminar I taught in the spring of 2009 twenty students used and in effect brought into being in concrete ways a range of philosophical research methods. By telling the students we would study philosophical research methods, I had engaged in a very deliberate performative speech act that sought to bring about what it seemed to describe. When I say the students 'brought philosophical research methods into being', I do not mean that they invented or created new methods, but rather that by naming their ways of thinking and writing as philosophical research methods, they made these ways of thinking and writing available for explicit consideration. The work of philosophers of education and philosophers more generally has not been without method, but this has not commonly been taught under the term 'research methods'.[1]

My choice of the term 'philosophical research methods in education' for the course was based on a pragmatic recognition of the omnipresence and weight of the term 'research' in universities across the English-speaking world. The university at which I work—like many other universities—identifies itself as 'research-intensive', and its faculty are evaluated on their contributions to 'research'. In the UK, the Research Assessment Exercise is called just that, the *Research* Assessment Exercise, and scholarly work that is not labelled 'research' is not counted. Although philosophers of education may be more comfortable thinking of their work as 'scholarship' or 'inquiry' rather than 'research', the discourse of 'research' is so pervasive that it has seemed to me prudent to examine and explain, rather than to deny, the research aspects of our work. In this I felt supported by the American

Philosophical Association, which has adopted the following statement on the profession:

> 'Research' has come to be employed in contemporary academic life as a generic term referring to forms of inquiry pursued in all the many disciplines, from the natural sciences to the humanities. In this broad sense of the term philosophers have been engaged in research throughout the entire history of philosophy, and continue to be so engaged today, together with their scientific and humanistic colleagues in the many other disciplines descended from philosophy in which the degree of Doctor of Philosophy is still granted. (American Philosophical Association, 1996)

But even if the idea of philosophy as research is palatable, what about method? Does this volume cave in to what Richard Rorty has called 'methodolatry', the uncritical worship of method (Rorty, 1999, p. xxi)?[2] I would like to think it does not, and one reason for that is that it employs a much broader conception of method than its Baconian conception as technique that 'can be applied reliably irrespective of the talent of the researcher' (Smith, 2006, p. 157). 'Methods' in this volume refers to the various ways and modes in which philosophers of education think, read, write, speak and listen, that make their work systematic, purposeful and responsive to past and present philosophical and educational concerns and conversations.

The impetus for this volume is the fact that many philosophers of education work not, or not only, in departments of philosophy but in faculties and schools of education. Research methods courses are uncommon in departments of philosophy where it is assumed that students learn to read and write philosophy by, well, reading and writing philosophy. Faculties and schools of education, however, are interdisciplinary environments where students generally do not have the same experience of being immersed in philosophical discourse. Moreover, education is commonly seen *as* a social science, rather than as a field of theories, policies and practices that can be approached in a variety of ways, with perspectives *from* the natural and social sciences as well as the humanities. One of the consequences is that philosophers of education are expected to be able to answer questions about their methods just as their social science colleagues do. Whether due to 'physics envy' or not, there seems to be a heightened concern with research methods in the social sciences. In addition, in faculties and schools of education, which may already suffer from 'status anxiety' in the academy, the desire to have one's work be regarded as sufficiently scientific can lead to an even greater emphasis on the articulation of methods.

The challenge, as I see it, is for philosophers of education to talk about their research methods without submitting to the paradigms and expectations of the social sciences—especially the emphasis on 'data', technique and the tripartite breakdown of method into data gathering, data analysis and data representation. Without succumbing to the anxious concern with method to which I referred above, how might philosophical work be articulated on its own, that is, *philosophical*, terms? How might we describe with precision and specificity the types of thinking and writing, of analysis, questioning, critique, interpretation and so on that philosophers of education engage in? What are our modes of thought and discursive operations?

The present collection complements two special issues of the *Journal of Philosophy of Education* published in 2006, entitled *Philosophy, Methodology and Educational Research*. These special issues focused largely on philosophy (or philosophies) of research in the face of empiricist tendencies and threats. This volume focuses not on philosophy *of* research but philosophy *as* research—a possibility included in Bridges and Smith's (2006) introduction to the first of the two special issues (p. 131) but not elaborated in detail. The essays in the current volume are not critiques of lack of philosophical self-awareness and solid conceptual frameworks in educational research, nor do they take on 'data-driven' or 'evidence-based' policy discourses. Rather, they provide articulations of particular modes of philosophical thinking, reading and writing that are of value for the elucidation or critique of educational questions.

WHAT IS TO BE GAINED? WHAT IS TO BE LOST?

I introduce this collection of essays with excitement, but also with some hesitation. Even if the project does not fall victim to 'methodolatry', might there be drawbacks to a focus on method in philosophy of education? An oft-heard objection by philosophers of education to requests for, for example, abstracts or keywords prior to the completion of an article is that they don't know what they'll write until they've written it. Likewise, 'selecting' a method or set of methods prior to actually using them in philosophical research is problematic. Although some philosophers of education may be able to articulate a particular operation— say the analytic differentiation of a concept from related yet distinct concepts— before approaching a new philosophical quandary, many others are able to identify their methods only in retrospect. This, however, need not be an insurmountable problem. The order in which a text is presented to the reader hardly ever represents the order in which the ideas were formed and the text was written. More importantly: the intentions of the author—methodological or otherwise—cannot contain the effects of the text. Jacques Derrida has observed that the foreword is 'essential' but also disingenuous, as it gives the impression that it was written before the rest of the text while it was more than likely written afterwards, and bound to fail, as it indicates the central theme or thesis that is presented in the text but cannot control what the reader will emphasise or de-emphasise in her or his reading:

> From the viewpoint of the fore-word, which recreates an intention-to-say after the fact, the text exists as something written—a past—which, under the false appearance of a present, a hidden omnipotent author (in full mastery of his product) is presenting to the reader as his future. ... This is an essential and ludicrous operation: not only because writing as such does not consist in any of

these tenses (present, past or future insofar as they are all modified presents); not only because such an operation would confine itself to the discursive effects of an intention-to-mean, but because, in pointing out a single thematic nucleus or a single guiding thesis, it would cancel out the textual displacement that is at work 'here'. (Derrida, 2004, pp. 6–7)

If philosophers of education believed that announcing a methodological nucleus or guiding methodology before the 'work itself' could contain the displacements the text incurs, we would similarly be mistaken. Philosophers of education may make explicit in what ways they have analysed a certain concept or critiqued an idea, but their readers may discern other, perhaps even more powerful, discursive operations at work in the text. If we keep the necessarily self-limiting nature of methodological delimitation in mind, however, and accept that the prefatory methodological statements required in certain professional communications (such as grant applications) are a 'false appearance', then I believe that we stand to gain from the methodological reflection these falsely prefatory statements can encourage.

A second concern philosophers of education may have is that research methods in philosophy of education cannot be divorced from content. It may be all well and good to study the design of questionnaires or the coding of interview transcripts as methods, these hypothetical objectors will argue, but this is not how thinking and writing in philosophy of education proceed. But if this is the concern, I wonder if we have grown a little too fond of our status as 'research outsiders' to recognise our similarities with other kinds of research. After all, good researchers do not select a method irrespective of their object of inquiry or theoretical framework. In good research, the methods have to be understood within a methodology or theory of method, and this needs to be congruent with the theoretical framework of the study, which in turn has to be pertinent to the research question.

Methodological statements about philosophy of education can perhaps be understood by analogy to artists' statements about their work. Artists' primary concern is to make art, yet most art academies also teach their students to communicate about their work through the medium of the artist's statement. It can be argued that the artist's explanation of what he or she has done and why does not enhance the work itself and may actually detract from it; at the same time, many viewers, especially those not expert in the particular discipline, appreciate the additional information or perspective the artist's statement provides. Derrida notes that works of art, *erga*, are surrounded by many *parerga*, a term he borrows from Immanuel Kant and that denotes elements that surround but are not, strictly speaking, part of a work of art, such as the artist's statement but also the frame, title and signature (Derrida, 1987). As I have written elsewhere (Ruitenberg, 2009), Derrida discusses the supplementary functioning of *parerga*. They are outside the work but at the same time contest the borders of the work and what can be counted as inside and outside of it: 'I do not know what is essential and what is accessory in a work. And above all I do not know what this thing is, that is neither essential nor accessory, neither proper nor improper . . ., for example the frame' (Derrida, 1987, p. 63). The artist's statement is neither essential nor accessory to the work of art itself; it *supplements* the work. At first glance, a supplement is an addition, but Derrida observes that 'the supplement supplements. It adds only to replace. It intervenes or insinuates itself *in-the-place-of*; if it fills, it is as if one fills a void' (Derrida, 1976, p. 145). The supplement is both complementary and compensatory (*suppléant*); it is not merely something that can be removed as easily as it was added but rather something that 'instills itself as a *natural* part of that which it supplements' (Bingham, 2002, p. 269). Although the 'work itself' is considered complete, once it has been supplemented with an artist's statement, this statement completes the work and, if removed, it will leave the work incomplete. The methodological commentaries that were invited as part of the chapters in this volume function perhaps as supplements to the 'real work' of philosophy of education. Although philosophy of education was considered sufficient unto itself, once methodological statements are added and readers grow used to such statements—in the way that art audiences have grown accustomed to artist's statements—their absence may be perceived as a lack in 'the work itself'. The point is not that this is either desirable or undesirable: it is just that it is a possibility.

There are, then, reasons for misgivings about the present project, and it would perhaps have been rash to have embarked upon it without considering these. Once these questions of philosophical method are broached, however, they generate real excitement. This was evident in my graduate seminar, it has been evident in conversations I have had with colleagues about the subject, and it is there to be seen in the various contributions to this collection. As a result, I believe now more strongly than when I started this process that there is something to be gained from an explication of philosophical work in methodological terms. So what did my students do? To give just two examples: Stefan Honisch, a trained pianist and composer, conducted a phenomenological inquiry into the lived experience of playing the piano. Through a stripping away of what he knew about playing the piano, he came to pay attention to his corporeal consciousness of the movement of his arms, the weight of his fingers and the sensation of his breath. This type of inquiry, he noted, is valuable but rare:

> The embodied connection to sound is attenuated too often in Western art music's (admittedly necessary) emphasis on technical fluency, stylistic propriety, and the general cultivation of perfection ... In observing my teachers and other pianists whom I admire, I focused on replicating the appearance of their gestures and failed to ask what their bodily experience of those gestures might be—all the more troubling given that, as a musician with a physical impairment, my embodied connection to music was likely considerably different from their own. (Honisch, 2009)

A second example comes from Lian Beveridge, who examined how children's picture books multiply the hermeneutic circles between reader and text, as both reader (child and adult) and text (words and images) are doubled. Analysing the ways in which text and image can reinforce or contradict each other, the ways in which the adult mediates the picture book, and the ways in which the book as read by the adult reinforces or contradicts the book as seen by the child, all helped her clarify the complex conditions of interpreting children's picture books. Such clarification is helpful, she argues, because:

> [c]hildren's literature is generally understood as an educational tool, teaching moral lessons, literacy, and how to engage in literary meaning making, among other things. Therefore, picture books can be reluctant to open themselves up to the play of meaning between text and reader, as they have a strong investment in a particular reading. (Beveridge, 2009)

These then were some of the inspired ways in which my students used philosophical methods in their research. I suspect methodological reflection on philosophical work was as uncommon for many of the contributors to this volume as it was for my students, and I sensed many a raised eyebrow on the other side of the correspondence I carried on with them about the unusual task I asked them to engage in. So let me say something about what the contributors have written about and how this collection is organised.

THIS VOLUME

The contributors to this volume demonstrate and explicate a wide—although, of course, not comprehensive—range of philosophical methods. The contributors work in Finland, Cyprus, Canada and the United Kingdom and draw on philosophical work that ranges from Plato to Hannah Arendt and from Israel Scheffler to Jacques Derrida (to name just a few). The collection is organised not by region or tradition but begins with essays that outline more recognisable methods and moves increasingly into terrain that is methodologically less usual. The first piece is by Katariina Holma, who has undertaken a retrospective reflection on a research project that entailed an analysis of the philosophical debate between Nelson Goodman and Israel Scheffler on constructivism and realism. Her chapter provides a peek behind the curtain of a piece of Anglo-analytic research focused on both analysis and synthesis and gives a detailed account of the many rounds of reading, categorising, and rethinking that were involved. In '"Anything You Can Do I Can Do Better": Arguing Across Paradigms in Philosophy of Education', Daniel Vokey uses dialectical argument of the kind elaborated by Alasdair MacIntyre to compare and analyse the relative merits of two competing approaches to teaching professional ethics. The common argumentative mechanisms of opposing, comparing and evaluating are made uncommonly visible here. Michael Bonnett offers a phenomenological commentary on recent work in which the nature of selfhood and subjectivity in education is at stake. He argues that the structural and abstract claims in such work do not necessarily hold up when tested against the rich and varied lived experiences of those actually involved in education. Bonnett's chapter combines phenomenological inquiry with critique and argument, thus illustrating how philosophers of education rarely use just one 'method'.

Andrew Davis's 'Examples as Method? My Attempts to Understand Assessment and Fairness (in the Spirit of the Later Wittgenstein)' shows an analysis of issues pertaining to assessment and fairness in a variety of educational settings. Davis's concern is with the role of examples in philosophical writing, and rather than seeing them as illustrations in a more general and linear argument, he uses them in this analysis to argue from the ground up, from the specific and complex to the more general. This chapter also illustrates how different genres of writing—in this case the addition of a 'Brechtian' voice that addresses the reader directly—are part of the philosophical repertoire. Gert Biesta, in 'Witnessing Deconstruction in Education: Why Quasi-Transcendentalism Matters', explains why decon-struction, in the Derridean tradition, cannot be understood or used as a method and argues that, instead, we must attempt to 'witness' deconstruction as it occurs. While 'witnessing' may be an uncommon term to include among the more common descriptors of what philosophers of education do and how they do it—such as analysing, questioning, arguing and interpreting—Biesta argues compellingly that witnessing the event of deconstruction in education opens up an ethico-political register that exposes education to newness.

Charles Bingham distills a method from his own work and the work of Jacques Rancière and names it 'presumptive tautology'. Having named a new method, he also raises provocative questions about what it means to operate with such a 'named' method, and how the name can be understood literally as well as metaphorically. In 'Distance and Defamiliarisation: Translation as Philosophical Method', I propose thinking of translation, both in the interlinguistic and interdiscursive sense, as one of the methods philosophers use. Translation can be said to be the 'philosophical condition' that prevents self-presence in all thought, but it can also be used more deliberately to shift a concept or text into a new linguistic or discursive environment where it raises new questions. Like 'witnessing' and 'presumptive tautology', 'translating' does not refer to a new method but is proposed as a new term to help philosophers of education think in more fine-grained ways about their work.

The final two pieces demonstrate methods and 'talk back' to the assignment of attending to philosophical research methods. Richard Smith in 'Between the Lines: Philosophy, Text and Conversation' provides us with a provocative dialogue, a fictionalised seminar that both demonstrates and troubles distinctions between speech and writing, between teaching methods and research methods, and between systematic and edifying philosophy. In 'Method, Philosophy of Education and the Sphere of the Practico-Inert',

Marianna Papastephanou incites philosophers of education to, as it were, become less dependent as philosophical importers and more confident as philosophical exporters. Calling into question the assumed subject and object connected by the genitive 'of' in 'philosophy of education', she argues that, while the transfer of more general philosophical categories and concepts to education is not without value, philosophers of education stand to gain from revaluing the singularity and everydayness of education and its disruption of philosophy.

To respond to R. G. Collingwood: I am not sure if 'great progress' can or should be made now that questions of method in philosophy of education have been asked and some answers to them given. I do believe, however, that greater methodological awareness can improve both the aim and communicability of philosophy of education. Moreover, it encourages reflection on the rich *methodological* inheritance that philosophical traditions have left us but that is easily ignored. As two of the fictionalised students in Richard Smith's contribution to this volume demonstrate:

> *Anna:* Descartes? Why Descartes?
> *Aisha:* His *Discourse* is the *Discourse on Method*, Anna. On *method*.

ACKNOWLEDGEMENTS

I am grateful to Paul Standish and the Editorial Board of the *Journal of Philosophy of Education* for giving me the opportunity to pursue this experiment, and for their support in the process. I also wish to acknowledge (in alphabetical order) Lian Beveridge, Mary Ann Chacko, Linda Dame, Lina Darwich, Catherine Dick, Graham Giles, Wendy Hartford, Donna Hill, Stefan Honisch, Jessica Jordan, Vanessa Liston, Angélica Maia, Joanne Martin, Gavin McDonald, Mylo Riley, Claire Robson, Annette Ruitenbeek, P. J. Rusnak, Mike Sorsdahl and Bhuvinder Vaid, whose enthusiastic study and discussion of philosophical methods were a great stimulus to this project.

NOTES

1. There has been little recent work that explicitly addresses philosophy of education in explicit methodological terms, but Frieda Heyting, Dieter Lenzen and John White's edited book *Methods in Philosophy of Education* is a notable exception. This edited collection stems from a symposium on methodological issues in philosophy of education, held in Amsterdam in 1998. With objectives similar to those of this volume, the symposium organisers and book editors sought to examine what philosophers of education do, to ask them to demonstrate the 'methods of working' of certain approaches, and to use this for the facilitation of 'the training of new researchers in the field' (Heyting, Lenzen and White, 2001, p. xi).
2. The term 'methodolatry' was used earlier in psychology by Rollo May (1958) and David Bakan (1967) to protest a similar 'reductionist confusion [of research] with a particular methodology' (Leitner and Phillips, 2003, p. 162).

REFERENCES

American Philosophical Association (1996) Statements on the Profession: Research in Philosophy. Online at http://www.apaonline.org/governance/statements/research.aspx (accessed 7 April 2009).

Beveridge, L. (2009) How to Read a Picturebook: A Hermeneutic Model, unpublished manuscript.

Bingham, C. (2002) I Am the Missing Pages of the Text I Teach: Gadamer and Derrida on Teacher Authority, in: S. Rice (ed.) *Philosophy of Education 2001* (Urbana, IL, Philosophy of Education Society), pp. 265–72.

Bridges, D. and Smith, R. (2006) Philosophy, Methodology and Educational Research: Introduction, *Journal of Philosophy of Education*, 40.2, pp. 131–35.

Collingwood, R. G. (2005) [1933] *An Essay on Philosophical Method* (revised edn.) (Oxford, Clarendon Press).

Derrida, J. (1976) [1967] *Of Grammatology*, G. C. Spivak, trans. (Baltimore, MD, The Johns Hopkins University Press).

Derrida, J. (1987) [1978] *The Truth in Painting*, G. Bennington and I. McLeod, trans. (Chicago, The University of Chicago Press).

Derrida, J. (2004) [1972] *Dissemination*, B. Johnson, trans. (New York, Continuum).

Heyting, F., Lenzen, D. and White, J. (2001) *Methods in Philosophy of Education* (New York, Routledge).

Honisch, S. (2009) For Now We Hear Through an Instrument, Dimly: A Phenomenological Experience of Musicking, unpublished manuscript.

Leitner, L. M. and Phillips, S. N. (2003) The Immovable Object Versus the Irresistible Force: Problems and Opportunities for Humanistic Psychology, *Journal of Humanistic Psychology*, 43.3, pp. 156–73.

Rorty, R. (1999) *Philosophy and Social Hope* (London, Penguin).

Ruitenberg, C. W. (2009) *The Hors D'Oeuvre in a Teacher Education Course (Response to M. Manson)*, in: R. Glass (ed.) *Philosophy of Education 2008* (Urbana, IL, Philosophy of Education Society), pp. 314–17.

Smith, R. (2006) As if by Machinery: The Levelling of Educational Research, *Journal of Philosophy of Education*, 40.2, pp. 157–68.

2

The Strict Analysis and the Open Discussion

KATARIINA HOLMA

INTRODUCTION

One advantage of philosophical research in education is its potential to bridge the gap between the extremes of theory and practice. One particular problem today in pursuing educational research is that, while the scope of education is as wide as human civilisation itself, the practice of academic research has tended to become more and more specialised. When particular, often narrowly focused research projects are evaluated by the criteria of measurable exactness and effectiveness, there is the danger of losing sight of the wider context of the phenomenon under study. This development implies an overemphasis on the gathering of research data without sufficient attention to their interpretation and implications.

Philosophy is an academic discipline specialised in analysing and under-standing the wider processes of the constructing of theories, questioning their hidden background premises, and revealing and examining the values affecting academic—as well as other—human practices. Furthermore, the perennial philosophical questions have straightforward connections to the world of education: for example the ethical questions of responsibility and humanity, as well as the epistemological questions of knowledge and its justification cannot be escaped in educational thinking. Philosophy of science, for its part, has an important role in evaluating the background theories of educational research. In my view, a philosophical approach is of great value in the broad and multidimensional field of educational research and practice.

In 2004 I published an article entitled 'Pluralism and Education: Israel Scheffler's Synthesis and its Presumable Educational Implications' (Holma, 2004). In this article I discussed, from an educational point of view, the philosophical debate on constructivism and realism conducted by two Harvard scholars, Nelson Goodman and Israel Scheffler, and especially Israel Scheffler's subsequent synthesis of this debate. The idea to investigate this topic derived from my observation that, although there was an ongoing conversation on constructivism and realism in educational philosophy, the insights of this Harvard debate were not exploited in this conversation.

In the present essay, I will focus on the methodological issues I confronted in this research project. Although I will approach the theme through this particular project, I assume that my concerns have much in common with other research projects in the same general area. The basic challenge of combining philosophical ways of analysing and arguing with the dialogical and pluralist way of thinking—which is certainly needed in educational research—relates this particular project to the wider concerns of philosophy of education.

In methodological terms, the crucial feature of my approach is an emphasis on the role of a thoroughgoing process of analysis and synthesis. I stress the significance of a deep understanding of the concepts, arguments, and ideas of the explored topic before entering into the dialogical, critical or supplementary part of the research. The process of disassembling and reassembling (i.e. the philosophical reconstruction) is, as I have experienced it, the way of gaining access to a new, more profound understanding of the issue, and it thus creates possibilities for achieving the researcher's own philosophical perspectives and insights on the topic under consideration.

In the following, I will first present the process of philosophical reconstruction as it developed in my research project on 'pluralism', a term coined by Scheffler, on which I shall elaborate below. I will then consider the issues related to the dialogical approach necessary in educational research.

PHILOSOPHICAL RECONSTRUCTION

My own experience as a student-in-training upon entering the Anglo-American philosophical tradition is that a strong emphasis is given to the rules of argument.[1] Although the books on philosophical research methods happened to mention that, before one's own criticism and argumentation is implemented, it is important to sympathetically explore and understand the philosopher under study (for example, Rosenberg, 1984, p. 95), the concrete methodological steps that could show the way to achieving this understanding, and thus develop the ability needed for participation in academic philosophy, were not so often clearly explicated. 'I have again reached the limits of what is teachable' (Rosenberg, 1984, p. 96), as I recall Jay F. Rosenberg repeating in one of the course books of my undergraduate studies in philosophy.

Like many others (for example Fisher, 1988), Rosenberg concentrates on the rules of valid argumentation, then touches slightly on the 'six ways to read a philosopher', where he rather soon reaches 'the limits of the teachable'. I am not denying that in philosophical research, or in academic research and realisation in general, there are components that cannot be taught. However, I believe that many students—as well as researchers—of philosophy could benefit from simple methodological procedures as tools for achieving new levels of understanding and argumentation. In this particular case, this methodological tool was systematic textual analysis. This method, as far as I know, is quite widely used in the tradition of Continental philosophy, but it is not as often stressed as a useful methodological tool also for an analytically oriented philosopher.[2]

The process of analysis and synthesis, or philosophical reconstruction,[3] is thus what I aim to explicate in this section. Roughly speaking, this process of reconstruction seeks: (1) to understand the concepts as they are used in this particular context, (2) to clarify the interconnections of these concepts, and finally, (3) to reconstruct the text for understanding and interpreting it from a new perspective.

The principal idea in this part of the research is to read the explored texts with the aim of understanding the author's thinking as such. Thus, this phase of research is not meant for the researcher's own criticism, argumentation, or any kind of application, but rather for capturing the thinking of this unique subject of interest as a whole. Richard Rorty, for example, speaks of 'historical reconstruction', which seeks to describe the views of the studied philosopher in her or his own terms, rather than those of the researcher (Rorty, 1984, p. 50). Moreover, Juhani Jussila, Kaisu Montonen and Kari E. Nurmi speak of 'immanent analysis', by which they refer to the researcher's special commitment to pursue understanding the wholeness of meaning, intrinsic to the texts being explored (Jussila, Montonen and Nurmi, 1989, pp. 198–200). In the three following sections, I will describe the practical steps in implementing the process of reconstruction.

INITIAL OPTIONS AND DECISIONS

Before reaching the point of exact philosophical analysis on a particular theme, there are many significant choices the researcher must make first. The choices related to the topic, perspective, demarcation and limitation are decisive for successful philosophical research and should thus be made by a process of conscious reflection.

In the beginning, there must be some exceptional feature or attribute that brings a particular theme to a researcher's attention. At the time I wrote my Master's thesis on rationality and education in the philosophy of Israel Scheffler, for example, there was a pivotal episode. In light of Scheffler's texts, I had come to the conception that Scheffler was both committed to ontological realism and ultimately very much of the same mind as his Harvard colleague Nelson Goodman. Then, one day, I happened to read about Goodman's radical disagreement with any version of realism.

As an insecure graduate student, my first thought was that I must somehow have misinterpreted Scheffler. Now unfolding in my mind was the twin horror of the huge flaw permeating my whole thesis and the extensive revisions I would have to undertake to correct it. Luckily, however, I immediately came across other texts on Scheffler, and later I came to the extraordinary realisation that my own interpretation had been correct after all! I now think that encountering this tension, and independently finding the answer, was my first real experience of doing philosophical research.

After securing my MA degree and entering the international field of educational philosophy as a doctoral candidate, I realised that the constructivism–realism issue was widely discussed (see, for example, Phillips, 2000; Matthews, 1998). In my native Finland, for its part, Tapio Puolimatka's book on constructivism and realism (Puolimatka, 2002) had just come out, and it had gained much attention. At this time, I noticed the absence of Scheffler's and Goodman's arguments from the conversation in education. In addition, I received around this time Scheffler's newly published contributions on the theme (Scheffler, 2000, 2001). The rewarding episode from the years of writing my Master's thesis, moreover, made this theme of special personal interest. In this way, two things came together that were crucial to the successful research project: the topicality of the theme, and my own personal interest in the topic.

The next decision to be made involved choosing a perspective on the theme, for this would later be essential in selecting texts for closer analysis. In the initial stage, I had masses of articles and books considering the theme, all of which were given equal status; the earliest sources were from the 1970s and the later ones from the 2000s. Furthermore, I was working with texts from two authors who needed to be understood in terms of their own frames of reference—that is, against the background of their philosophical work as a whole. In addition, the latest texts on Scheffler, although they were closely related to the theme, differed crucially from the other texts, since Scheffler wrote them after Goodman's death, and they could not, therefore, be considered as a part of the debate proper. Thus, there were at least three sets of texts requiring their own 'immanent analysis': Goodman's texts belonging to the debate, Scheffler's texts belonging to the debate, and Scheffler's synthetic texts produced after Goodman's death, which in consequence did not belong to the debate proper.

I decided to start from 'plurealism', which was Scheffler's later, synthetic contribution to the theme. There were three central reasons backing this choice. First, plurealism was a new philosophical idea that combined the best aspects of the two debated positions, and this made plurealism of special philosophical interest. Second, plurealism initially seemed to fit the complex reality of education (perhaps Scheffler's own background as an educational philosopher had had its effects on this position). Third, at a personal level, I had studied and examined Scheffler's philosophy earlier, which naturally added to my possibilities of accurately understanding and interpreting his philosophy.

Scheffler had published two articles on plurealism (2000, 2001), but in light of my initial reading it was evident that they had made so much reference to the earlier debate with Goodman that they could not be adequately understood without exploring the debate as a whole. I decided to begin with the initial analysis of plurealism and then, on this basis, turn to the further analysis of the earlier debate.

THE PRELIMINARY STUDY OF THE PLUREALIST ARGUMENT

The main argument on plurealism was spelled out in Scheffler's two articles 'A Plea for Plurealism' (Scheffler, 2000) and 'My Quarrels with Nelson Goodman' (Scheffler, 2001). At this initial phase of analysis, my task was to extract Scheffler's major lines of argumentation. As a result, I needed to formulate an outline for focusing on the further, more detailed conceptual analysis. I will next describe my operations in this matter on the very practical level.

I organised the texts from two articles in various ways, collecting into separate passages all that Scheffler wrote on particular themes, ideas, or persons. Thus, under such rubrics as 'Peirce', 'Kuhn', 'Goodman', as well as 'realism', 'irrealism',[4] 'physicalism', 'monism', 'pluralism', 'reductionism', 'plurealism', and so on I collected all the notes from both these articles concerning the theme in question. One passage could thus be repeated under various rubrics, in case it was simultaneously related to several of the main themes. To take a simple example, Scheffler's concluding statement: 'I take it as a bonus of plurealism that it weds the strong points of two of the greatest of modern philosophers, uniting the realism of C. S. Peirce with the pluralism of Nelson Goodman' (Scheffler, 2000, p. 172) belongs under the rubrics of 'Peirce', 'Goodman', 'realism', 'pluralism' and 'plurealism'.

The resulting texts of this process were, in one sense, both overly long and very disorganised. One might ask, why break into pieces the carefully built structure of the original author? There are two answers to this question. First, the process of disassembly is a useful tool for finding out whether the original author is speaking coherently. Any contradictory statements are relatively easy to discover when they are written one after another in the same passage. By contrast, the carefully assembled structure of the original text may quite easily hide particular incoherencies. Second, this process, as laborious as it is, has the benefit of familiarising the researcher with the original line of argument. And this, if anything, opens up the further possibilities of offering further, philosophically relevant comments on the issue.

As a result of this brief analysis, I formed an outline of Scheffler's argument. My simplification of the argument looked like this:
Scheffler claims:

(1) There is a real (not only an apparent) disagreement between Goodman and himself.
(2) That disagreement comes to a head in the meaning of the term 'worldmaking'. This disagreement reflects the difference in opinion in relation to the constructivism–realism issue.

(3) Nevertheless, realism and pluralism can be united in a coherent view. This new conception solves the earlier disagreement.

The third point condensed the new argument, which could be disassembled as follows:

(1) Goodman fallaciously assumes that a 'realist' must be a 'monist'.
(2) In rejecting 'realism', and in defending 'pluralism', Goodman actually rejects 'monism' but not necessarily pluralist realism (plurealism).
(3) 'Realism' can be accepted without 'monism' and in conformity with 'pluralism'.

Along the lines of this outline, I next turned to the selection of the texts for closer analysis. For example, the following questions arise from this outline: What is the exact meaning of 'worldmaking'? On what basis does Scheffler argue that Goodman is actually rejecting monism, not realism? What version of pluralism does Scheffler accept? These kinds of questions now needed answers, and these could be drawn from the texts of the earlier debate.

Since it was the birth of plurealism that was my main subject of interest, I decided to remain focused on Scheffler's texts. In light of Scheffler's own references, the following texts were selected as subjects of the further analysis: 'Epistemology of Objectivity' (Scheffler, 1996),[5] 'World Features and Discourse Dependence' (Scheffler, 1997),[6] 'Worlds and Versions' (Scheffler, 1997)[7] and 'Worries about Worldmaking' (Scheffler, 1997).[8] The two plurealist articles were naturally also taken into consideration.

THE SYSTEMATIC ANALYSIS

Systematic analysis (see, for example, Jussila *et al.*, 1989) extracts all the uses of the relevant terms from the corpus. This idea presupposes the possibility that the real usage of a term may be different from an author's own explicit definition.

How was this done? As a simple first step, I picked up the concepts and their definitions as I encountered them in the reading process. Whenever I encountered any (at least possibly) essential term with some expression clarifying its meaning and usage, I typed this term as a heading, along with the related expression and its reference under this heading. It quickly became evident that, perhaps owing to the fact that these texts were a part of the debate, the terms were usually defined not only in keeping with their positive definitions, but also, and more often, by describing what was *not* referred to by them. This was essential if I was to understand the usages of any particular term from which Scheffler wished to distance himself. For example, in his use of the term 'world' Scheffler stresses that he is *not* 'defending some doctrine about the world—arguing that there really is one world or that the world is a touchstone of truth, or independent of mind, or the like' (Scheffler, 1997, p. 197).

My first notebook broke down the various concepts under the following rubrics: 'the versional interpretation', 'the objectual interpretation', 'discourse-dependence', 'nulls and non-nulls', 'the auxiliary', 'certainty', 'words not worlds', 'coherence', 'constructivism', 'subjective idealism', 'the referential nature of language', 'the plurality of conceptual schemes', 'the question of independent facts', 'what makes a version right?', 'conflicting right versions?', 'no structural similarity' and 'clash-realism'. From this material I extracted the following key terms: 'world(s)', 'version(s)', 'monism', 'physicalism', 'the reducibility', 'pluralism', 'the convergence', 'plurality', 'versional', 'objectual' and 'worldmaking', and I then identified what was crucial to their meaning for the purposes of later reconstruction and discussion.

Naturally the key concepts were not used independently of each other, but rather in a network of conceptual interrelations. The task following the analysis of the singular concepts on the singular level was the mapping of their interrelations. For example, 'physicalism' appeared to be a subspecies of 'monism'—that is, 'physicalism' is a version of 'monism', but 'a monist' does not need to be 'a physicalist'. The concept of 'reducibility' is connected to these two concepts in a way that the 'physicalist' is one who is committed to the reducibility of all science (and all human knowledge) to physics, whereas a monist in general supports the idea of reducibility to one single system, which can be the system of physics or some other system of description.

As an intermediate result of the work of analysis, I condensed the meanings and interrelations of the concept that were crucial for understanding the debate and, especially, for understanding plurealism. In addition to these explicit written results, this process had naturally deepened my knowledge and understanding of the whole philosophical issue. One important thing that I had realised during the process of analysis was how careful and well-grounded the arguments were that were used to defend the three positions in question: constructivism, realism, and plurealism. I had also realised how all these notions would offer interesting viewpoints with regard to educational concerns. The nature of the debate, however, tended to hide the wholeness of each conception by concentrating on particular disagreements and, furthermore, concentrating on correcting the misunderstandings and alleged misguidedness of the opposite side. In the hope of understanding the intrinsic logic of each position as well as its possible bearings upon education, I reconstructed the texts from the three perspectives on the basis of the three independent notions of constructivism, realism and plurealism.

This decision, however, naturally required closer analysis of Goodman's writings, since it would have been altogether unfair to construct Goodman's views on the basis of Scheffler's account of these. This task of analysis differed, however, from that of earlier analysis, since I now had a far more focused subject of interest: I was interested solely in adequately reconstructing

Goodman's constructivism. I thus implemented a local and focused analysis of Goodman's concept of constructivism, along the lines of the analysis described earlier. The texts of Goodman that were analysed were the relevant parts of the books *Ways of Worldmaking* (Goodman, 1978) and *Of Mind and Other Matters* (Goodman, 1984) and the articles 'Words, Works, Worlds' (Goodman, 1996a) and 'Comments' (Goodman, 1996b).

THE RECONSTRUCTION: CONSTRUCTIVISM, REALISM AND PLUREALISM

The process had now come to the phase of reassembling (or reconstruction). During the analysis, I had come to understand that the three philosophical positions defended during the debate all had strong reasons for their acceptance as well as, naturally, their own problems and weaknesses. In the original texts, constructivism and realism were not presented in a way that would collect the components of each view into the same context, but, in contrast, as fragmented pieces depending on what was needed in order to provide a rejoinder to the latest counterclaim of the opposite side. The original debate thus cast much attention upon the particular disagreements, often aiming to correct misinterpretations of the opposing side, whereas I decided, through the reconstructive process, to search for the positive and constructive understanding of three views as they each existed as a whole in their own contexts. Plurealism, however, differed from the other two positions as a result of Scheffler's analysis and synthesis of the earlier debate and, moreover, as a result of his suggestion to solve the problems that the two earlier notions had confronted. It was not evident, in any case, that this synthesis succeeded in solving the earlier disagreement. Thus, I found it reasonable to reconstruct all three views as independent philosophical positions and to evaluate their strengths and weaknesses from both the philosophical and educational angles. In the following, I will present, as examples, brief parts of these reconstructed notions.

Constructivism, on Goodman's interpretation, is based on the claim that we cannot describe the world except by using our systems of description. Even when we explain how our language describes 'reality' we do so by means of our language, and we do not have any way of describing reality independently of our language. In Goodman's view, we construct the worlds by describing them, and different and equally true symbol systems lead to different and irreducible descriptions of reality. The description of reality that is true in one symbol system may be incommensurable with the true description of some other system. Therefore, according to Goodman, 'there is no way things really are' and 'worlds are made rather than found' (Elgin, 1998).

The version of realism that Scheffler defends against Goodman is a minimal one. This is to say that Scheffler is suspicious, for example, of taking the concept of reality as a primary educational idea. Instead, he emphasizes that in education we should respect the constraints of inquiry into reality and strive to adopt them.[9] The only disagreement with Goodman, which makes it impossible for Scheffler to accept constructivism, is that he cannot accept the idea that 'we create or shape the things to which our words refer' (Scheffler, 1997, p. 196). In Scheffler's view: 'In making the true statement that there were stars before men, we do not also make the stars that were there then' (ibid.). Or, as he also states: 'Neither Pasteur nor his version of the germ theory made the bacteria he postulated, nor was Neptune created by Adams and Leverrier by their prescient computations' (Scheffler, 1997, p. 200). It is this one single point that differentiates these two philosophers.

The main idea of plurealism, for its part, is to preserve Goodman's pluralism in terms of systems of description without refuting the minimal realism that Scheffler defends. This becomes possible by refuting 'monism' and accepting in its stead 'pluralism'. Plurealism 'agrees with [Goodman] in rejecting the notion of one world, but disagrees with him in that it holds whatever worlds there are to be independent of their corresponding versions' (Scheffler, 2000, pp. 165–6). Thus as pluralists, '[w]e have to reckon with a variety of domains of entities' (ibid.), but we do not have to think that we have literally made the things our systems of description refer to.

Due to the process of analysis and synthesis, I thus gained a new understanding of the philosophical basis and argumentation of two Harvard scholars on three notions crucial to the constructivism–realism issue. It was finally time to turn to wider considerations.

THE DIALOGUE

The field of educational philosophy has its own peculiar questions also in terms of research methodology. The reason for this is not that these two fields of study, philosophy and education, do not have common interests or investigational intersections. On the contrary, the problems confronted in education are closely related to the questions considered in academic philosophy. The questions concerning the possibility and limits of knowledge, the justification of values and ethical beliefs, as examples, are philosophical questions having an effect on everyday educational choices. The special problems of this field of research derive from the complexity and multi-dimensionality of this field. First, the academic research in the field of education in general is multidisciplinary: psychology, sociology, the neurosciences, and so on, have their own perspectives and practices in educational research. Even in more narrowly focused philosophical approaches to educational research, the representatives from various philosophical traditions participate in the same conversation. Second, even if we could approach educational phenomena from the point of view of one single philosophical tradition, the world of education would still be multifarious, with different disciplinary approaches each playing their role.

Thus, to enter into philosophical dialogue in such a multidimensional field is not a simple task.

In contrast to the previously described, relatively rigorous procedure of analysis and synthesis, the dialogical part of the research project cannot follow such strict methodological rules or procedures. It should, nevertheless, avoid slipping into the superficial everyday expression of opinion and, on the contrary, be able to contribute to the field with new, philosophically grounded insights.

My reconstruction of constructivism, realism and pluralism functioned as a basis for opening various levels of discussion concerning philosophy, educational theory and educational practice. The style of discussion depends naturally on who one is discussing things with: on the philosophical level, the validity of the arguments in the strict logical sense is central; in participating within the context of educational theory, valid argumentation must come to terms with the wider understanding of the educational realm, the empirical context in which the argument will have its purchase; and, finally, in discussing the possible practical educational implications of the notions that have been explored, the open and contemplative style of questioning would serve much better than any enterprise attempting to present watertight arguments.

To take just one example of the first, philosophical way of arguing, I addressed a conceptual problem following from constructivist epistemology. The constructivist position denies that our theories or systems of description refer to anything 'real'. I presented this idea along the lines of Richard Rorty,[10] who argues that we should not take our conceptions in terms of science, morality, and so on, as being in any sense 'real', but we still ought to teach the content of our Western science for the simple reason that it is *ours* (Rorty, 1997, p. 530). I questioned the philosophical tenability of Rorty's argument from two angles:

> First, if Rorty means that we should teach our science because we do not have anything better (which is a truism, of course), his argument that we, for this reason, *ought to* teach it is a flawed conclusion from 'is to ought.' Second, if Rorty means that we should adopt something solely because it is *ours*, this position entails the loss of any criteria for accepting some things and leaving other things out ... the most perverted and harmful ideas that sometimes happen to cross my mind may all be interpreted as products of *our* culture and *our* society. (Holma, 2004, p. 425)

This kind of philosophical argument has its place in educational philosophy, but it does not in itself offer very much to real educational problems. The second level of the dialogical part of my article was to discuss these conceptual issues dealt with in the educational constructivism–realism conversation in light of Scheffler's and Goodman's thinking. In this educational conversation I discovered some conceptual confusion in terms of the relations of educational ideas to the philosophical conceptions. As a philosopher versed in this particular theme, I had the possibility to use the tools of philosophy for clarifying and solving these confusions.

For example, cognitive constructivism (the idea, based on present-day learning theories, that an individual constructs her or his own cognitive system) was often fallaciously taken as requiring constructivist metaphysics (the idea that *everything* is constructed by human beings, individuals, or communities) as its philosophical background. Likewise, philosophical realism (the idea that *something* exists independently of human beings) is sometimes fallaciously equated with the views that presuppose human certainty or some kind of 'metaphysical realism', which assumes that our knowledge and symbol systems directly reflect the structure of reality.

Thus, contrary to the preconceptions of 'metaphysical realism' I was able to show that from Scheffler's minimal version of realism, it follows only that we should respect the constraints of inquiry into reality (Holma, 2004, pp. 426–7). This position is one that requires no kind of commitment either to certainty of knowledge or to 'metaphysical realism' (p. 421). Or, as Nicholas Burbules and Michael Matthews have also argued (Matthews, 2000, p. 187; Burbules, 2000, p. 326), constructivist pedagogy does not require philosophical commitment to constructivist metaphysics.

To assess the possible implications of philosophical conceptions to educational practice is naturally a complicated task. Although it is clear—in light of the educational practices of different cultures, as well as in different eras of history—that ultimate conceptions of the world, knowledge and humanity do have their effect on educational practice, these connections are far from straightforward and depend on the whole complexity of the overall circumstances. While keeping this in mind, I still see it as being relevant to address these questions. The following examples demonstrate my examination of this issue.

Goodman's constructivist ideas seemed to have important implications for the role of art education: his idea of different and irreducible symbol systems in worldmaking places a strong emphasis on the creative cultivation of the symbol systems of visual arts, dance or music, naturally alongside the symbol system of language. Realism, by contrast, stresses the responsibility of the educator to expand the student's conception of reality in order to increase her chances of living a rewarding life (Holma, 2004, p. 427). Plurealism, as a synthesis of these two, enables the appreciation and value of different and concurrent systems of description without slipping into the voluntarism and relativism of philosophical constructivism[11] (p. 430). The general perspectives offered by these thoughts are, in my view, of obvious significance for the reasoned direction of further educational research.

CONCLUSIONS

Dialogue between the most theoretical issues in philosophy and such a practical enterprise as education is plainly a worthwhile endeavour. The philosophical debate on 'worldmaking', which deals with ontology, episte-mology and philosophy of language, turned out not to be as far removed from educational concerns as one might at first glance have thought.

In philosophical research, especially in the tradition to which this research belongs, the question of methodology is not normally raised but usually taken as being somehow self-evident or best left implicit. Although it is indeed true that the way the philosopher discusses and argues in relation to her topic may not normally warrant explication (at least, amongst those familiar with the particular paradigm), I have found it a worthwhile exercise to make explicit how I conducted my research and how I produced the published outcome.

The ancient idea of disassembling and reassembling (sometimes called analysis and synthesis, or reconstruction) was the methodological key to this particular research project. In my view, this more or less technical part of the research was crucial in deepening my own understanding of the issue. This deeper understanding opened the way to the discussion of education and, specifically, to an elaboration of the educational implications of the conceptions defended during the philosophical debate.

The basic—often unconsciously accepted—conceptions underlying the choices, decisions and solutions of everyday education are, in the final analysis, philosophical conceptions. It is academic philosophy that studies the questions of what exists, what we can know and what the relation of our language to all this is. These questions have direct connections to the educator's thinking regarding what to teach, how to teach it and what an adequate justification for doing so might be. Although many educators are not conscious of the influence of such underlying assumptions on their educational choices, to become conscious of them and to reflect upon their grounds is one of the benefits that philosophy of education can offer to educational theory and practice. In this essay I have presented one example of how to carry on this kind of academic conversation.

NOTES

1 My experience naturally derives only from my own studies at the University of Helsinki, where the books of Rosenberg (1984) and Fisher (1988) served as entrance requirements in the undergraduate and graduate seminars of theoretical philosophy. Although I take these books as being both outstanding and beneficial, I would now suggest, additionally, orientation in textual analysis.

2 The term 'analytical philosophy' as referring to the contemporary Anglo-American philosophical tradition is, as a matter of fact, misleading, since there is no consensus on the reference to the notion of 'analytical philosophy' in contemporary philosophy (Raatikainen, 2001). In this essay, this term is used in a broad sense, referring to the Anglo-American philosophical tradition as distinct from, for example, Continental philosophy.

3 The term 'reconstruction' is used both as referring to the whole process of analysis and synthesis, and as referring to the latter, synthetic part of the process. I would prefer the

latter usage, but as the former is also well established in philosophy, this chapter uses the term both ways, depending on the context.

4   'Irrealism' is Goodman's own term for his constructivist position. I decided to label the position 'constructivism' in order to call attention to the similarity between Goodman's irrealism and what we now term constructivism (Holma, 2004, p. 421).

5   This piece is originally from Scheffler's *Science and Subjectivity* (1982, first published in 1967).

6   This piece was first published in *Inquiries* (1986, pp. 82–6) and is also published in *Starmaking* (McCormick, 1996) under the title 'Reply to Goodman' (pp. 161–4).

7   This article first appeared in *Synthese* (1980) as 'The Wonderful Worlds of Goodman' (pp. 201–9), and it is reprinted also in *Starmaking*, pp. 133–41.

8   This piece appeared almost in the same form in *Starmaking* as 'Worldmaking, Why Worry,' pp. 171–7.

9   In contrast, the defender of the stronger version of realism could, for example, propose that an important task of education is to help children encounter reality and learn to understand it.

10 Rorty's argument was chosen as an example because Rorty, in contrast to Goodman, discusses also the educational implications of constructivist epistemology. In relation to the philosophical argumentation, I am also acquainted with the broader philosophical conversation of this particular debate, for example Hilary Putnam (1992, pp. 108–33), Harvey Siegel (1984a, b), and Catherine Elgin (1984) who have contributed to the philosophical conversation on the topic. Since my own interest in relation to the theme was educational, these texts did not play a significant role in the final version of the chapter.

11 The term 'voluntarism' here refers to Goodman's suggestion that right versions, made by us, make worlds. As Scheffler puts it: 'My argument is not with Goodman's pluralism or relativism but his voluntarism … "We make versions," says Goodman, "and right versions make worlds." But I say: we make versions but we do not make them right' (Scheffler, 1997, p. 206, in Goodman 1984, p. 42). 'Relativism' refers not to the relativity of our systems of description but to the relativity of what they describe.

REFERENCES

Burbules, N. C. (2000) Moving Beyond the Impasse, in: D. C. Phillips (ed.) *Constructivism in Education: Opinions and Second Opinions on Controversial Issues* (Chicago, NSSE), pp. 308–30.

Elgin, C. Z. (1984) Goodman's Rigorous Relativism, *Journal of Thought*, 19.4, pp 36–45.

Elgin, C. Z. (1998) Goodman, Nelson, in: E. Craig (ed.) *Routledge Encyclopedia of Philosophy* (London, Routledge), online at http://www.rep.routledge.com/article/M045SECT1 (accessed 19 August 2003).

Fisher, A. (1988) *The Logic of Real Arguments* (Cambridge, Cambridge University Press).

Goodman, N. (1978) *Ways of Worldmaking* (Hassocks, Harvester Press).

Goodman, N. (1984) *Of Mind and Other Matters* (Cambridge, MA, Harvard University Press).

Goodman, N. (1996a) Words, Works, Worlds, in: P. McCormick (ed.) *Starmaking: Realism, Anti-Realism, and Irrealism* (Cambridge, MA, MIT Press), pp. 61–77.

Goodman, N. (1996b) Comments, in: P. McCormick (ed.) *Starmaking: Realism, Anti-Realism, and Irrealism* (Cambridge, MA, MIT Press), pp 160–67.

Holma, K. (2004) Pluralism and Education: Israel Scheffler's Synthesis and its Presumable Educational Implications, *Educational Theory*, 54.4, pp. 419–30.

Jussila, J., Montonen, K. and Nurmi, K. E. (1989) Systemaattinen analyysi kasvatustietei-den tutkimusmenetelmänä [Systematic Analysis as an Educational Research Method], in: T. Gröhn and J. Jussila (eds.) *Laadullisia lähestymistapoja koulutuksen tutkimuksessa* [Qualitative Approaches to Educational Research] (Helsinki, Department of Education, University of Helsinki).

Matthews, M. R. (ed.) (1998) *Constructivism in Science Education: A Philosophical Examination* (Dordrecht, Kluwer Academic Publishers).

Matthews, M. R. (2000) Appraising Constructivism in Science and Mathematics Education, in: D. C. Phillips (ed.) *Constructivism in Education: Opinions and Second Opinions on Controversial Issues* (Chicago, NSSE), pp. 161–92.

McCormick, P. (1996) *Starmaking: Realism, Anti-Realism, and Irrealism* (Cambridge, MA, MIT Press).

Phillips, D. C. (ed.) (2000) *Constructivism in Education: Opinions and Second Opinions on Controversial Issues* (Chicago, NSSE).

Puolimatka, T. (2002) *Opetuksen teoria: Konstruktivismista Realismiin* [The Theory of Teaching: From Constructivism to Realism] (Helsinki, Tammi).

Putnam, H. (1992) *Renewing Philosophy* (Cambridge MA, Harvard University Press).

Raatikainen, P. (2001) Mitä oli analyyttinen filosofia? [What was Analytic Philosophy?], *Ajatus*, 58, pp. 189–217.

Rorty, R. (1984) Historiography of Philosophy: Four Genres, in: R. Rorty, J. B. Schneewind and Q. Skinner (eds) *Philosophy in History* (Cambridge, Cambridge University Press).

Rorty, R. (1997) Hermeneutics, General Studies and Teaching, in: S. M. Cahn (ed.) *Classic and Contemporary Readings in the Philosophy of Education* (New York, McGraw-Hill), pp. 522–36.

Rosenberg, J. F. (1984) *The Practice of Philosophy: A Handbook for Beginners*, 2nd edn. (Englewood Cliffs, NJ, Prentice-Hall).

Scheffler, I. (1982) *Science and Subjectivity*, 2nd edn. (Indianapolis, Hackett Publishing Company).

Scheffler, I. (1986) *Inquiries: Philosophical Studies of Language, Science, and Learning* (Indianapolis, IN, Hackett Publishing Company).

Scheffler, I. (1996) Epistemology of Objectivity, in: P. McCormick (ed.) *Starmaking: Realism, Anti-Realism, and Irrealism* (Cambridge MA, MIT Press).

Scheffler, I. (1997) *Symbolic Worlds: Art, Science, Language, Ritual* (New York, Cambridge University Press).

Scheffler, I. (2000) A Plea for Pluralism, *Erkenntnis*, 52.2, pp. 161–73.

Scheffler, I. (2001) My Quarrels with Nelson Goodman, *Philosophy and Phenomenological Research*, 62.3, pp. 667–77.

Siegel, H. (1984a) Goodmanian Relativism, *The Monist*, 27.3, pp. 359–75.

Siegel, H. (1984b) Relativism, Realism, and Rightness: Notes on Goodmanian Worldmak-ing, *Journal of Thought*, 19.4, pp. 16–35.

3

'Anything You Can Do I Can Do Better': Dialectical Argument in Philosophy of Education[1]

DANIEL VOKEY

It is a central task of philosophy of education to assess the comparative strengths and limitations of the conceptual frameworks that educational scholars and practitioners employ to 'interpret experience, express purposes, frame problems, and conduct inquiries' (Coombs and Daniels, 1991, p. 27). In some cases, this means critically comparing the competing sets of fundamental philosophical and other beliefs ('worldviews') that accompany radically different conceptions of the proper ends and means of education.[2] In other cases the conceptual frameworks in question can have a more narrow scope, such as when advocates of critical pedagogy debate which way of conceiving the student–teacher relationship is most consistent with and conducive to their emancipatory aims.[3]

My goal in this chapter is to illustrate how a case for the advantages of one conceptual scheme[4] over another can be made through *dialectical argument* (or *dialectic* for short). I first encountered the use of this term to describe a distinct form of critical inquiry when studying Bernard Lonergan's (1973) treatise on method in theology, in which *dialectic* refers to one among eight distinct theological tasks or 'functional specialties'. However, it is to another modern interpreter of Thomas Aquinas that my intellectual debts in this area are principally owed: Alasdair MacIntyre and his account of the *rationality of traditions* (Vokey, 2001, pp. 49–65). The 'method' of dialectic is introduced in the first section below, with references to my critical appropriation of MacIntyre's account of non-foundational justification for those seeking the elaboration of distinctions and arguments that a brief introduction cannot provide. The practice of dialectic is demonstrated in the second section, where I compare the advantages of my metaethical position to a popular contemporary alternative in relation to teaching courses in professional ethics. The conclusion offers reflections upon the conditions under which dialectical encounters are likely to be productive.[5]

INTRODUCING DIALECTICAL ARGUMENT

There is no context-free 'view from nowhere' from which we could impartially evaluate the respective strengths and limitations of alternative conceptual schemes. Rather, we engage in philosophical inquiry equipped (and sometimes saddled) with assumptions and interests shaped by the particulars of our personal biographies, social locations, political contexts, and more. In MacIntyre's terms, we engage in dialectical argument from standpoints internal to one or more historical traditions and corresponding communities of inquiry and practice. This holds true whether we engage in dialectic as an advocate of one among two competing conceptual frameworks or whether we compare two rival schemes from the perspective of a third. However, to thus assert that argument and assessment are necessarily situated entails no troubling relativist conclusions. MacIntyre described and demonstrated dialectic precisely to show how the standards of rational judgement internal to particular communities of inquiry and practice can themselves be rationally justified in a non-circular and non-foundational way (Vokey, 2001, pp. 66–97).

Conceptual schemes are candidates for dialectical assessment when they represent alternative ways of conceiving and pursuing similar objectives regarding the same domain of human experience. That they have overlapping fundamental interests helps explain why the perspectives of rival communities of inquiry and practice sometimes converge (pp. 97–102). Even so, just because there is no 'view from nowhere', there is no tradition-neutral description of the shared or overlapping intentions by virtue of which alternative paradigms are rivals. For example, although we can recognise traditional Chinese and modern Western traditions of medical inquiry and practice as having similar objectives, they work with incommensurable conceptions of *health* and *disease* corresponding to their respective worldviews. Thus, the terms in which the aims of such practical initiatives as health care and education are best conceptualised is itself a matter for dialectical debate that, amongst much else, considers the relative merits of competing worldviews.

When advocates undertake to demonstrate the advantages of their conceptual framework over an alternative through dialectic they set themselves two argumentative tasks. The primary task is to show that their framework has the conceptual resources to:

(a) make progress on one or more theoretical and/or practical problems that representatives of the alternative position recognise as important, but cannot adequately address within the limitations of their conceptual framework;
(b) identify what is lacking in the alternative scheme that accounts for their failure; and
(c) offer some explanation for the alleged blind spot(s) or lacunae within the alternative scheme.

The second task that advocates undertake is to show that their conceptual framework shares all the advantages of the alternative scheme, and so is not vulnerable to a similar kind of argument from the alternative point of view. Typically, this involves explaining why the criticisms that have been or could be made by one's dialectical interlocutors are either relatively inconsequential or entirely off the mark.

Engaging in dialectical argument is an integral part of seeking the overall most satisfactory conceptual framework possible to inform some practical initiative in some particular time and place. Encountering what appears to be a different perspective than one's own is taken as an opportunity for learning from what is brought into focus by the new conceptual 'lens'. Different perspectives are not always complementary, however. Dialectical argument properly selects for attention differences that make a difference, on the assumption that some conceptual frameworks will serve human interests better than others (Lonergan, 1973, p. 130). To take the commitment to social justice for example: Iris Marion Young appreciates what the distributive conception has to contribute to this cause in contemporary pluralistic liberal democracies, but advocates an alternative paradigm by undertaking to show why 'it is a mistake to reduce social justice to distribution' (Young, 1990, p. 15).

The 'method' of dialectical argument is not a formula and does not guarantee results—and this is not just because our attachments to our beliefs can make us blind to the advantages of alternative points of view and immune to rational persuasion. Elsewhere, when considering the different ways in which one conceptual scheme can be considered to have advantages over another, I have proposed that the generic virtues of a theoretical framework are that it is:

- intelligible (suffers no problems arising from ambiguity);
- internally coherent (suffers no problems arising from logical or performative contradictions);
- plausible (suffers no problems reconciling its empirical beliefs and normative commitments with what is widely accepted to be true); and
- successful in practice (suffers no problems related to persistent lack of progress in relation to one or more of the purposes for which it was developed).

This means that competing conceptual schemes can be assessed according to different kinds of expectations, and that a theoretical framework has strengths in one area is no guarantee that it will not exhibit limitations in another. Dialectic is not formulaic, then, because the issue of what relative weight should be assigned to the different assessment criteria—internal coherence versus pragmatic success, for example—is itself open to debate (Vokey, 2001, pp. 92–7). What might this 'method' of dialectic look like in practice?

NASH'S 'POSTMODERN MORAL PRAGMATISM' AND 'THE ETHICS OF TRANSCENDENT VIRTUE'

Given the limited scope of this book chapter, this illustration will take up only the first of dialectic's two tasks. In other words, I will occupy myself with arguing that the set of beliefs I refer to as 'the ethics of transcendent virtue' has the conceptual resources to make progress on some problems recognised as important but not adequately addressed by a competing conceptual scheme; I will identify what is lacking that accounts for its failure; and I will offer some explanation for the alleged 'gaps' in the competing scheme. I will not undertake dialectic's second task of showing how the ethics of transcendent virtue shares all the advantages of the competing scheme and so is not vulnerable to a similar kind of argument from its point of view. More specifically, I will argue that the ethics of transcendent virtue has important advantages for teaching courses in professional ethics over the 'constructivist-postmodern-moral-pragmatism' informing Robert J. Nash's *'Real World' Ethics: Frameworks for Educators and Human Service Professionals*. Nash's text is widely known and used in North America, but I have chosen to examine it here for more weighty reasons than its popularity. One important reason is that Nash and I have similar objectives for our courses; in particular, we both aspire to help teachers and other professionals enhance their abilities:

1. to make sound practical judgements on the moral issues that arise in the complex contexts of professional practice;
2. to articulate the basic beliefs shaping their moral perception, feeling, thought, and action;
3. to appreciate the commitments of people representing very different moral traditions *in their own terms*, identifying any points of agreement as well as any points of conflict; and
4. to engage respectfully, sensitively, and open-mindedly in conversations about contentious moral issues, seeking enough moral agreement to achieve solidarity across differences in the name of justice and peace (Nash, 2002, pp. 179–80), without ignoring real conflict in the name of consensus.

Another reason for choosing this book is that it represents Nash's efforts over many decades of teaching professional ethics to formulate a framework that is both theoretically and pedagogically sound. As such, it is a worthy representative of the 'multiple languages' approach to professional ethics instruction that has emerged in response to perceived limitations of the previously dominant 'principled-reasoning' approach (pp. 106–15; Vokey, 2005). Finally, I have chosen Nash's book because I wish to show how dialectic functions in my own academic work, and that currently includes reading texts on professional ethics looking for points of significant agreement and disagreement between the authors' assumptions and my own as a way to test the set of beliefs that inform my teaching.

THE ETHICS OF TRANSCENDENT VIRTUE[6]

As I use the term, *moral* education encompasses programs of character, citizenship, environmental, peace, religious, and anti-oppressive education in addition to courses in ethics for educational professionals. By definition, in my view, moral *education* programs should enable their participants to appreciate and assess reasons for and against particular moral commitments, particularly those commitments that the programs have been designed to promote. Accordingly, I agree with Dwight Boyd that education is not possible in any domain in which humans exercise judgement if those judgements are not open to correction (Boyd, 1989, pp. 81–9). To investigate whether and if so how moral judgements are open to correction I have turned to moral philosophy, focusing on the metaethical question 'To what kind of arguments, reasons, and/or evidence should we appeal to support a moral commitment or to resolve disputes when moral judgements conflict?' Here, in greatly compressed form for the purposes of this exercise, is the set of provisional metaethical assumptions that inform my scholarship and practice:

1. **Some actions and events are, to greater and lesser degrees, intrinsically morally good (or right) and others are, to greater and lesser degrees, intrinsically morally bad (or wrong).** *Intrinsically* here means *independently of human needs, desires, and interests.* To assert that something is intrinsically good in this sense is to assert that it *merits* being recognised as such regardless of whether it happens already to be valued or not. Not all intrinsic values are moral values, and not all moral values are intrinsic values, but at least some moral values are intrinsic values (Vokey, 2001, pp. 207–13). *Intrinsic value* is an odd notion, to be sure: It is not immediately clear what it could *mean* to say that something *merits* being recognised as intrinsically morally good or *merits* being valued for its own sake independently of human interests. Nevertheless, references to intrinsic value, moral and otherwise, appear in conversations and texts inside as well as outside academic contexts, such as when the inherent worth of non-human species is affirmed in discussions of ecological justice. To me, this suggests that the language of *intrinsically good* and *intrinsically bad* serves to communicate something important about human moral experience.

2. **The 'highest', most accurate form of knowledge is direct, 'intuitive' insight; that is, an immediate, non-conceptual grasp of the true nature(s) of things.** This claim is based in part upon the belief that conceptual and other frames of reference are superimposed upon a primordial experience that is prior to language, and that can never be perfectly represented in language in part because unmediated experience does not observe the law of the excluded middle. According to this non-dualistic world view (Loy, 1988), all truth

claims (yes, even this one) share the partial and limited character of the conceptual frameworks in the terms of which they are expressed (Vokey, 2001, pp. 214–22).

3. **We all have an innate potential capacity to apprehend what is intrinsically good and bad, right and wrong, through the depth and quality of** (for lack of a more elegant phrase) ***cognitive–affective experience.*** Appreciating moral goodness is not so much like grasping the solution to a puzzle or the conclusion of an argument as like being stirred in the soul by the infinity of stars in a cloudless night sky. Accordingly, when we dig down into the roots of our moral commitments, we typically find experiences in which we were *profoundly moved*, both positively (for example, by acts of kindness, generosity, courage, honesty, solidarity, and compassion) and negatively (by acts of cruelty, greed, and wilful ignorance). Saying that 'we' can be profoundly moved by what is genuinely good and bad is both correct in a relative sort of way *and* slightly misleading, because intrinsic value is apprehended in the non-dualistic 'I–Thou' (Buber, 1970) state of experiencing that is prior to the superimposition of conceptual frameworks, including the most basic dualistic framework of *self* and *other*. In other words, apprehensions of intrinsic value arise prior to distinctions between the experien*cing*, the experien*ced*, and the experien*cer*. That its apprehension occurs before the superimposition of our usual dualistic subject–object frames of reference fits well with the notion that *intrinsic value* is not relative to human desires and interests. That it is apprehended intuitively also helps explain why the meaning of *intrinsic value* eludes definition—hence the perennial popularity in ethics of references to our 'reasons of the heart' (Vokey, 2001, pp. 227–45).

4. Ethical decision-making typically involves much more than relying upon intuitive apprehensions of what is intrinsically right and wrong. This 'more' can include consequentialist calculations, deductive reasoning from general principles, harkening to emotions, appeals to shared ideals, considering legal and other regulatory injunctions, and reasoning by analogy to paradigm cases. However, **no account of practical judgement can be complete if the contributions of our 'reasons of the heart' are not recognised**.

5. The ability to retain the insight and perspective of non-dualistic experiencing while working with(in) dualistic conceptual frameworks is the fruition of a process of unlearning habits of self-centred perception, feeling, thought, and action ('ego' for short). **Because ethical decision-making must reflect an accurate apprehension of intrinsic value to be sound, we grow in practical wisdom by following a spiritual path, defined very broadly as a journey to connection with 'something larger and more trustworthy than our egos'** (Parker, 1998, p. 6). Those who are highly realised spiritually—Saints, Sages, Elders, Masters, Buddhas, Bodhisattvas, and Philosopher-Kings, whether recognised as such or not—by virtue of access to an unconditioned source of insight and compassion, manifest the insight to know without deliberation and the motivation to do without hesitation whatever

action is appropriate given the particulars of the situation. Because unconditioned insight and compassion is always already there—albeit usually obscured by deeply-rooted habits of self-preoccupation—everyone from time to time has the experience of knowing and doing 'the right thing' without deliberation. This helps explain why appeals to *moral intuition* never completely disappear from moral philosophy, even during periods when knowledge tends to be identified exclusively with the output of the intellect (Vokey, 2001, pp. 172–73).

6. **Intrinsic goodness is what we all most fundamentally desire.** Ultimately, then, human fulfilment lies in knowing and doing what is genuinely virtuous for its own sake. The intellectual and moral virtues are not only or even primarily a *means* to realise the human *telos*. Rather, actualising our potential for practical wisdom *is* fulfilment (pp. 186–205).

7. The intellectual culture of the modern 'Western' world continues to be shaped by the mechanistic (materialistic, deterministic, atomistic, reductionistic) worldview and associated positivistic epistemologies. More often than not, experimental scientific research is taken to be the most (if not only) reliable source of knowledge, and what cannot be validated according to its methodological canons still tends to be received sceptically if not dismissed or ignored. With the rise of secular institutions and instrumental rationality, the worldviews of the 'wisdom traditions' invoked in the six statements above have either been relegated to the margins of, or been entirely banished from, the public domain. Even so, some of their concepts and ideals survive as remnants in public discourse.[7] Assuming it is true that intrinsic moral and other value is apprehended 'intuitively' in the depth and quality of cognitive-affective experience, **what is most important about ethics cannot easily be articulated in the terms either of mechanistic worldviews or of rationalistic post-enlightenment moral and political philosophies.** This helps explain why, in modern liberal democracies, we lack agreement on a satisfactory response to the argument that moral relativism is the best explanation for the fact of moral pluralism.

8. **Appealing to apprehensions of intrinsic value**—either directly, or indirectly via the particular moral judgements and actions that such apprehensions inform—**is an important feature both of moral education and of *moral discourse***, meaning the dialectical engagements and other conversations through which people with very different moral standpoints seek to identify and extend their common ground (Vokey, 2001, pp. 276–83). One form these inquiries and arguments can take is the search for reflective equilibrium between general moral principles and particular moral intuitions.

Much more would have to be said, of course, to establish that the ethics of transcendent virtue summarised above measures up reasonably well against the generic criteria of intelligibility, internal coherence, plausibility, and practical success. What of its advantages for teaching professional ethics in comparison to Nash's metaethical views?

'REAL WORLD' ETHICAL FRAMEWORKS FOR EDUCATIONAL AND HUMAN SERVICE PROFESSIONALS

Robert Nash wrote *'Real World' Ethics* with two main objectives in mind corresponding to two intended audiences. For the benefit of students preparing for professional practice, he describes a variety of 'problem-solving frameworks' that he promises will help them identify and solve ethical dilemmas (Nash, 2002, pp. 2, 10–11, 17). For the benefit of instructors and students in professional ethics courses, Nash describes the particulars of his classroom pedagogy so we might learn from what has worked well over his years of teaching and what has not (p. 13). The core of Nash's conceptual framework for both doing and teaching professional ethics is his account of what he calls our First, Second, and Third Moral Languages; respectively the languages of Background Beliefs, of Character, and of Principle (pp. 22–3). Nash uses these three categories to organise the wide variety of moral vocabularies and discourses found in our modern pluralistic democracies. The central claim of his book is that we have the best chance of making sound professional judgements on moral matters when all three languages feature in our deliberations. The core of my dialectical argument is that, because it lacks an account of intrinsic moral value and its apprehension, Nash's three-fold schema lacks an adequate response to the challenge of moral relativism, and so provides only part of the conceptual resources he needs to help his students make progress toward his own course objectives. I will build my case in three parts, beginning with a closer look at Nash's account of our First Moral Language, followed by observations about the limitations of the problem-solving frameworks associated with his Second and Third Moral Languages. With this discussion as background, in part three I offer an explanation and critique of what I interpret as a shift in Nash's metaethical position from the first to the second edition of his text.[8]

The Language of Background Beliefs

In Nash's terms, our First Moral Language is the set of deeply rooted assumptions and commitments that shape our moral perceptions, feelings, thoughts and actions as individuals, whether or not we have taken time to bring these 'bedrock' beliefs to conscious awareness. By definition, then, our background beliefs are 'the most fundamental assumptions that guide our perceptions about the nature of reality and what we experience as good or bad, right or wrong, important or unimportant' and are 'the 'ultimate' bases by which we make our ethical decisions' (pp. 36–7). Once he convinces his students that they should undertake to formulate their most fundamental beliefs about morality in a systematic fashion, Nash offers them a series of questions or 'metaphysical probes'—the Background Beliefs Framework—to help them accomplish this unfamiliar task. He also supports them by introducing the specialised vocabulary that moral philosophers use to describe their different positions on the issue of moral truth, terms such as rationalist, intuitionist, emotivist, naturalist, secularist, and the like (p. 47).

Nash requires participants in his courses to articulate their First Moral Language because, according to his analysis, background beliefs 'underlie and drive the entire decision-making process' and 'exert perhaps the most powerful influence on all of ... moral thinking' (p. 23; also p. 39). He asks students to identify what if anything they rely upon as sources of moral authority, introducing them to the debate between *moral objectivists*, who believe that 'there are moral truths "out there" waiting to be discovered'; and *moral constructivists*, who believe 'that moral truths are created "in here"' (p. 27). He reports that, in any given year, course participants typically span the full range of positions for and against the possibility of truth in moral matters, with the majority occupying the subjectivist end of the objectivist-constructivist continuum. However, Nash does not require his students to produce arguments supporting their fundamental assumptions about morality: different positions are described and compared, but *not* defended.

> I try to keep the questions open-ended, thoughtful, and even a bit playful ... to get them in the mood to asseverate freely about their fundamental moral beliefs. I stress that there are no right or wrong answers to any of the questions. After all, I remind them, their metaphysical beliefs are grounded in 'unprovable sources'. The purpose of the First Language is not to 'prove' or to 'justify' anything; it is to 'locate' ethical judgments, decisions, and actions in a Background Language that deepens, explains, and reveals. (p. 40)

Nash's statements here echo his remarks earlier in the text that 'all people, including my students, cling to "unprovable sources" of moral authority' and that 'ultimate questions about meaning, purpose, and being ... cannot finally be resolvable on rational grounds, because they are fundamentally undemonstrable' (p. 38). The relativistic '*de gustibus non est disputandum*' flavour of these statements is further intensified by how Nash characterises his own background beliefs when he joins his students in 'coming out of the metaphysical closet':

> One of my First Language Beliefs is that the world of ethics is an endlessly interpretable world, and rarely is there a final or definitive response to an ethical dilemma. In this sense, I am an unrepentant ethical constructivist, perhaps even a moral postmodernist. For me, the goal of a hermeneutical approach to ethics is to determine what morality means to each of us in the present, to interpret and translate this understanding in our own idiom, and to give concrete expression to this interpretation by our daily ethical actions. (pp. 56–7)

Self-identifying as a moral constructivist in his chapter on background beliefs involves Nash in three apparent contradictions, which appear like cracks in the foundation of his conceptual scheme. First, it appears to contradict his claim that his Three Moral Languages schema enables him to transcend the opposition between objectivist and constructivist perspectives on moral truth (p. 28) and 'navigate a middle course between the two contrasting viewpoints' (p. 50). Second, Nash cites a text by Mary Midgley in which she challenges the easy assumption of the moral sceptic that 'nobody can ever be in a position to question the morality of others, because nothing at all can ever be known with any degree of certainty about morality' (p. 42). Nash endorses Midgley's epistemological point that, because such moral scepticism is itself a substantive moral position, it becomes self-refuting. Citing Midgley while asserting that fundamental moral commitments are not open to correction seems to leave Nash in the position of simultaneously rejecting and embracing moral scepticism. Third, as we have seen, Nash asserts that our moral perception, feeling, thought, and action are shaped through and through by our background beliefs (p. 23). However, if the latter cannot be rationally justified, then the former are ultimately indefensible as well. This conclusion casts doubt on Nash's ability to deliver on his promise to students that they will learn, not only to resolve their ethical dilemmas (pp. 2, 17), but also to justify their decisions to others. In order to make progress toward his educational objectives, then, Nash's account of our Second and Third Moral Languages must provide him the resources to avoid moral relativism that the Languages of Background Beliefs does not.

The Language of Character, the Language of Principle, and Ethical Bricolage

Our Second Moral Language, in the terms of Nash's scheme, is the set of moral concepts, norms, and ideals that we share with the other members of the particular communities that we inhabit by chance or by choice. Like MacIntyre, Nash observes that particular communities and traditions provide the necessary resources for the development of our moral characters, including the development of our fundamental assumptions about the nature of morality itself (pp. 59–61). To the description of our moral standpoints that the First Language of Background Beliefs provides, the Second Language of Moral Character adds the temporal dimension of a work-in-progress, for it assumes that each decision we make and action we take shapes as well as expresses who we are and who we aspire to be as moral agents: 'Every ethical choice is always a choice about what kind of character to become, about what choice will best preserve . . . moral integrity in such a way that . . . actions will fit [our] best moral images' (pp. 62–3).

According to Nash, assessing the two horns of an ethical dilemma from a Second Language standpoint means asking '*Which decision has the most integrity in terms of the kind of person I either perceive myself to be or am striving to become?*' (p. 63). The corresponding problem-solving framework that Nash offers his students is his Second Language Moral Brief, a list of questions designed to bring into sharp focus the manifold elements of character and context that bear upon a particular ethical decision. It is a long list. Jonathan, the moral protagonist of the case Nash constructs to illustrate Second Language decision-making, assesses his options in the light of (i) the moral ideals of his family and of his religious community; (ii) the virtues he considers central to his character; (iii) the moral narratives from which he draws inspiration; (iv) the feelings aroused by the people and events in the case before, during, and after the incident giving rise to the dilemma; (v) the rules he was taught while he was training to become a professional; (vi) the written and unspoken norms of his workplace; (vii) the expectations associated with his particular workplace role; and (ix) the codes of ethics of his professional association. Which of these many considerations prove decisive, and why? At the end of Jonathan's deliberations, says Nash, 'Jonathan trusts his initial intuitions and feelings, and he decides to do what "feels" right. His heart goes out to Sam' (p. 100).

As this case shows, the difficulty with Nash's Second Language problem-solving framework is not that it provides no reasons to choose one out of a range of possible responses to a difficult ethical situation. The difficulty is that it provides a very wide variety of *different kinds* of considerations without guidance on which should be assigned more or less weight in light of the situation at hand. In the end, students are left to rely on their gut feelings about the right thing to do. Furthermore, as Nash himself observes, critics of this approach will argue not only that it is 'too dependent on intuition and feelings,' but also that the 'thick' moral languages associated with particular religious, philosophical, political, and/or cultural communities are 'too location-, time-, and person-bound' for the purposes of justification in a secular, pluralistic public realm (pp. 103–4).

For a less context-bound basis for ethical decision-making Nash turns to the Third Language of Moral Principle, which aspires to be the 'thin' public language that would enable conversation between 'moral strangers' (pp. 106–109). However, the corresponding Third Language Moral Brief fares no better than its predecessor as a problem-solving procedure. Regina, the protagonist in Nash's Third Language case, looks for moral principles to cite for and against the choices she contemplates, ending up with a long list that includes *fidelity, gratitude, non-maleficence, beneficence, autonomy,* and *justice* (pp. 130–8). The rules, principles, and theories that Nash's Third Language framework brings to bear on an ethical dilemma serve exceptionally well to highlight a wide range of considerations possibly relevant to finding a solution. Again, however, determining which considerations in what combination should take precedence is left up to the judgement of the individual facing the dilemma. Again, the case Nash carefully constructs to demonstrate his problem-solving framework serves to illustrate the very objections that would be levelled by its critics: 'moral principles seem arbitrary because . . . in those cases where principles may be in conflict with each other, it is left exclusively to a person's intuition to find a resolution' (p. 144; cf. p. 9).

The solution that Nash recommends to the limitations of each of the Three Moral Languages taken on its own is to combine them in *moral bricolage*: 'I attempt to integrate the various moral languages into a structured whole so that they form one usable ethical language. I argue that every ethics educator must become a "bricoleur" who engages continually in the "selective retrieval and eclectic reconfiguration" (Stout, 1988, p. 76) of various moral languages' (Nash, 2002, p. 14). Although Nash sometimes uses the term 'integration' to describe how background beliefs, considerations of character, and matters of theory and principle should be combined in ethical decision-making, he offers no explanation or illustration *how* reasoning, feeling, and intuition might be combined to achieve 'reflective equilibrium' among the many considerations he lists in his moral briefs (p. 205). The essential difficulty with his as with any 'multiple ethical languages' approach to teaching professional ethics is the *problem of conflict*: the different perspectives represented by the core concepts of different moral traditions (justice, care, utility, duty, *eudaimonia*, grace, compassion, piety) are as likely to be contradictory as complementary, as likely to complicate as facilitate the process of deciding among alternative courses of action (Vokey, 2008, pp. 298–9).

From Constructivism to Pragmatism

The closest Nash comes to a description of the kind of practical wisdom required for moral bricolage to work is when he borrows the notion of *discernment* from a work in *theological* ethics:

> The final discernment is an informed intuition; it is not the conclusion of a formally logical argument, a strict deduction from a single moral principle, or an absolutely certain result from the exercises of human 'reason' alone. There is a final moment of perception that sees the parts in relation to a whole, expresses sensibilities as well as reasoning, and is made in the condition of human finitude. In complex circumstances it is not without risk. (Gustafson, 1981, p. 338, cited in Nash, 2002, p. 168)

In Christian as in other wisdom traditions, *discernment* is the fruit of spiritual practice, so the sudden appearance of this notion on the last page of the first edition of *'Real World' Ethics* represents a *deus ex machina* resolution to the problem of conflict. Nash's richly textured account of the many considerations relevant to practical judgement portrays the complexity of professional practice exceptionally well. What his three moral languages schema does not provide is moral grounds for maintaining that one practical judgement can be better or worse than another in any sense other than being faithful to an individual's considered (but ultimately indefensible) moral convictions. It is for this reason—or so I surmise—that in the question-and-answer epilogue added to the second edition of his text Nash revisits the question of moral truth in response to a reader's concern about the relativistic flavour of his constructivist leanings in the first edition (pp. 176–7). As before, Nash rejects both 'anything goes' moral relativism *and* any form of moral absolutism or objectivism that asserts 'universal, unchangeable, and exceptionless' laws dictated by God, Biology, or Reason. He then proposes an *ethic of pragmatic moral consensus* in which moral principles and ideals would be justified in terms of their contributions to 'the good life for everyone'. Such a naturalistic metaethics is an improvement, in my eyes at least, over free-floating ethical constructivism. Since I also maintain that sound moral judgement and human flourishing are closely connected—not least because personal fulfilment lies in knowing and doing what is genuinely virtuous and good—I agree with Nash that those representing different religious, philosophical, political, and cultural traditions are well advised to seek common ground by comparing their accumulated wisdom on what ways of life conduce to human well-being. Why, then, do I find it necessary to posit such imponderables as *intrinsic moral value* and *moral intuition*, and to defend the moral realist side of the objectivist-subjectivist debate?

I see three main advantages to the ethics of transcendent virtue over Nash's naturalistic pragmatism. First, an instrumentalist or consequentialist metaethics cannot do justice to considered convictions that some things are just plain morally right or morally wrong (slavery and genocide, to borrow Nash's examples, p. 177), and these convictions are not limited to Kantian Deontology and Deep Ecology. In his discussion of the Language of Moral Character, Nash cites with approval the Aristotelian view that there are 'objectively desirable states of character' that 'every rational being has good reason to acquire' and that 'these dispositions define the fulfilled rational being' (p. 105). However, the Aristotelian conviction that the fully virtuous person properly loves virtue for its own sake is one piece with the conviction that some actions are and are not inherently 'noble and fine', and this metaethical view cannot be captured in consequentialist terms (pp. 192–6).

Second, if intrinsic moral value is apprehended in the depth and quality of unmediated cognitive–affective experience, then it makes sense that intuition would be integral to ethical decision-making. Conversely, it is not clear how Nash can coherently adopt the Catholic notion of *discernment* to describe the pinnacle of practical wisdom if decisions are ultimately to be justified in terms of their consequences for individual or collective human flourishing, for this would suggest something more like a deductive utilitarian calculus. Whatever the capacity to make sound ethical decisions is called—judgement, intuition, discernment, or some cognate term—the key educational question is how it can be improved. Although *the ethics of transcendent virtue* does not provide a complete answer, it affords two helpful perspectives on education for sound practical judgement, both related to the important role that it assigns to direct experience. By identifying the right thing to do with what would be done by someone liberated from ego's fixations, it reaffirms the contemporary relevance of the time-tested disciplines and practices through which members of various philosophical and religious 'wisdom traditions' cultivate the intellectual and moral virtues upon which individual *and* collective discernment depend. The importance of this contribution is evidenced by the growing number of workshops, retreats, conferences and publications devoted to integrating contemplative practices in secular institutions of higher education—and, more generally, to balancing 'educating the mind' with 'educating the heart'.[9] By underlining the importance of direct perception, it also reaffirms the relevance to education for sound practical judgement of aesthetics and the arts.[10]

Third, navigating a middle road between moral relativism and absolutism requires reconciling belief in the possibility of reaching some measure of moral truth with the fact of persistent moral disagreement. Like Nash, I believe that:

(a) persistent disagreement even among those who embrace some notion of moral truth can be explained in part by our embeddedness in particular 'personal histories, cultural contexts, and interpretive frameworks' (p. 179; Vokey, 2001, pp. 230–3);

(b) efforts to identify and extend common ground among different moral perspectives should begin with appreciating them as much as possible in their own terms, the challenges that this represents notwithstanding (Nash, 2002, p. 180; Vokey, 2001, 274–5); and

(c) the potential to reach agreement through argument is limited so long as conflicting practical judgements are rooted in radically opposed moral points of view.

It is a measure of the shift from the first to the second edition of his text that Nash enjoins us in his epilogue 'to strive together to reach some kind of moral consensus' and 'to take ethical positions and defend them' (Nash, 2002, p. 180). His book offers much to help us clarify our basic moral beliefs, religious or otherwise, but has little to say about their defence or about how progress toward even partial moral consensus is possible. The ethics of transcendent virtue, by combining the generic expectations of intelligibility, coherence, plausibility, and practical success with an account of the fundamental interest that makes alternative moral conceptual frameworks *moral*, is able to specify appropriate criteria for moral discourse (Vokey, 2001, pp. 250–6). In addition, by calling attention to what moves us most profoundly, the ethics of transcendent virtue highlights the indispensable roles of symbols and stories in communicating the experiences without which the beliefs and commitments of alternative moral points of view cannot be adequately understood (pp. 257–63). As Aristotle points out, it is precisely because what is intrinsically 'noble and fine' is apprehended through the felt quality of human response that moral arguments will have no effect upon those unfortunate souls who, through lack of proper education, 'have not even a conception of what is noble and truly pleasant, since they have never tasted it' (*NE* 1179b15).

I do not imagine that the assessment of Nash's metaethical position offered above represents a 'knock-down' argument against naturalism. My hope is that it would open rather than end conversations with those who find moral realism untenable. I also hope that, its abbreviated nature notwithstanding, this case for the advantages of the ethics of transcendent virtue illustrates the form of dialectical argument introduced in the first section.

CONCLUDING THOUGHTS ON DIALECTICAL ARGUMENT

For dialectic to be productive—indeed, possible at all—a variety of material and cultural conditions must be fulfilled. Like any form of rational inquiry and argument, dialectic presupposes that active communities of inquiry and practice exist into which we can be initiated, learning to take up their concepts, standards, and arguments as our own. Such communities and corresponding traditions are only sustained by people exercising a broad range of virtues such as fairness, generosity, diligence, courage, creativity, and open-mindedness or 'epistemic humility'. Lonergan's (1973) account of functional specialisations within theological 'method' illustrates how, before dialectical argument can even begin, texts must be published, translated, interpreted, and re-interpreted in light of historical, sociological, and other studies of circumstances of their origins. It also illustrates how the efforts of specialists in dialectic are properly understood as contributions to larger theological inquiries and initiatives. Similarly, I think arriving at more and more satisfactory conceptual frameworks via the interplay of theory and practice is a long-term collaborative process involving many forms of research and scholarship, including many forms of philosophy (conceptual analysis, hermeneutics, and deconstruction to name just a few). In this view I find support for Ernst Boyer's (1994) arguments that institutions of higher education will better serve human needs when the scholarship of discovery is complemented by the scholarships of integration, application, and teaching.

Ideally, the pursuit of truth in discourse is not compromised by strategic interests. Ideally, those with whom we disagree are considered *allies* or at least *adversaries* (to borrow a term from Chantal Mouffe, 2002), but never *enemies*; and dialectic is an exercise in mutual education rather than winner-take-all intellectual warfare. To this end I think it helps to keep shared fundamental interests in mind (better health, more justice, deeper learning and so forth) when engaging with dialectical interlocutors and to recognise that alternative conceptual frameworks can be related in a variety of ways including compatibly, incompatibly, paradoxically, obliquely, genetically, antagonistically, or complementarily (Vokey, 2001, pp. 74–9).[11] 'For me or against me' are by no means the only two options.

While affirming the ideal of expanding horizons through respectful dialogue and debate, I also accept that there is no 'neutral ground' on which to stand, literally and metaphorically, in relation to ongoing histories of oppression and colonisation. On this view, it is a mistake to do philosophy as if class, race, gender, sexual orientation ... does not matter,[12] and engaging responsibly with those representing alternative standpoints entails being mindful of the privileges we do and do not enjoy by reason of our social locations in contexts of domination.

NOTES

1. This is the opening line of the song 'Anything you can do' from the American film comedy *Annie Get Your Gun* (Sidney, 1950). A movie clip showing the tongue-in-cheek quality of the contest can be viewed at http://www.youtube.com/watch?v=JY7Hh5P-zELo.
2. Examples of conceptual frameworks in this very broad sense are provided by Miller and Seller (1985) in their characterisation of competing 'curriculum perspectives'.
3. For one example, see Margonis, 2007.
4. For definitions of *conceptual framework* and *conceptual scheme* and related terms such as *paradigm* and *tradition of inquiry and practice*, see Vokey (2001), pp. 2–4, 28–30.
5. In referring to the 'method' of dialectic, it is not Socratic questioning that I have in mind, although it can also serve to demonstrate the limitations of a conceptual framework.
6. 'Transcendent' here refers to a source of insight and compassion beyond ego, but not outside human experience in 'this world'.
7. One notable contemporary illustration of this was the opening ceremonies, invocations, prayers, and speeches at President Obama's inauguration, including his own inaugural address (http://www.cbc.ca/world/story/2009/01/20/obama-speech-text.html).
8. The first six chapters (Nash, 2002, pp. 1–168) were originally published in 1996 under the same title; the seventh chapter (pp. 169–206) is a 'Question-and-Answer Epilogue' added for the 2002 second edition.
9. Sources of information on such publications, workshops, and conferences include the websites of the Center for Contemplative Mind in Society (http://www.contemplative-mind.org/), the Center for the Advancement of Contemplative Education (http://www.naropa.edu/cace/index.cfm), the Dalai Lama Centre for Peace and Education (http://www.dalailamacenter.org/), and the Mind & Life Institute (http://www.mindan-dlife.org/current.conf.html). See also Duerr, Zajonc, & Dana, 2003.
10. See Carr (2004); cf. Vokey (2001, pp. 229–30) for a discussion of the power of perception, honed by art and poetry, to apprehend *intrinsic value* in the context of environmental education.
11. Lonergan suggests that horizons are related complementarily, genetically, or dialectically (Lonergan, 1973, pp. 236–7). To create this list I reformulated his original categories and added four more. Even this list may not be exhaustive.
12. On this point, and particularly the 'dot dot dot' problem, see Boyd (1998).

REFERENCES

Aristotle. *Nicomachean Ethics* (various editions).
Boyd, D. (1989) Moral Education, Objectively Speaking, in: J. Giarelli (ed.) *Philosophy of Education 1988* (Urbana, IL, Philosophy of Education Society), pp. 83–100.

Boyd, D. (1998) The Place of Locating Oneself(ves)/Myself(ves) in Doing Philosophy of Education, in: S. Laird (ed.) *Philosophy of Education 1997* (Urbana, IL, Philosophy of Education Society), pp. 1–19.

Boyer, E. (1994) Scholarly Work: New Definitions and Directions, in: L. J. N. Mangieri and C. C. Block (eds) *Creating Powerful Thinking in Teachers and Students: Diverse Perspectives* (Fort Worth, TX, Harcourt Brace), pp. 187–94.

Buber, M. (1970) *I and Thou* 2nd edn., R. G. Smith, trans. (New York, Charles Scribner's Sons).

Carr, D. (2004) Moral Values and the Arts in Environmental Education: Towards an Ethics of Aesthetic Appreciation, *Journal of Philosophy of Education*, 38.2, pp. 221–39.

Coombs, J. and Daniels, L. (1991) Philosophical Inquiry: Conceptual Analysis, in: E. Short (ed.) *Forms of Curriculum Inquiry* (Albany, State University of New York Press), pp. 27–41.

Duerr, M., Zajonc, A. and Dana, D. (2003) Survey of Transformative and Spiritual Dimensions of Higher Education, *Journal of Transformative Education*, 1.3, pp. 177–211.

Gustafson, J. M. (1981) *Ethics from a Theocentric Perspective,* Vol. I (Chicago, University of Chicago Press).

Lonergan, B. (1973) *Method in Theology*, 2nd edn. (London, Dartman, Longman, and Todd).

Loy, D. (1988) *Nonduality: A Study in Comparative Philosophy* (New Haven, CT, Yale University Press).

Margonis, F. (2007) Seeking Openings of Already Closed Student-Teacher Relationships, in: D. Vokey (ed.) *Philosophy of Education 2006* (Urbana, IL, Philosophy of Education Society), pp. 176–84.

Miller, J. and Seller, W. (1985) *Curriculum Perspectives and Practice* (New York, Longman).

Mouffe, C. (2002) *Deliberative Democracy or Agonistic Pluralism* (Vienna, IHS).

Nash, R. J. (2002) *'Real World' Ethics: Frameworks for Educators and Human Service Professionals*, 2nd edn. (New York, Teachers College Press).

Parker, P. (1998) *The Courage to Teach: Exploring the Inner Landscape of a Teacher's Life* (San Francisco, Jossey-Bass).

Sidney, G. (1950) *Annie Get Your Gun*. Online at: http://en.wikipedia.org/wiki/Annie_Get_Your_Gun_%28film%29 (accessed 8 April 2009).

Stout, J. (1988) *Ethics After Babel* (Princeton, NJ, Princeton University Press).

Vokey, D. (2001) *Moral Discourse in a Pluralistic World* (Notre Dame, IN, University of Notre Dame Press).

Vokey, D. (2008) Hearing, Contemplating, and Meditating: In Search of the Transformative Integration of Heart and Mind, in: C. Eppert and H. Wang (eds) *Cross-Cultural Studies in Curriculum: Eastern Thought, Educational Insights* (New York, Lawrence Erlbaum), pp. 287–312.

Young, I. M. (1990) *Justice and the Politics of Difference* (Princeton, NJ, Princeton University Press).

4

Education and Selfhood: A Phenomenological Investigation

MICHAEL BONNETT

In this chapter I wish to examine a burgeoning approach to education that invites us to question a cluster of ideas that have been widely influential in educational discourse at various times. The approach that I wish to examine can be read as a critical commentary on the nature and importance of selfhood, here intending by this term broadly what constitutes one's sense of individual existence as a person, one's sense of personal identity, one's sense of self. Notwithstanding that arguably in recent years selfhood has received rather little emphasis in educational policy and practice, I will develop the claim that the notion has a central place in educational debate and will explore some ways in which its reinterpretation—or indeed, perhaps rejection—fundamentally affects the terms of that debate.

The chapter falls into three sections:

(1) a brief introduction that sketches a traditional view of selfhood;
(2) the outline of a view that rejects this understanding of selfhood and that, in very general terms, is taken to exemplify a growing strand in current thinking;
(3) a set of comments and questions that this view provokes.

1.

Historically, the relationship between ideas of education and of the development of the individual or self has been of enduring importance and has found expression in a number of influential educational philosophies, ranging from those of Plato, through to *Bildung*, and to progressive education. The character of this relationship seems particularly apt for phenomenological investigation as the idea of experience is central to both education and selfhood. Indeed, many have conceived the individual precisely as a centre of conscious experience and as one of the poles around which the idea of education is to be articulated (for more recent examples of this, see Dewey, 1972; Peters, 1970, Chapter 2; and Freire, 2000). And certainly it would be difficult to understand education without some reference to individual experience. Even traditional approaches to education that were based on a *tabula rasa* view of the mind derived from Locke recognised this. The structure and character of experience as it is understood in relation both to selfhood and to education is, therefore, of considerable concern.

Yet if education is of necessity concerned with the experiences of individual selves, it need not be so in a way that is respectful. One reading of much contemporary educational practice is that its chief concern is to shape the selves of its learners in accordance with what are perceived to be current economic imperatives rather than, say, with what arises from their sense of their own existence. And whether or not this is true, much education is heavily conditioned by sets of standards and objectives determined quite independently of individual learners, and indeed, their teachers. With regard to respecting selfhood, this is not a promising situation.

But what is the self? What, if anything, is its value? And what would be involved in respecting it?

I will begin by giving a characterisation of such matters drawn from English literature and that I take to convey something of our everyday view. In the novel *Tess of the d'Urbervilles* Thomas Hardy tells the story of the developing and ultimately tragic relationship of the young parson's son Angel Clare and a farm-girl, Tess Durbeyfield. As their acquaintanceship grows, Clare is brought to consider the situation that is arising:

> Despite his heterodoxy, faults and weaknesses, Clare was a man with a conscience. Tess was no insignificant creature to toy with and dismiss; but a woman living her precious life—a life which to herself who endured or enjoyed it, possessed as great a dimension as the life of the mightiest to himself. Upon her sensations the whole world depended to Tess; through her existence all her fellow creatures existed, to her. The universe itself only came into being for Tess on the particular day in the particular year in which she was born.
>
> This consciousness upon which he had intruded was the single opportunity of existence ever vouchsafed to Tess by an unsympathetic First Cause—her all; her every and only chance. How then should he look upon her as of less consequence than himself; as a pretty trifle to caress and grow weary of; and not deal with the greatest seriousness with the affection which he knew that he had awakened in her—so fervid and impressionable as she was under her reserve; in order that it might not agonize and wreck her? (Hardy, 1992, pp. 178–9).

Here we have an eloquent expression of a sense of the selfhood of another and the responsibilities that it entails. The self portrayed here has a number of salient interrelated features: it is enduring, having its own life, identity; while shaped by its environment, it is not simply some sort of concrescence of that environment—it has an internal unity of its own and therefore a perspective on the world that is unique; it has feelings and a basic apprehension of its own existence—its experiences have the quality of 'mineness' and of privacy; it is finite, having only one life to live and this life is the sum of all that is possible for that individual. In these regards it is therefore worthy of a respect that cannot simply be trumped by the desires of another; a sense of responsibility pervades the self and its relationships.

The conception of selfhood portrayed here sits loosely in the tradition of liberal-humanist theory of an on-going pre-existing self that lies at the centre of its world. And this shares something of a Cartesian turn in that the direction of movement for meaning-giving and for the disclosure of the self is from the inner to the outer, from the private to the public. While this conception has had a strong following in educational debate (notably in strands influenced by Romanticism), it is periodically challenged—often in ways that essentially seek to reverse this flow of meaning-giving from inner to outer. For example, writers such as Richard Peters (1970), Michael Oakeshott (1972) and Elliot Eisner (1998) in their different ways have placed weight on the cultural formation of mind, the public nature of the concepts that structure—that is, significantly constitute—the mind of the individual and the experience of which each is capable.

While in an important sense related, it is a distinctively different challenge that I wish to discuss in this chapter: one that moves beyond an acknowledgement that there are important senses in which the self as an individual centre of consciousness is necessarily structured, at least in part, by a social and cultural inheritance to the position of undermining and emptying the very notion of the self as a centre of consciousness.

2.

In a number of recent educational texts we are invited to see the self as existentially constituted by factors that are external to it, and as possessing little or no internally maintained steady identity. For example, there are those influenced by Michel Foucault and Judith Butler who see individual subjectivities as heavily and continuously constituted by discourse and the performative utterances and gestures of others, or who, influenced by Hannah Arendt and Emmanuel Levinas, see us as constantly entering the world by the grace of others who give us meaning. Here the direction of flow of meaning-giving and disclosure is from the outer to the inner. So to speak, it is not simply the outer but the 'other' that is posited as at the centre and as originative of selfhood. In this way the self becomes both decentred in the sense of losing its central epistemic position and de-nucleated in the sense that any supposed core or essence is removed. I wish to examine this radical evacuation of the interiority of the self and some of its educational implications.

It is my intention in this short essay to begin to open up some of the issues raised by such a flow reversal by initially referring to one well worked through example of its portrayal in an educational context. In his book *Beyond*

Learning: Democratic Education for a Human Future, Gert Biesta investigates the important issue of how we should conceive the subjectivity of the learner. In what initially one might construe to be a rather Heideggerian stance, he expresses an interest in the opportunities that educational institutions offer for individuals to 'come into presence' and sets out as his central premise that this coming into presence occurs when we initiate actions that are taken up by others who are capable of initiating their own actions. 'Action' here is meant in a particular sense taken from Hannah Arendt. It is distinguished from repetitive 'labour', on the one hand, and artefact producing 'work', on the other, and is conceived as 'the only activity that goes on directly between men without the intermediary of things or matter' and through which, by taking the initiative, beginning something anew, we reveal our unique personal identities (Biesta, 2006, p. 47). We reveal ourselves most fundamentally through those of our actions that directly affect others, and that by choice or necessity are taken up by them in some way (including, presumably, in responses of rejection).

But it must be noted that this is not conceived as the revelation of some *pre-existing* identity. On this account, the self only becomes clear for the other and for the self *in* the action. To quote Biesta:

> If I would begin something, but no one would respond, nothing would follow from my initiative, and, as a result, my beginnings would not come into the world and I would not *be* a subject. I would not come into the world. When, on the other hand, I begin something and others do take up my beginnings, I *do* come into the world, and in precisely this moment I *am* a subject. (p. 133)

This makes the domain of action—and, therefore, coming into presence—boundless and inherently unpredictable. It will always entail risk. We come into presence in a world of ever-arising beginnings and beginners. To initiate or pursue our own beginnings we always have to rely on the actions of these other beginners. Hence, coming into presence means coming into a world of plurality and difference. 'Our coming into the world structurally relies on the activities of others to take up our beginnings, yet others will always do so in their own, unpredictable ways' (p. 92). This constitutes the 'worldly space' by virtue of which we come into presence, and it gives us a way of thinking about our being with others in which plurality is not conceived as something to be overcome so that common action can become possible, but that makes our own being and our being with others possible and real in the first place. And although, in a sense, this situation frustrates the 'purity' of our beginning, following Arendt, it is held that this 'impossibility to remain unique masters of what [we] do' is at the very same time the condition—and the only condition—under which our beginnings can ever come into the world. Action, as distinguished from fabrication, is never possible in isolation. Arendt argues that 'to be isolated is to be deprived of the capacity to act' (cited in Biesta, 2006, p. 84).

It is important to note here that such occurrences are considered to be stymied by participating in 'strong' (i.e. norm-governed) communities such as a rational community, for it is held that here one slips into becoming a mere representative of its categories and norms rather than being a unique individual. This points to a fundamental tension within educational institutions, for notwithstanding this antagonism Biesta acknowledges that it is the legitimate business of schools to develop a rational community and thus it would appear that it is only when lapses and discontinuities of this occur that coming into presence can occur. Its location only in the interstices of school life raises questions as to how plausible phenomenologically it is for a worldly space to be maintained, given that Biesta portrays the superordinate environment in such antagonistic terms. While I will return to this point, it is worth noting here that it focuses attention on an issue that is fundamental to education: how to think the interface between the individual and what is to be learnt—and indeed, whether it is best thought as an interface at all, but rather in terms of some sort of continuity, the boundary between self and world in a significant sense having been dissolved. That is to say, the question of the character of educational engagement is raised.

To return, now, to the *leitmotif* of the thesis: the concern throughout is with the coming into the world of unique, singular beings whose thoroughly relational nature means that such entry is not be confused with mere self-expression. Rather, it involves entering the social fabric and thus responding to—and being responsible for—what and who is other, the question of the other *and the other as a question.* Overall this entails an essentially non-instrumental receptivity on the part of the learner—a listening and attentiveness to the other *as* other - and a certain violation of the sovereignty of the learner as they are challenged by difficult questions and difficult encounters entailed in entering a community of, as Biesta puts it, borrowing from Alphonso Lingis (1994), 'those who have nothing in common'. That is to say, those of whom one is to assume nothing, can know nothing, for presuming to anticipate others' beginnings would be to reify them and is necessarily hegemonic. This all means that education—along with all other genuine human interaction—is *inherently difficult* and at times discomforting. And for the teacher there is the additional challenge of responsibility without knowledge, for it would seem that she must take responsibility for the subjectivity of a learner that she does not and, indeed, cannot know. This view holds that the basic posture of education should be one of openness to different ways of being human; it therefore has to be *experimental* and *experiential*. The question of the humanity of human beings has to be taken up as a *practical* question, a question that requires a response with every new manifestation of subjectivity (Biesta, 2006, p. 106). It is not something to be determined by some pre-existing notion of human essence that posits a norm of humanness. The key question in genuinely human encounters is not *what* is present but *who* is present.

On this view, then, our being-with-others is primordial in that we are with others before we are with ourselves and furthermore it is ethical in that (following Levinas) it is characterised by a primordial responsibility—a responsibility that is held to be 'older than the ego' and that is not a matter of our choice, but is already identified from outside: we are *called* to be a responsible self. And the call is not to human being in general, it is *me* who is called by the other. The subject as a unique and singular being, as a 'oneself', comes into presence because it finds itself in a situation where it cannot be replaced by anyone else. There is a fundamental sense in which I exist in my service to the other; my subjectivity is a subjection to the other. Following Levinas, 'the subject is subject' (cited in Biesta, 2006, p. 52).

While certainly, on this view, it is not the sole task of education to maintain a space where freedom to come into presence can occur; it is one central task. And this space will need to be one of encounter and difference—indeed, following the logic of the argument, for Biesta, the ideal educational space will have the *urban qualities* found in Herman Hertzberger's conception of the 'city'—a space where we 'are continually preoccupied with measuring, mirroring and pitting ourselves against each other' because 'it is not we that determine who we are, but mainly others'. The 'aim' of the city is therefore 'to provide the opportunity for us to inspect, assess, keep an eye on and bump into one another' (p. 112). On this view we need schools built to facilitate such encounters that constitute the 'worldly space' in which we can come into presence as unique individuals.

3.

It seems to me that the above presents an internally consistent account that provokes a timely re-evaluation of what it would be for education to take seriously the subjectivity of students. The idea of a self as a coming into presence through initiating action taken up by others is seminal in a number of respects, for example, clearly having extensive implications for educational institutions from ethos to architecture. In foregrounding the relational nature of subjectivity and how growing as a subject is enriched by diversity of encounter, it brings out the disturbance and difficulty that are internal to education properly understood. True education is not a comfortable business. It is not about indulging the proclivities of some pre-existing fixed self. Nor is it the role of educational institutions to determine the selfhood of individuals through some heavily prescribed curriculum, but to create a space where, indeed, in some sense they can come into presence (see Bonnett, 1976; 1978).

The account also addresses a very pressing question: How to live with others who, in many significant respects, are not like us? Clearly at one level this is an issue of ever-growing importance as societies become more multi-cultural, and in the context of the ever more significant global society where we constantly encounter difference and the need to work *with* it. Biesta's account might be seen to provide a rather neat response by claiming that the other is a necessary condition of our own coming into the world and that we have a non self-chosen fundamental responsibility to respect the other, enable it to come into the world. Though the subjectivity of the other is something essentially unpredictable and beyond our control, we depend upon it for our own subjectivity. Yet the point goes deeper than this, for it draws attention to the need to recognise the otherness of those who, because of their familiarity, can too easily appear to be knowable, 'just like us'. Hence, essentially it seeks to imbue education with a sense of the unknown rather than the known. Again, this latter seems to me to be a very healthy attitude. Elsewhere, I have argued for the importance in education of being attentive to the fluid presencing of individuals on the grounds that such de-reification sensitises us to subtle qualitative aspects of an individual learner's current engagement with—that is, inherence in—the world and that this is a prerequisite of effective pedagogy (Bonnett, 2009b).

And certainly there is something highly persuasive about the key notion that takes seriously that human existence is 'being-with' and that the significance of our selves must at least in part be the product of the diversity of ways in which our initiations are taken up by others. Indeed, there would appear to be something stultifying about a life in which one's intentions ruled absolutely, one's plans were never disrupted, one's expectations never confounded, where routine ruled supreme, no difference or disruption ever occurring. A life insulated from all contingency, unpredictability and uncertainty—a life devoid of risk—would be a severely impoverished life; perhaps no life at all.

But what is it to come into the world—to 'come into presence'? Does it simply *mean* to have one's actions taken up by other agents? Are there not other ways in which one's subjectivity can receive recognition? And is there not an issue about the *way* in which others take up one's beginnings, from what perspective? Furthermore, exactly what is one to be open to in responding to another if the meaning of any action is in such a strong sense always deferred? Let me refine these concerns through a series of more specific points.

On the question of what is necessary for us to come into presence: can I not come into presence for myself in moments of self-awareness, and if so, in what sense do I require the otherness of others? The portrayal of Tess referred to in Section 1 recognises important dimensions of interiority and privacy to selfhood. It is one thing to make the participation of others a *formal* requirement in the sense that in principle the recognition of myself—me— requires a public language and culturally produced horizons of significance, and these are the product of others. It is quite another thing to make it an *occurrent* requirement—empirically my actions must be recognised by others on every occasion for me to come into presence on that occasion, as Biesta does. This would seem to be in flat contradiction with experience. And regarding this latter, while it is certainly true that one may experience a heightened sense of self-awareness when one feels oneself to be in the presence of others—one might indeed become, as we say, 'self-conscious'—equally there can be occasions when for some at least, solitude is as, if not more, effective in this regard. This also invites the question as to whether the other in her or his otherness always engenders self-revelation rather than self-concealment. Even when the other does not seek domination, but is simply making her or his own responsive 'beginning', this might be experienced as in some sense threatening. Experiencing the charisma or authority of others can readily become overweening and result in passivity and sometimes subjugation. A Levinasian claim that a certain uniqueness attaches to one's subjectivity through its irreplaceability in responding to the call of the other does little to ameliorate this.

Furthermore, are there not experiences of coming into presence in relation to the natural world—both in terms of a certain quality of being that can be experienced by the individual, and the quality of the entry into the world of nature as *quintessentially* 'other'? The towering anthropocentrism that seems to run through accounts of this kind needs to be appraised. The experiences of surprise and inherent mystery that encounters with aspects of nature can provoke and that can convey a heightened and humbling sense of one's own being are well attested and perhaps deserve greater provision in the activities and environment of the school than is often the case (Bonnett, 2009a). Such considerations lead to the question: do such, in a certain sense, performative accounts of subject constitution privilege the perspective of a particular 'cosmopolitan', 'urban', perhaps, 'extroverted' personality type? A thought lent weight in Biesta's case by the characteristics of Hertzberger's city that he uses to exemplify the qualities of a worldly space necessary to becoming a subject.

This relates to a further question: In what sense can the stranger's recognition bring me into presence in a fuller way than my neighbour or friend—that is, subjectivities characterised by what they share with me, what they have in common with me? Perhaps the stranger sees a new 'angle', but what of depth and intensity? Might not one who, say, is understood as having shared a traumatic experience with me, be able to recognise and respond to aspects of me—affirm me—in a way that those with whom I 'have nothing in common' cannot? Of course it would be presumptuous, and seriously limiting of subjectivity, if others attempt to *define* me by such things that they think they share with me. But this is not what is being said. The point is that on occasion someone characterised as friend might be better able to recognise my action for what it is than those with whom I have 'nothing in common'.

To be sure, a response to this last point might be that the idea of identifying an action for 'what it is' is one of the ideas that a view such as this seeks to challenge on the ground that its meaning is always deferred. Ideas of 'the death of the author' might readily be deployed. But surely what the initiator intended by her action is not to be completely dismissed in characterising it. While of course she cannot control how it is seen or taken up by others, what it meant to her is an important aspect of its being *her* action, an act of unique self-expression, having the quality of 'mineness'. This experience of agency is central to one's sense of one's existence and of 'inserting' oneself into the world, making oneself 'count'. It is part of the tragedy of *Tess* that her actions are frequently misconstrued and her own voice silenced in her encounters with others. Here again a point of considerable educational significance arises: the desirability of allowing a space for the (owned) voice of the student to be heard and respected, such that the perspectives that arise from her own emplaced life-world are allowed to play into the life of the school—that is to say, allowed to contribute to the conditioning of the worldly space that it offers.

But perhaps an even more fundamental question is now raised: To what extent is 'everyday phenomenology' of the above kind relevant to the argument? Biesta's account can be considered phenomenological insofar as it appeals to us to recognise what it describes in terms of our own experience—including our own sense of what is morally right—rather than exclusive appeal say to formal logic, etymologising, semantic meaning, or everyday usage. Yet, it might be claimed that the argument is intended to be understood as deeply structural—that is, as operating at an ontological level, say, on a par with Heidegger's ontological 'existentials' of *Being and Time*. This might be seen to render it immune to a phenomenological critique. It might be argued that all phenomenological descriptions reflect antecedent interpretations and thus are incapable of providing anything sufficiently primordial. On what basis is one to privilege one such description over another? Of course, a 'phenomenological reduction' of the kind once advocated by Edmund Husserl might be seen as a way of dealing with this criticism. By bracketing all everyday asssumptions of, say, the existence of what is perceived and focussing on the pure phenomenological content—intentionality—of what is given apodeictically in experience all such prejudices are eschewed and we truly get back to—apprehend—'the things themselves'. But this strategy has two problems. First, its ultimate destination, as Husserl (1969) recognised, is a transcendental meaning-giving subjectivity (i.e. transcendental idealism). But the positings of such a subjectivity become purely formal and hence unable to sustain—reconsti-tute—the things that we actually encounter in everyday experience. Second, and related to this, such a strategy represents an arbitrary prejudice against one of the most luminous and primordial qualities of experience: fundamentally we apprehend things (including ourselves) always as already in a world. Our consciousness is ineluctably 'worldly'. The everyday, in this sense, is not something to be circumvented or transcended in order to reach something more primordial, it is the raw 'data' with which ultimately all accounts have to accord. It is never to be dismissed. Taken from a different perspective—that of the nature of learning—that great advocate of the importance of experience in education, John Dewey, was surely right to require of education that the formal content of the logical disciplines be 're-clothed' in the experience of learners (Dewey, 1956). In *Being and Time*, Heidegger shows how his ontology accommodates the phenomenology of the everyday—indeed, that in a certain sense it is a necessary condition of such everyday experience. Whatever else coming into presence signifies, it cannot be something that denies everyday experience, and it should be something that either enriches or illuminates it.

The 'de-nucleating' of subjectivity in the presence of the other is intimately related to the matter of the banishing of the idea of a human essence. This now is an oft-encountered sentiment. But should the quarrel be not so much with the idea of a human essence *per se* as with totalising versions of what this might be? For does not any account of humanness assume or extol some version of human essence? Either it is legitimate to say that when we speak of a human being we refer to an entity that, for example, is capable of thought and feeling, has some sense of self-awareness and responsibility for its actions, or it is not. If it is not, how in the first place do we identify those entities that we encounter in the world that are deserving of the particular responsiveness that we should extend to human beings? To be sure, it is not that normally this identification is experienced as a conscious choice or decision, rather it is an implicit recognition that primordially structures our way of being in the world. But, because it must presuppose some (non-totalising) notion of essence in order to get off the ground, an account that denies such an essence—and despite itself—is in danger of increasing its operative power by positioning it beyond questioning.

Furthermore, the displacement of the idea of a grounding identity from the idea of subjectivity by a focus on spontaneity and openness to the other raise issues for the idea of authenticity. How is *my* openness to be distinguished from that of someone else? Are we in danger of being left with a sea of essentially ephemeral, un-rooted, actions? Sober reflection on one's history— the sediments of one's previous experiences and one's track record on particular matters—may play a significant role in becoming an authentic subject, and would be important to an education that takes seriously the idea of personal growth. Without this, is there not the possibility that what one takes to be one's openness—one's spontaneous action—is little more than a reflection of what Heidegger has called the 'they-self' (Heidegger, 1973, Sections 26–27, 35–37)? A danger exacerbated by an encouragement to read oneself off from the ways one's actions are taken up by others at large, which might in fact be 'crowd' responses? Heidegger provides an array of cautions concerning being grounded in such publicness. Overall, an account that eschews the idea of identity by de-nucleating the self renders ideas of being true to oneself either redundant or deeply mysterious, and in so doing both again dismisses a well-attested aspect of human experience and runs counter to the intuitive account of selfhood outlined in Section 1.

A move to criticise Enlightenment humanism for having too limiting (i.e. reifying) an understanding of what it is to be human is supported phenomenologically by the wide range of non-rational experiences—such as, on occasion, those of love, faith, compassion, repugnance, whose felt presence and power are not simply to be assessed rationally or summoned up and deployed, and that as modes of awareness and action can open up more than can be pre-conceived. Certainly education must beware imposing rigid and limiting conceptions of what it is to be 'more fully human' through pre-specified aims and objectives of the sort found in many 'rationally justified' curricula. There are many varieties and nuances of goodness. The teacher needs to be guided by her feel for an interplay of complex non-outcome defining values rather than aims of the foregoing kind. But a view that attributes so much of the character of the self to the other results in a very *thin* conception of subjectivity, attenuated, strung out across the myriad beginnings of others. Plurality in those who take up one's beginnings will mean that these beginnings will get taken up in a wider range of ways—that one comes into presence more richly in the sense of more diversely—but also, perhaps, more superficially. And ultimately what is the point of it? —Of becoming *dispersed* in such a way? What regard would and should we have for the 'other' conceived merely as passing actions rather than someone with an enduring identity? What are we to make of an individual whose existence is conceived only in terms of what we and others attribute to her actions and how we take them up—that is, has no identity independently of this?

Even in its own terms, an individual's recognition of another's action as one that does indeed take up *her* beginning is highly problematic. *What counts as taking up someone else's beginning?* How are we to know when it has or hasn't (perhaps, despite appearances) happened? Whose story is to be privileged? And if none is, if ultimately anything can count as taking up someone's action, does not the idea become vacuous? Talk of 'responsibility' for the other, listening to the other responsively, similarly eddies off into a disconnected circularity if the 'meaning' of the action amounts to no more than how a stranger takes it (up), however sincerely. This is a central issue to those forms of pedagogy that seek to relate to pupils as individuals, seeming to evacuate the idea of education of the individual of intelligibility.

All this returns us to a fundamental issue previously alluded to. Education needs to have values, a sense of what it is worthwhile introducing pupils to and inviting them to participate in and of what potentially counts as their development as a person. That is, it involves a sense of 'strong community'. I have noted that Biesta accepts this, but sees it as something that somehow proceeds separately from the coming into presence of the subject. But arguably participation in such worthwhile activities is not something to be juxtaposed to coming into presence, rather it is to be understood as an essential part of it. I have in mind here Michael Oakeshott's (1972) claim that self-disclosure and self-enactment occur through engagement with a civilised inheritance of enduring traditions of thinking. A view that separates development of self—capacities for coming into presence—from initiation into a strong community of cultural discourse would seem to herald a certain solipsism of its own. It also mystifies experiences of coming to feel that one has made aspects of one's culture one's own, and denies the legitimacy of an educational aspiration to develop in pupils a sense of the personal significance of what is learnt—a feeling for how it should affect their outlook and their sense of their own existence. This is an unfortunate outcome.

Early in this chapter I said that a phenomenological approach is apt to the topic of selfhood and education because of the salience of experience in understanding such phenomena. This is true in a way not demanded by understanding, say, abstract notions such as those of 'triangle' or 'quark'. Taking seriously the experiences of those involved in education, their own, usually implicit, sense of their human condition and the environment in which they find themselves, the meanings that their understandings have for them and drawing upon the rich range of resources that testify to this is a rebuttal of the quasi-scientific and managerial models of education that threaten to objectivate all and render invisible the fluid and felt realities of what is occurring in educational institutions. In addition, the general requirement that an educational analysis be at least consistent with—and better, illuminative of— everyday experience (which is not to deny that it might problematise it) can provide a brake upon theories and analyses that take off into a world of their own. It also acts as an impetus to students to evaluate what they read in terms of their own existence and the existence of others known to them by whatever means, and thus to engage personally with the issues at stake. Over recent years philosophy of education has been greatly enriched by attention to the writing of a much extended range of luminaries. Such openness is to be applauded. But sometimes the result has been too exclusive a focus on descriptive exegesis and history of ideas with relatively scant critical evaluation of the content of views from outside their own mutually supporting terms of reference—or, alternatively, where a series of compare and contrast exercises stands substitute for personal engagement. The dead hand of scholarship can lie heavy upon the fertile mind, diverting it from actively confronting issues through the enervating insinuation that yet more of what others have written must be absorbed before one can be in a proper position to articulate a view of one's own, and that a point is to be substantiated by the authority of some luminary rather than with arguments that one is willing personally to stand behind and defend—and that draw upon the wealth of experience that most are able to bring to bear if so encouraged. Phenomenology of the kind that I have adopted intimately involves the subjectivity of the thinker and is resistant to philosophy by proxy.

At this point, I hasten to add that the above are intended as general considerations, and are not directed in any wholesale way at the view that I have been examining in this chapter. And I have previously noted that it has phenomenological elements. But arguably its underlying preoccupation with a certain set of abstract normative ideal notions and aspirations without sufficiently referring them to experience in places risks vitiating potentially important insights. In particular, with the emphasis on the diffuseness, transience, ephemerality and sheer contingency of the occurrence of subjectivity through initiating action taken up by others, the dismissal of reification and essentialism that in certain senses is to be welcomed, seems on this and allied 'performative' understandings of selfhood to be achieved at the expense of anything sufficiently centred to be intelligible as a 'self', with the upshot that education must be cast as an essentially empty enterprise.

The issue of the presencing of unique subjectivities in their intimate relation with the presencing of others is seminal for education. It has profound significance for understanding the quality of space—intellectual, volitional, emotional, bodied—that occurs within schools as educational institutions, that is to say their qualities as *places* of education. But realisation of the rich potential of the exploration of schools conceived in this way requires the inclusion rather than the occlusion of the interiority of the individual. Proper account needs to be taken of what one might term the 'phenomenological self', with its own felt intentionality and intelligence that is both always potentially transformatively engaged and subtly existentially enduring.

ACKNOWLEDGEMENT

I am grateful to Claudia Ruitenberg for her very helpful comments on an early version of this chapter.

REFERENCES

Biesta, G. (2006) *Beyond Learning: Democratic Education for a Human Future* (Boulder, CO, Paradigm Publishers).

Bonnett, M. (1976) Authenticity, Autonomy and Compulsory Curriculum, *Cambridge Journal of Education*, 6.3, pp. 107–21, reprinted in N. Norris (ed.) (2008) *Curriculum and the Teacher: 35 Years of the Cambridge Journal of Education* (London, Routledge Education Heritage Series).

Bonnett, M. (1978) Authenticity and Education, *Journal of Philosophy of Education*, 12, pp. 51–61.

Bonnett, M. (2009a) Systemic Wisdom, the 'Selving' of Nature, and Knowledge Transformation: Education for the 'Greater Whole', *Studies in Philosophy and Education*, 28, pp. 39–49.

Bonnett, M. (2009b) Schools as Places of Unselving. An Educational Pathology?, in: G. Dall'Alba (ed.) *Exploring Education Through Phenomenology: Diverse Approaches* (Oxford, Wiley-Blackwell), pp. 28–40.

Dewey, J. (1956) *The Child and the Curriculum* (Chicago, University of Chicago Press).

Dewey, J. (1972) *Experience and Education* (New York, Colllier).

Eisner, E. (1998) Minding the Arts, Lecture given at University of Denver, Denver, CO.

Freire, P. (2000) [1970] *Pedagogy of the Oppressed* (New York, Continuum).

Heidegger, M. (1973) *Being and Time* (Oxford, Blackwell).

Hardy, T. (1992) [1891] *Tess of the d'Urbervilles* (Ware, Wordsworth Classics).

Husserl, E. (1969) *Ideas* (London, Allen & Unwin).

Lingis, A. (1994) *The Community of Those Who Have Nothing in Common* (Bloomington, University of Indiana Press).

Oakeshott, M. (1972) Education: The Engagement and its Frustration, in: R. Dearden, P. Hirst and R. Peters (eds) *Education and the Development of Reason* (London, Routledge & Kegan Paul), pp. 19–49.

Peters, R. S. (1970) *Ethics and Education* (London, Allen & Unwin).

5

Examples as Method? My Attempts to Understand Assessment and Fairness (in the Spirit of the Later Wittgenstein)

ANDREW DAVIS

> We can easily imagine people amusing themselves in a field by playing with a ball so as to start various existing games, but playing many without finishing them and in between throwing the ball aimlessly into the air, chasing one another with the ball and bombarding one another for a joke and so on. And now someone says: The whole time they are playing a ball-game and following definite rules at every throw.
>
> (Wittgenstein, 1958, # 83)

INTRODUCTION

Wittgenstein urges philosophers to scrutinise examples. 'Don't think, but look!' (Wittgenstein, 1958, ## 66–7). He believes that they should embrace the fine grain of events and processes rather than forcing phenomena to fit preconceived theories. The context is his famous discussion of family resemblance. We cannot discover something common to all games. Hosts of complex similarities obtain between pairs and small groups, with no unifying thread. Similarly, our linguistic activities are richly diverse, and we should not expect them to share any one feature. In this chapter I pursue my inquiries in the spirit of these injunctions. However, I also engage in argument of a more structured kind than that favoured by the later Wittgenstein. My explorations here revolve around the following questions: What forms of educational assessment are fair to all, and in what sense or senses?

I am going to comment on some of my philosophical manoeuvres. These observations are italicised. Sometimes I adopt a more informal tone than in the body of the chapter. Occasionally it was difficult to decide whether certain passages belonged in the main text or in this commentary.

For me, the opening epigraph from Wittgenstein sums up the intellectual situation at the heart of many philosophical problems, including some of those lurking behind policy issues in education. A number of educators and policy makers seem to think that definite rules are, or should be adhered to when we play the 'game' of fair educational assessment. Closer examination reveals that no such rules are or could be followed, and also casts light on some of the reasons for this.

Some Wittgenstein scholars may be inclined to point out that I am doing something different from Wittgenstein. There is little doubt that I am. Saul Kripke famously or infamously offered 'Wittgenstein's argument as it struck Kripke' (Kripke, 1981). He wanted to credit Wittgenstein with a very important set of reflections about the possibility of a private language, and yet he knew that Wittgenstein might well have rejected the interpretation concerned. Now in this chapter I am not offering my own 'versions' of Wittgensteinian arguments. However, my philosophical approach emphasises the detail of specific contexts and is often uneasy with overarching theory. I feel that this owes much to Wittgenstein.

The anti-essentialism of Wittgenstein's game example has a specific role in his later philosophy. It inspires me on a broader front to look at the detail and fine grain in educational assessment practices, and to take account of the complexities and inconsistencies to be found there.

When I speak of a 'more structured kind' of argument than that practised by the later Wittgenstein I don't mean that there are no deep and robust arguments to be found in his work. On the contrary. All I am saying here is that the style in which, for instance, the Investigations *is written is far removed from the step by step approach to argument development favoured by plenty of philosophers writing in the analytic tradition in the last few decades.*

Founding my inquiry on examples is shown to be especially important when examining these issues, given the wide range of situations to which they can be applied. I discuss a number of case studies involving assessment procedures, noting how they are criticised and sometimes changed for selected groups in the light of concerns about fairness. I work with a broad notion of 'example', where each case includes an assessment context, together with the cultural and political circumstances in which it is embedded. I refer to the overt and tacit values behind related policies and practices.

I also have an audience in mind. As a philosopher who often writes for a non-philosophical audience, I want to inform policy. My intended audience includes many people in educational research who interest themselves in questions of assessment and fairness. I am also concerned with those who devise assessment policies, whether at the school or Higher Education level. My style of philosophising is meant to be clear and accessible to them. Examples are particularly important, then, in bringing more complex points to light and exposing the kinds of confusion that can arise, especially where our thinking about these matters becomes too theoretical and abstract.

By attaching such importance to contexts I do not mean to imply that my approach 'leaves everything as it is' (Wittgenstein, 1958, # 124) (or, indeed, that Wittgenstein himself implied that everything is in order with our concepts and language). The function of examples in my writing reminds me of the role Wittgenstein accords to his primitive language games in his observation that

'The language games are . . . set up as objects of comparison which are meant to throw light on the facts of our language by way not only of similarities, but also of dissimilarities' (Wittgenstein, 1958, # 130).

This chapter says a good deal about *normative* aspects of assessment, and I do not think that all is well, normatively speaking, with current policies and practices. As far as I am concerned, real world attempts to secure fairness in assessment procedures may involve confusion, inconsistency and lack proper justification. Yet current practices comprise vital data for exploration, and must be examined on their merits rather than being marginalised in the interests of predetermined theories of fairness and justice.

So here I begin with examples but then develop some abstract lines of philosophical reasoning. The latter incorporate a critique of some of the jargon employed by empirical researchers and policy in relation to assessment. These terms include 'construct validity' and 'accommodation'. This feature of the chapter is typical of much of my writing in philosophy of education. I am constantly on the lookout for unwarranted certainties, both normative and conceptual, especially where such confidence damages the interests of students and teachers.

I pursue some negative theses about the application of fairness verdicts to educational assessment. I contend that no wholly coherent and consistent approach is possible. The opposite is sometimes assumed by those bringing accusations of unfairness. Moreover, even where the fairness of a given assessment process seems to have a significant value, the latter will often need to be weighed against other concerns when taking practical decisions about assessment policy. I discuss provision at the level of Higher Education, but also examine practices involving children at the primary stage. Themes and challenges that emerge from the first case study at university level re-appear in later contexts, but I do not expect any neat or codifiable results in terms of fairness and justice. Indeed, I anticipate tensions and even contradictions in how these ideas are applied.

DISABILITY ACCOMMODATIONS

I begin with familiar attempts to offer fair assessments to students thought to suffer from learning disabilities. For example, 'accommodations' are frequently given to 'dyslexic' students. Sometimes a rationale is supplied:

> - a variation in assessment methods should be allowed for a student who can achieve the specific learning objectives but is prevented by disability or specific learning difficulty from demonstrating this through the usual assessment methods. (University of Brighton, 2009)

The above is, of course, a quotation from a university's policy on assessment methods. It has no bearing on the reflections I offer during this chapter concerning my own philosophical 'methods'.

Such thinking seems to underlie most accommodations even where it is not made explicit. Now what is supposed to be 'unfair' about subjecting a dyslexic student to the same assessment process as other students? At first sight, this is a concern about the validity of the assessment process. It is believed that conventional forms of assessment fail to measure a dyslexic student's knowledge and understanding of the intended learning outcomes. Validity lapses can, apparently, be instances of unfairness.

I would argue that a necessary condition of the very coherence of this approach is that there is a clear difference between the actual possession of knowledge and understanding and the mere manifestation of it by means of successful test performance. The conventional concept of *construct validity* fits in nicely here. I understand construct validity in the usual way: a test is valid to the extent that it succeeds in measuring a relevant 'construct'.

> [A] question like Are IQ tests valid for intelligence? can only be posed under the prior assumption that there does exist, in reality, an attribute that one designates when using the term intelligence; the question of validity concerns the question of whether one has succeeded in constructing a test that is sensitive to variations in that attribute. (Borsboom, Mellenbergh and van Heerden, 2004, p. 1065)

So an intelligence test has construct validity if it measures how much intelligence a student has. 'Intelligence' itself is the construct. Constructs in the context of educational assessment are often conceptualised as 'traits', as unobservable but persisting aspects of mental life.

The view that validity failures linked to disabilities can be instances of unfairness sees students as possessing varying 'amounts' of relevant learning when tested. Conventional tests can detect the learning of most students. However, a minority labour under certain disadvantages associated with familiar disability labels such as dyslexia. The disadvantages block the usual manifestations of learning. Hence standard assessment devices cannot sample relevant performances and so fail to 'measure' cognitive achievement.

Often enough, fair treatment provisions seem eminently sensible so long as we embrace the idea that manifestations of a construct can be separated from the actual possession of that construct. Consider, for instance, the use of special spell checks, tinted glasses, a PC with software designed to support those with access problems, extra time, rest breaks, scribes and someone to read the exam questions. All this is consistent with the postulation of underlying cognitive traits whose manifestations are sometimes masked by specific constraints associated with learning disabilities.

However, the posited division between construct and manifestation is put under severe strain by some proposed accommodations. Markers may be advised to discount poor spelling and grammar. This assumes that such aspects of performance are separable from the cognitive achievements the assessments are supposed to be probing. Yet 'grammar' issues could range from the relatively superficial to matters impinging on the very coherence of the thinking in an answer. Now coherence of thinking is unlikely to be regarded as an optional component of any kind of cognitive achievement. 'Grammar' is represented in proposed accommodations as an aspect of manifestations only. Nevertheless, on closer examination it threatens to invade the territory of the relevant constructs themselves.

So does a sharp divide really exist between mere manifestations of knowledge comprising an underlying 'construct' and the construct itself? I think not. The 'gap' between putative manifestations and the underlying construct varies from case to case. It will always be a matter of degree. I speak metaphorically here, and arguably the very notion of a 'gap' is open to criticism. Whenever we judge a piece of behaviour to be a manifestation of knowledge or ability we are interpreting it as having qualities that are bound up with mental functioning underlying it. The supposed manifestation/construct divide represents just the kind of supposed opposition between the 'inner' private mental states and the 'outer' signs of these that Wittgenstein did so much to combat. For instance, saying that a pupil answers an arithmetic problem correctly is an interpretive judgement of an agent whose thought processes cannot be stripped away from the interpretation.

Admittedly a swimming test, for instance, does seem to sample the desired skills very 'directly'. Nevertheless, underlying the swimming performance *now* is, surely, a persisting complex of muscular and psychological states without which the performance would not be swimming. (Mere bodily movements might keep the body afloat, but not all bodily movements are swimming.) If the supposed divide between manifestation and underlying construct is not absolute but rather is a matter of degree, then arguably the conception of fairness as linked to construct validity is itself questionable. This is a serious threat to some standard rationales for accommodation.

Some guidelines for marking in Higher Education go even further than the typical accommodations just outlined. For example:

> For a very small number of severely dyslexic students there will be a continued difficulty with presenting their work in standard academic formats, such as the continuous argument of the essay. It may be more appropriate for some dyslexic students to present their work using bullet points . . .

And:

> The majority of students with dyslexia can . . . learn to present coursework in appropriate academic formats. However, within those forms, dyslexic students will continue to have difficulties with logical sequences of ideas and with moving smoothly from one point to another. We would ask that . . . markers do not penalise work of dyslexic students. (University of Greenwich, 2009)

Higher Education institutions may grant exceptions to accommodations of these kinds where it can be established 'which learning outcomes justifiably constitute competence standards, in which case the duty to make reasonable adjustments may not apply' (Bristol University, 2009). For instance, the statement from the University of Greenwich implies that in exceptional cases academic departments may be able to justify claims that providing 'continuous argument' is an essential feature of their learning objectives and so establish that they should not be expected to set this element aside in the interests of treating *any* minority group 'fairly'. However, Greenwich gives us to understand that normally, dealing with and presenting logical sequences of ideas can be detached from the knowledge, understanding and abilities sought by any given academic module and hence relevant accommodations can be offered.

Could Greenwich really put up a defence for that word 'normally'? What value could learning objectives possibly have when separated from logical sequences of ideas? Even if we put these doubts to one side for a moment, is it not obvious in any case that certain features of some learning programmes are bound to trump considerations relating to justice and fairness? Consider a non-academic example:

There is no duty in UK law to make 'reasonable adjustments' to the driving test for people with impaired vision. It is perfectly legitimate to expect satisfactory test performance from all putative drivers. Fairness considerations carry no weight here. Surely some programmes in Higher Education, especially those with a vocational focus might well be in a similar position. Suppose, for instance, despite strenuous efforts, it turned out to be impossible while accommodating certain kinds of disability to assess medical students' possession of knowledge and skills essential for their future role as doctors. In such a situation it is obvious that accommodations should be refused. Health concerns trump those relating to fairness in the sense under consideration.

Some readers may be surprised at the sudden departure from educational contexts here. My instinct is to assume that there is no sharp division between assessment practices within education and those obtaining elsewhere. Some situations outside education exemplify in an especially vivid fashion just how 'fairness' may be weighed against other values and found wanting. In the driving case, health and safety wins hands down. We return to education with a clearer view of the possible range of verdicts that can result from weighing 'fairness' against other concerns.

In any event, such policies depend in part on sustaining a distinction between test *modification* and test *accommodation* (Hollenbeck, 2002). Hollenbeck characterises modification as altering the test so much that the construct it assesses is changed. He cites a reading comprehension test where students read the items. Accordingly the test is said to involve the construct of 'silent reading comprehension'. If the test were changed so that the items were read aloud for the candidates then the new construct would be 'listening comprehension' (p. 396). I now argue that the distinction between modification and accommodation is conceptually insecure.

In our attempts to understand both accommodations and modifications we are actually disadvantaged by our capacity to coin phrases purportedly referring to constructs. Our hazy and indefensible intuitions suggest that linguistic differences between one phrase and another mark differences between the constructs to which they refer. So we may well think, with Hollenbeck, that the construct identified by 'reading comprehension' differs from that picked out by 'listening comprehension'. But how do we arrive at a criterion for deciding what counts as one construct rather than another? The ancients believed that 'the morning star' identified a different object from 'the evening star'. Astronomical science eventually remedied their error. Arguably there is nothing waiting in the wings capable of bringing off a similar feat for constructs. Some might hope that neuroscience could play this role, but I have elsewhere raised serious objections to this proposal (Davis, 2009). The arguments cannot be rehearsed here.

The widespread provision of extra time for students allegedly suffering from conditions such as dyslexia assumes that accommodation can be distinguished from modification and that we are dealing with accommodation. In the light of this it is disconcerting to discover that a reasonably persuasive argument can be developed for the claim that we are really dealing with modification here. I now develop this point.

I suspect that the next move may be particularly difficult for some non-philosophers to follow, but philosophers quite often engage in the kind of argument strategy I am about to offer. It involves pitting arguments against each other, with the intention of bringing out conceptual problems underlying current practice and the distinctions it assumes. I have already established that, according to current practice in educational assessment, the provision of extra time is supposed to be accommodation rather than modification. To test the robustness of this assumption, I mount a defence of the claim that it is, in fact, modification and not accommodation. It turns out that this contention looks quite plausible, but cannot be definitively evaluated, any more than the assumption it counters, namely that extra time is accommodation. When, in the course of philosophical explorations, we end up in this kind of confusing situation, we have made progress of a kind, or at least so I believe. We have good reason to suspect that shared underlying assumptions made by both sides of the argument are confused. Here, then, is the manoeuvre in question.

Speed of thought and response is often prioritised in ability tests developed in the West. Some other cultures take the opposite view, according to which rapid responses to a problem may well be a sign of stupidity rather than intelligence (see, for example, Sternberg, 2003). When we talk in this fashion we are, on the face of it, identifying a construct that can be separated from other aspects of cognition. According to the story, certain societies value selected cognitive functioning *and* speedy intellectual processing, while others prefer the cognitive functioning without the speed. If our attempts to make such references are coherent then extra time might well involve modification. Within a narrative pointing to modification rather than accommodation, tests with extra time measure constructs relating to cognitive thinking. They do not measure constructs for speedy thinking. So the provision of extra time means that the original test has been modified.

A counter-argument might run as follows. In just those cases where disabilities threaten the validity of the conventional test, modification is *not* involved after all. The candidate with the disability is held to be in possession of such and such a level of cognitive capacity. In the conventional test the disability prevents responses from providing a valid measure. With extra time, the disability is disarmed and the test can probe the relevant cognitive capacity. Any constructs relating to *speed* of cognitive response simply do not figure. They have no chance to play any role in generating test performances. On the other hand, according to this counter-argument under review, were candidates *without* the disability to be given extra time then mental speed traits would have a chance to influence performance. Suppose non-disabled groups in possession of equal cognitive capacities other than those to do with speed were compared. Imagine that Group A has a significant construct for speedy thinking, while Group B does not. If some of Group A are given extra time, they should perform no better than the rest of A who have the usual time. The former can think quickly and so do not benefit from having more time than their peers who also have the quick cognition construct. However, where candidates from Group B are given extra time, they might well do better than their Group B peers without the time allowance. For those lacking the speedy thinking construct, more time might well prove very helpful.

Needless to say, there are many obscurities in this rehearsed debate, not least the key idea of a construct responsible for speedy cognitive functioning. We have now reached a point where we can ask the final crucial question: How could the dispute between the verdict of accommodation and of modification possibly be settled? I do not think that this question can be answered. These problems are surely *conceptual* and stem from principled difficulties with ideas of 'construct' and the supposed distinction between accommodation and modification.

Let us continue to play around with the ideas of test validity and fairness for a little longer, despite our growing unease with the whole project of making sense of fairness in terms of test validity. Do other personal traits, over and above those attributable to learning disabilities, also threaten validity? For instance, some students are very anxious under test conditions. Moreover, a minority even have serious difficulties with handwriting. Cambridge University (2008) makes allowances for poor handwriting but only if this is 'caused by a disability or medical reason' (*sic*). We can only speculate on their thinking here. One account might run as follows: 'normally' a tacit component of *all* constructs tested at university level is the capacity to write by hand, for most examination candidates handwrite their answers. However, such a component is not regarded as central to university programmes and so can be set aside in certain circumstances. Failing to test for handwriting might even count as modifying the test. All the same, it is not thought to be important.

But why should poor handwriting 'caused' by a disability be regarded as an excuse, when the same degree of incompetence lacking a cause of this kind is not? If the disability is deemed to be an excuse because the candidate *cannot help it* then surely many other non-medical cases of poor handwriting are equally beyond the control of the individuals concerned. Similar questions arise in connection with the University of Wales (2006) suggestion that students may have 'additional exam arrangements' if suffering from 'increased anxiety as they have an underlying mental health issue'. Many would react sympathetically to this, feeling that this is 'fair' to such students because it ensures that the assessment process has the greatest chance of measuring what they know and understand. Yet, once again it is unclear why *only* states of anxiety linked to health issues trigger special treatment. A plausible case can be made that people become anxious in a wide range of situations, most of which cannot be said to involve medical conditions, and at least some of which are not under their control.

Another familiar criticism of accommodations is that they are unfair because they threaten the *reliability* of the assessment process. The special treatments offered to certain types of candidate may well not be applied consistently. If a candidate is having her question read for her, one reader may use much more appropriate expression than another (Pitoniak and Royer, 2001). Moreover, in so far as we can make sense of learning disabilities such as dyslexia, such conditions are not all or nothing. People suffer these afflictions with varying degrees of severity. It is arguably 'unfair' to give a severely dyslexic student the same amount of extra time as another who is only mildly afflicted. Some dyslexic students need 'more' accommodation than others. Needless to say, it is even *more* unfair to highlight disabilities such as dyslexia if we cannot in principle be clear about what counts as suffering from such a condition, or if related existence claims lack adequate empirical evidence. I cannot pursue this issue further here.

My interim conclusion is that if accommodation policies rest on ideas of fairness linked to test validity then they are open to serious philosophical criticism. The salient concept of 'construct' is flawed, and the assumed divide between the performances sampled by a test and the underlying construct supposedly measured, cannot be sustained. Moreover, even if accommodation policies based on fairness as validity could be defended, practical educational decisions must still be informed by other values too, values that sometimes outweigh fairness considerations. This is something that defenders of the 'rights' of disability groups do not always seem to recognise.

I am ready to move to another worked example. I have chosen one involving motivation; my examples and explorations began with constructs focusing on cognitive achievement and ability, but the reflections on student anxiety are already pointing up the crucial importance of the affective domain for fairness issues in the context of assessment practices.

UNFAIRNESS AND THE MOTIVATION OF CANDIDATES

Seven years ago the National Curriculum Key Stage 2 reading tests for eleven-year-olds in England were described by the National Primary Heads Association as 'biased' and unfair on the following grounds: the text was factual, presented in a magazine format and offering 'bite-sized chunks' (Henry, 2001). Two years earlier, similar complaints had been made about the spider-related content, and the inclusion of cartoons. Sudden improvements in boys' scores over girls were attributed to the incorporation of material held to be more appealing to boys than girls.

First of all I will attempt to run the standard validity narrative as a way of explaining and justifying the complaint of the Primary Heads: The tests are unfair to girls in the following way: Let us assume that male and female students possess equal amounts of the relevant reading construct. The girls' lack of enthusiasm for the content prevents their performances from fully manifesting their reading competence. In this account, lack of enthusiasm functions similarly to a learning disability.

This account is very obviously open to challenge. Why choose the explanation in terms of a deficit? Perhaps we should instead be talking about the boys' unfair advantage. Why not speak of test validity being threatened by the boys' enthusiasm for the content—they perform *too well?* This is counter-intuitive, to say the least, but if performance is still seen as separable from underlying construct, how can it be ruled out?

The very possibility of alternative stories here gives us a major problem. How are we supposed to choose between one verdict according to which girls have an affective deficit that undermines the capacity of the test to measure their reading abilities, and a second verdict crediting boys with an affective advantage that also damages the validity of the test? The difficulty here again points to conceptual confusions embodied in how the situation is being characterised. I suspect that the villain of the piece is the construct–manifestation division.

So this is yet another example of a philosophical strategy that I have already highlighted; rehearsing the possibility of plausible defences of each of two incompatible claims, and explaining the lack of a route to a verdict favouring either one of the claims. Again, I draw the conclusion that hidden incoherence underlying both claims is the source of the difficulty in taking either side in the dispute.

Arguably there are more ways in which the original complaints could be articulated. For instance, it could be said that the test was *modified* by the presence of the boy-friendly content, the latter changing the construct concerned. After all, there is no reason why constructs should not include stable or relatively stable aspects of motivation, interest, and dispositions to find given material enjoyable. The boy-friendly test picks up on certain of these affective elements, and, unsurprisingly there are changes in the relationship between boys' and girls' scores in comparison with the results of the reading tests in previous years. (To consider this possibility at all we have to set aside the problems with the accommodation/modification distinction already rehearsed.)

Such a change in construct might be good or bad, but is it obviously *unfair* and, if so, in what sense? Some might concede that altering the tests in the light of boys' predilections does indeed count as a modification, and that the modified test is an improved test. Others might dispute this improvement verdict, though it is not at all clear how they could do so on the grounds that it was *unfair* to modify it. We might concede this much to critical commentators: any verdict that boys really had improved their reading in comparison with girls in the year of the 'boy-friendly' material would be open to serious question.

Let us try again on behalf of the primary heads. If, in a particular culture, there are some motivational patterns associated with boys, and others associated with girls, then is a test catering for masculine rather than feminine motivation obviously unfair? I cannot see why. It could be urged instead that differential performances linked to gender should be tackled during schooling so that the group lacking certain motivations and interests 'catch up' with the other group. (Which group should 'catch up' would depend on value judgements other than those relating to fairness.)

Yet another problem with this whole approach is the arbitrariness of the categories and performance differentials picked out for concern. Gender is, of course still a high profile political issue. Nevertheless, we might find that other factors such as geographical origin, wealth or position in family also figured in how interesting children found given content.

Again, the upshot of this discussion is that conceptual problems rule out the very possibility of articulating clearly and defending convincingly some everyday verdicts about the fairness of educational assessment. This simply echoes the results of our treatment of the accommodation issues.

UNFAIRNESS IN MUSIC CONSERVATOIRES

I continue my strategy of exploiting distinctive examples: I am eager to compare recruitment processes of specialist conservatoires with those of Higher Education more generally. Should conservatoires weigh the fairness of assessment processes against other values differently from conventional universities? If they do not, are there grounds for suggesting that they should?

Over the last few years there have been complaints about the fact that students at Britain's music conservatoires such as the Royal Academy of Music and the Royal College of Music do not represent society at large. There is talk of 'under-represented groups', and pressure on these institutions to widen participation. Several conservatoires combine outreach activities, junior music schools, targeted scholarships and other initiatives to combat the 'problem'. However, they also argue that there is really very little they can do. Aspiring musicians need the benefit of resources and cultural capital in their families from the very beginning.

The Royal Northern College is reported to offer auditions to every applicant to ensure that potential rather than achievement is assessed (Morris, 2006). This worthy aim is highly controversial. On the face of it, the supposed distinction between potential and achievement is particularly hard to support here, since, arguably, applicants' potential is very closely linked to their existing achievements. Their 'velocity' on application plays an important part in their subsequent musical accomplishments. (The very coherence of this point, of course, depends on the possibility of making sense of 'potential', 'velocity' and so on.)

Compare this with selecting for conventional academic courses in Higher Education. Institutions such as Bristol University take account of applicants' schools' track records in addition to standard performance indicators such as 'A' level grades. They are presumably trying to identify 'potential', construed as some kind of general academic ability. Perhaps, or so the thinking behind such a policy might run, certain independent schools are too good at generating high exam scores in their students, thus successfully masking rather modest 'academic potential'.

Can we run a parallel account for musicians? Does it make really make sense to suggest that some instrumental teachers have been too successful with their pupils, thus interfering with the capacity of conservatoires to identify true *potential* for top-flight performance across applicants from all sectors of society?

We need to return to the phrase 'under-represented groups', and the implication that the conservatoires are not 'fair' to applicants in some sense. Terms such as 'elitist' and 'middle class' are often used, as if these were serious criticisms. If the composition of the student bodies does not reflect society at large, but is skewed towards the rich and away from the offspring of those lower in the socio-economic stakes, this is held to be 'unfair'.

Now it should be noted that, rightly or wrongly, those conservatoires committed to outreach have already conceded at least two points: first, that it is appropriate to construe unfairness as failure to tap 'potential'; second, that unfairness of this kind is at work in some fashion in the processes through which people in the United Kingdom become, or fail to become, professional musicians. However, in making these concessions the conservatoires need not be acknowledging a lack of fairness in their assessments of applicants. Instead they may be endorsing the criticism of the whole education system's role in developing musicians.

Why would it be 'fairer' if a group of putative professional violinists matched society at large? Does this apply to *all* professions and other employments? Should judges match the rest of us in terms of gender, ethnicity, socio-economic background and so on? Some have argued just this. But what about nurses, shop assistants, carers in homes for the old folk, refuse operatives, bus drivers and estate agents?

So even within an in-depth consideration of an example of assessment—that is, the assessment for recruitment into music conservatoires, I have recourse to an almost surreal variety of sub-examples in order to give advance notice of serious problems in the application of some of the conventional notions of fairness. My particular target at this stage turns out to be the idea of meritocracy. I want to show that rival conceptions of fairness need to be given house room.

Let us turn for a moment to the long debated idea of meritocracy (Young, 1958), of 'careers open to talents' and some notion of equality of opportunity to compete for desirable employment, associated economic success and status. As I noted above, the conservatoires could perhaps be construed as sharing this kind of aspiration for society in their attempts to 'make up' for earlier deficits by offering outreach activities of various kinds.

If we accept the 'fairness' of a meritocracy, and Higher Education's key role in channelling those with suitable merits into rewarding jobs, we might begin to generate an argument to the effect that the student mix in Higher Education should reflect society at large. Crucial assumptions here are, of course that conceptions of 'merit' and 'potential' make sense and that groups classified according to ethnicity or culture do not possess inherent and fixed differences in terms of 'merit' or 'potential'.

Perhaps this was one element in the thinking of the University of California in the famous Bakke case (Oyez Project, 1978). Given the racist history of the United States, relatively few ethnic minorities found their way into prestige professions such as medicine, and hence the university felt it was 'fair' to attempt to tweak their assessment of applicants in favour of, for example, African Americans. The latter, on this interpretation of the policy, had just as much potential to become doctors as any other group, and hence whatever was needed to ensure that potential was realised should be done.

Becoming a professional musician in the UK may not be the most obvious example of a route to economic success; yet, on some kind of meritocratic perspective, fair competition for this career might still be thought to be an important symptom of a just society. So on this view the distribution of violinists in a conservatoire should, ideally, mirror that of groupings in society at large.

Even so, many types of employment are unlikely to inspire similar arguments. This very point could be argued to be profoundly depressing. Indeed, it could be urged that it constitutes an *objection* to fairness construed as 'merit' winning through. It should be noted that it is perfectly possible to envisage society embodying laws and customs in which the less attractive employment roles are distributed equitably. This would be 'fair' in some sense, but not fair in the conventional sense of a meritocracy where the talented secure the 'best' jobs. In a fair society that did not construe fairness as meritocracy, a scientist might have to spend some time as a refuse operative, a company director serve for a period as a hospital ancillary dealing with bed pans, and so on. The novelist Ursula Le Guin (1974) explores an idea along these lines. Such thought experiments challenge the fairness of a meritocracy.

Literature, and especially science fiction often provides an important source of thought experiments that can fruitfully be deployed in the course of philosophical reflection. Le Guin's world in The Dispossessed *does not exist, and hence in a literal sense this is not an example. Nevertheless, her imaginary universe is extremely convincing and robust because of her qualities as a writer. Accordingly, it supplies something akin to real-world examples. When we engage with her 'subcreation' (Tolkien, 1964) we realise that there* could *be societies where fairness and justice worked very differently from the way they do in our own, even if it is supposed that in this fictional society people retain much of their real-world psychology and aspirations. We can test our normative intuitions and reasoning by taking these thought experiments seriously.*

It is important to note, however, that philosophy has often been criticised for using bizarre thought experiments as 'intuition pumps' (Dennett, 1993)—the term is pejorative, and refers to fictions carefully devised and presented by philosophers to evoke intuitive agreement from their readers. Those fantasies most open to objection are very obviously far removed from the world in which we live. Such abuses of thought are not recent; they have a very long history in philosophy. John Locke (1690), in investigating personal identity, wondered what the situation would be ' . . . should the Soul of a Prince, carrying with it the consciousness of the Prince's past Life, enter and inform the Body of a Cobbler as soon as deserted by his own Soul . . . '.

In Wittgenstein's later philosophy he also offers us a wealth of imaginative illustrations, some of which are 'real world' examples while others have varying degrees of fantasy built into them.

There is another familiar problem about linking fairness to 'appropriate' representation of all groups in prestige professions. Critics of affirmative action policies have long pointed out the serious dangers of inappropriate essentialisms about the groups singled out for special treatment. If we are thinking of the Bakke case or others flowing from it in the USA we should not think of African Americans as invariably of low-economic status and with limited educational aspirations for their offspring. On the contrary, families of many African Americans are comfortable middle class people with plenty in the way of worldly goods and strong expectations that their children will pursue higher education. It is 'unfair', or so the critics of group essentialisms argue, to identify applicants *as members of particular groups.*

Opponents of affirmative action often say that individuals should be treated on their own merits. Moreover, individual members of favoured groups are as likely to be concerned about special treatment as anyone else. They may well wish to be admitted to higher education on the basis of their own talents. Note, however, that such sentiments prioritise fairness as equality of opportunity in a meritocracy. We have already recognised that other understandings of fairness are possible.

Moreover, the 'equality of opportunity' associated with meritocracy is often claimed to be mere 'formal equality of opportunity', ensuring that places in Higher Education and in high status professions are open to all applicants who satisfy clear and transparent criteria. People are supposed to succeed on 'merit'. Such equality of opportunity differs significantly from 'equality of fair opportunity' (Rawls, 1971) in which people should not be disadvantaged by gender, ethnicity or socio-economic background. However, even on the Rawlsian view, 'native talent' is still supposed to win through, whatever the person's background. So it is still a matter of luck—children do not deserve their 'potential', and hence even this might still be regarded as 'unfair'. Why is the word 'merit' used *at all*? (See, for example, Nagel, 2003 for discussion.)

Needless to say, if we allow ourselves to raise more radical doubts about the justice of a meritocratic society, then this undermines associated verdicts about fairness in those educational assessment practices linked to 'careers open to talents'. Classic unease relates to qualms about the distribution of rewards and esteem among various types of employment and between those who are employed and those who are not. Some are unemployed by their own folly while others are made redundant through no fault of their own, are unable to work because of health problems, or cannot work because they have serious learning difficulties. The important point here is that equality of opportunity comes in a range of guises. Moreover, it is not the one and only self-evident account of fairness and justice in society and in how educational assessment should be framed.

What emerges from the discussion of this section is that criticisms of conservatoires on the grounds that their recruitment is 'unfair' are not only highly contestable but, what is worse, reliant on notions of justice in society about which there is no consensus and for none of which exist definitive arguments. Moreover, the standard accounts of the situation still make much use of contestable and obscure ideas of 'potential' and 'talent'. As in the earlier discussion, conceptual difficulties abound, together with unjustifiable and ambiguous notions of fairness and justice.

UNFAIRNESS IN 11-PLUS SELECTION

In the UK the 11-plus exam has long been argued to facilitate social mobility. Supporters point to famous achievers who have risen from humble origins via their local grammar school, and who otherwise would have been 'trapped' by their social antecedents. Despite fierce criticism of the system over many decades, some pupils still take this examination at the end of the primary stage, hoping to attend one of the remaining grammar schools. Recent research points to the examination involving 'social selection' (for instance, Atkinson, Gregg and McConnell, 2006). Middle-class children receive more coaching than their working class peers. Coaching boosts scores, and enhances chances of gaining the coveted grammar school places. Terms such as 'bias', 'elitist' and 'skewed selection' are used in connection with this phenomenon. The defence of the exam asserts or implies an association between the identification of potential and the promotion of social mobility.

First thoughts suggest that we are confronted once again with fairness as validity, an idea that we have already understood to bristle with difficulties.

Test performances of heavily coached candidates do not afford valid measures of the qualities required of grammar school students. Social mobility is highlighted because it is believed that where proper account is taken of pupils' *potential* (probably, and contestably conceived of as some kind of generic intelligence in the context of the 11-plus) then pupils from poor backgrounds will sometimes join the professional classes.

However, we may wonder whether this account does justice to the concerns of the critics. Is there some sense in which they value social mobility for its own sake? Is movement from low socio-economic backgrounds into 'high status' employment *per se* thought to be a mark of a fair society? Is it felt to have an inherent value, regardless of validity questions relating to the exam? Earlier we made a passing reference to the Bakke case and noted a meritocratic interpretation of the University of California's policy. There is a non-meritocratic understanding too. It attributes intrinsic value to a distribution of groups in higher education and prestige professions that mirrors the population at large, a value that is, on this alternative construal, held to be independent of the *potential* of the people concerned. Ronald Dworkin notes: 'our schools have traditionally aimed to improve the collective life of the community ... by helping to make that collective life more just and harmonious' (Dworkin, 2000, p. 403).

Similarly, critics of 11-plus coaching may be concerned about the distribution of 'kinds' of people in society, at any one time and over a period of time. However, it is difficult to pin down and justify such social ideals. In the Bakke case the whole issue of race was to the fore, together with the history of the United States in that regard. Social mobility in the United Kingdom in 2009 is not about race. Why should it be considered inherently valuable for upward mobility to be promoted regardless of whether it has anything to do with 'talent winning through'? Moreover, when seeking to promote the mobility of different kinds of people, how can we justify highlighting any one way of categorising them, given that our options include geographical origin, socio-economic status, appearance, gender, sexual orientation and religion? Perhaps different categories should have a higher profile than they do now. What about short people, those with ginger hair or those with summer birthdays[1]? And the difficulties do not end here. Evidently, encouraging mobility linked to some of these categories may not be compatible with a different kind of mobility rooted in other categories.

CONCLUSION

Applications of 'fairness' to educational assessment reveal a rich minefield of conceptual and normative obscurities and inconsistencies.

This, I believe, vindicates the style of philosophising from contexts and examples.

Confident verdicts about what is and what is not fair often depend on other ethical and political assumptions that are hard to justify and are in tension with each other. The value concerns that emerge from an examination of contexts exhibit features of Wittgensteinian family resemblance; similarities between cases can be strong, but no dimension of fairness links *all* of them. Equality of Opportunity resembles, but also differs from Equality of Fair Opportunity, which in turn resonates in some ways *but not in others*, with notions of diversity and mobility in society.

The conceptual issues may be summarised as follows. I have questioned whether there is a clear division between underlying knowledge and understanding, on the one hand, and its manifestation in tests, on the other. Yet I also showed that this division is vital for the very coherence of fairness construed as securing the validity of assessment processes for minorities with disabilities. Moreover the notion of a construct, and whether it should be restricted to cognition rather than affect has also been shown to raise intractable difficulties. Furthermore, I was unable to defend any kind of robust distinction between accommodation and modification, even though this is required if fairness is to be linked to the construct validity of tests.

Turning to the domain of the ethical and political: it emerged that judgements about the fairness of assessment hinge on verdicts about justice in society, and these, of course, are deeply contested, though this is rarely conceded explicitly by those bringing accusations of unfairness. Ideas of potential, talent and merit are often assumed by proponents of fairness but they are obscure and controversial. Hence there cannot be any kind of 'self-evident' verdicts about the fairness of the assessments themselves.

Fundamental difficulties in clarifying and defending judgements about fairness rehearsed in this chapter cannot be overcome by improving assessment processes. The problems have two main sources. The first is in the realm of conceptual confusion.

To the extent that this chapter has been about psychological constructs as well as moral and political ideas, I note Wittgenstein's observation at the end of the Investigations: 'For in psychology there are experimental methods and conceptual confusion' (Wittgenstein, 1958 p. 232). The problem with 'constructs' in psychology triggers a further Wittgensteinian aphorism: 'Misleading parallel: psychology treats of processes in the psychical sphere, as does physics in the physical' (Wittgenstein, 1958, # 571).

The second is the proliferation of over-simplified normative judgements that lack the self-evidence their protagonists sometimes assume. None of this points to the death of educational assessment, but it strongly suggests that it should be as 'low stakes'[2] as possible.

NOTES

1. In the UK and some other countries, children with summer birthdays have less time in school than their classmates with birthdays nearer to the beginning of the academic year in September. Much research indicates that summer birthday children suffer long-term disadvantage.

2. 'Low stakes' contrasts with the familiar 'high stakes assessment'—that is to say, tests whose results crucially affect the medium and long-term future of those who are subjected to it, and/or of those who are held to account for its results. In England, schools and even individual teachers are subjected to assessment with this flavour. So 'low stakes' assessment, by way of contrast, could be 'assessment for learning' rather than 'assessment for accountability'.

REFERENCES

Atkinson, A., Gregg, P. and McConnell, B. (2006) The result of 11+ Selection: An Investigation into Opportunities and Outcomes for Pupils in Selective LEAs. Centre for Market and Public Organisation, Bristol. Online at: http://www.bristol.ac.uk/cmpo/publications/papers/2006/wp150.pdf (accessed 29 January 2009).

Borsboom, D., Mellenbergh, G. and van Heerden, J. (2004) The Concept of Validity, *Psychological Review*, 111.4, pp. 1061–1071.

Bristol University (2009) Code of Practice for the Assessment of Students on Taught Programmes: 8 Assessment and Disability. Online at: http://www.bristol.ac.uk/esu/assessment/codeonline.html#disability (accessed 29 January 2009).

Cambridge University (2008) Undergraduate Examination Allowances: Information for Candidates. Online at: http://www.admin.cam.ac.uk/offices/exams/students/allowances_and_warnings_2008.pdf (accessed 29 January 2009).

Davis, A. (2009) Ian Hacking, Learner Categories and Human Taxonomies, in: R. Cigman and A. Davis (eds) *New Philosophies of Learning* (Oxford, Wiley-Blackwell), pp. 83–97.

Dennett, D. (1993) *Consciousness Explained* (London, Penguin Science).

Dworkin, R. (2000) *Sovereign Virtue* (Cambridge, MA, Harvard University Press).

Hollenbeck, K. (2002) Determining when Test Alterations are Valid Accommodations or Modifications for Large Scale Assessment, in: G. Tindal and T. Haladyna (eds) *Large Scale Assessment Programs for all Students* (Mahwah, NJ, Lawrence Erlbaum Associates), pp. 395–425.

Henry, J. (2001) Boy-friendly Tests Unfair, Say Heads, *Times Educational Supplement*, 25 May.

Kripke, S. (1981) Wittgenstein on Rules and Private Language, in: I. Block (ed.) *Perspectives on the Philosophy of Wittgenstein* (Oxford, Blackwell), pp. 238–312.

Le Guin, U. (1974) *The Dispossessed* (New York, Harper and Row).

Locke, J. (1690) *An Essay Concerning Human Understanding*, Book 2, Chapter 27, Section 15 (London, Penguin Classics).

Morris, S. (2006) Conservatoires: Can They Shake Off Their Inaccessible Image?, *The Independent*, 23 March.

Nagel, T. (2003) Rawls and Liberalism, in: S. Freeman (ed.) *The Cambridge Companion to Rawls* (Cambridge, Cambridge University Press), pp. 62–85.

Oyez Project, (1978) Regents of the University of California v. Bakke, 438 U.S. 265 (1978). Online at: http://www.oyez.org/cases/1970-1979/1977/1977_76_811/ (accessed 29 January 2009).

Pitoniak, M. and Royer, J. (2001) Testing Accommodations for Examinees with Disabilities: A Review of Psychometric, Legal, and Social Policy Issues, *Review of Educational Research*, 71.1, pp. 53–104.

Rawls, J. (1971) *A Theory of Justice* (Cambridge MA, Harvard University Press).

Sternberg, R. (2003) *Wisdom, Intelligence, and Creativity Synthesized* (Cambridge, Cambridge University Press).

University of Brighton (2009) Disability and Dyslexia Examinations and Assessments. Online at: http://www.brighton.ac.uk/disability/assessments.php?PageId = 352 (accessed 29 January 2009).

University of Greenwich (2009) Guidance for Lecturers Marking the work of Students with Dyslexia. Online at: http://w3.gre.ac.uk/students/affairs/dd/staff/marking.htm (accessed 29 January 2009).

Tolkien, J. (1964) On Fairy Stories, in *Tree and Leaf* (London, Unwin Books).

University of Wales (2006) Exam Protocol: Additional Provision and Support for Disabled Students and Students with Dyslexia. Online at: http://www.uwic.ac.uk/disability/students/Exam_protocol_students.htm (accessed 29 January 2009).

Wittgenstein, L. (1958) *Philosophical Investigations* (Oxford, Blackwell).

Young, M. (1958) *The Rise of the Meritocracy* (London, Thames and Hudson).

6

Witnessing Deconstruction in Education: Why Quasi-Transcendentalism Matters

GERT BIESTA

> Deconstruction is not a method and cannot be transformed into one.
> (Derrida, 1991, p. 273)

INTRODUCTION: THE END(S) OF DECONSTRUCTION

If 1967 was the year when Jacques Derrida burst onto the philosophical scene with the publication of three texts that became important reference points for late-20th-century philosophy—*De la grammatologie (Of Grammatology)*, *L'écriture et la différence* (*Writing and Difference*) and *La voix et le phénomène (Speech and Phenomena)* (Derrida 1967a; 1976; 1967b; 1978; 1967c; 1973)—1997, when Woody Allen released his film *Deconstructing Harry*, was perhaps the year when the word that made Derrida famous became firmly established in popular culture and, through this, in everyday language. Indeed, nowadays many seem to use the word 'deconstruction' as little more than a synonym for critical analysis,[1] without being aware of the very specific meaning the word has in Derrida's work. The Oxford English Dictionary is no exception to this as it defines 'deconstruction' as a 'strategy of critical analysis associated with the French philosopher Jacques Derrida ... directed towards exposing unquestioned metaphysical assumptions and internal contradictions in philosophical and literary language'.

Although Derrida has questioned the very possibility of defining what deconstruction is—claiming that 'all sentences of the type 'Deconstruction is X' or 'Deconstruction is not X' *a priori* miss the point, which is to say that they are at least false' (Derrida, 1991, p. 275, emphasis in original)—my problem with the depiction of deconstruction as a form of critical analysis is not so much that it tries to pin things down.[2] It is rather that equating deconstruction with critical analysis misses one of the main points of Derrida's work; namely, his questioning of the traditional philosophical gesture in which the philosopher positions himself on some safe ground outside of the scene of analysis. As Derrida has put it in an interview with Richard Kearney, one of the main questions that has motivated his writing has precisely been 'from what site or non-site (*non-lieu*) philosophy [can] as such appear to itself as other than itself, so that it can interrogate and reflect upon itself in an original manner' (Derrida, 1984, p. 108). This is why we cannot simply depict deconstruction as a form of critique because 'the instance of *krinein* or of *krisis* (decision, choice, judgement, discernment) is *itself* ... one of the essential "themes" or "objects" of deconstruction' (Derrida, 1991, p. 273, emphasis added). Deconstruction always aims 'at the trust confided in the critical, critico-theoretical agency, that is, the deciding agency', which means that in this regard 'deconstruction is deconstruction of critical dogmatism' (Derrida, 1995, p. 54; see also Biesta and Stams, 2001).

Starting, then, from Derrida's statement that deconstruction 'is not a method and cannot be transformed into one' (Derrida, 1991, p. 273)—which may be bad news for all the 'deconstructionists' and aspiring 'deconstructionists' out there—I will try to argue in this chapter that the 'end' of deconstructionism as a method or technique is actually good news as it paves the way for a different relationship with deconstruction. Following Geoffrey Bennington's suggestion, I will refer to this relationship as *witnessing* and, more specifically, as witnessing metaphysics-in-deconstruction (Bennington, 2000, p. 11). Witnessing metaphysics-in-deconstruction not only hints at a set of activities that is different from 'critical analysis' but also suggests a different attitude, one that is affirmative more than destructive and that is ethico-political more than that it operates on the plane of cognition and rationality.[3] In what follows I will try not only to indicate what it might entail to witness deconstruction in education and education-in-deconstruction, but also to make clear how and why this matters educationally. In the final section of this chapter I will turn to the question of philosophy of education, not only to articulate more explicitly how philosophy of education might be 'done' if it wishes to take inspiration from Derrida's writing, but also to hint at some reasons why philosophy of education may also need to be 'undone' a little. Let me begin, though, with some words about deconstruction.

METAPHYSICS-IN-DECONSTRUCTION: A WITNESS REPORT

One way to start reading Derrida is through his critique of metaphysics—bearing in mind that the meaning of 'critique' will be displaced in the attempt. Derrida has argued that the history of Western philosophy can be read as a continuous attempt to locate a fundamental ground, a fixed centre, an Archimedean point, which serves both as an absolute beginning and as a centre from which everything originating can be mastered and controlled (see Derrida, 1978, p. 279). He has suggested that ever since Plato this origin has been defined in terms of *presence*—that is, as an origin that is self-sufficient and fully present to itself; an origin that simply 'exists'. For Derrida the 'determination of Being as *presence*' is the very matrix of the history of metaphysics, a history that coincides with the history of the West in general (see Derrida, 1978, p. 279). This is why he has argued that it could be shown 'that all the names related to fundamentals, to principles, or to the center have always designated an invariable presence' (ibid.). Here we should not only think of such apparent fundamentals as 'God' or 'nature'. For Derrida *any* attempt to present something as original, fundamental and self–sufficient— and for Derrida such origins include both 'consciousness' (for example, in Kant or Hegel) and 'communication' (for example, in pragmatism or Habermas)—is an example of what he refers to as the *metaphysics of presence* (see Derrida, 1978, p. 281). The metaphysics of presence includes more than just the determination of the meaning of being as presence. It also entails a *hierarchical axiology* in which the origin itself is designated as pure, simple, normal, standard, self–sufficient and self–identical, so that everything that follows from it can only be understood in terms of derivation, complication, deterioration, accident and so on.

Why is the metaphysics of presence a problem? This is actually quite a difficult question to answer and in a sense Derrida's whole oeuvre can be seen as a series of attempts to develop an answer this question *and*—and the 'and' is very important here—to reflect on how and from where an answer can be given. One line in Derrida's writing centres on the observation that presence always requires the 'help' of something that is not present; that is, something that is absent. What is 'present' is therefore constituted 'by means of [the] very relation to what it is not' (Derrida, 1982, p. 13). 'Good', for example, only has meaning because it is different from 'evil'. One might argue that 'good' is originary and that 'evil' is secondary and has to be understood as a lapse or fall, as the absence of good—and there are powerful narratives in Western culture that indeed follow this pattern. But as soon as we try to define 'good' without any recourse whatsoever to a notion of evil, it becomes clear that the presence of 'good' is only possible because of its relationship to what is not good; namely, 'evil' (for this example see Lucy, 2004, p. 102). This shows that 'good' does not exclude 'evil' but is necessarily contaminated by it. Stated in more general terms, it reveals that the 'otherness' that is excluded to maintain the myth of a pure and uncontaminated original presence is actually constitutive of that which presents itself as such (see also Bennington, 1993, pp. 217–8). We could say, therefore, that the 'thing' that makes 'good' possible (i.e. 'evil') is the very 'thing' that also undermines it and makes it impossible. Or in more philosophical terms: that the condition of possibility of 'good' is at the same time a condition of *im*possibility. It is this strange—or in more technical terms: quasi-transcendental—'logic' to which Derrida sometimes refers as 'deconstruction'. Whereas transcendental philosophy aims to articulate conditions of possibility and leave things there, deconstruction concerns the 'oscillation', the necessary *and* impossible combination of conditions of possibility and conditions of impossibility (see also Caputo, 1997).

Looking at it this way shows that deconstruction is not the activity of revealing the impossibility of metaphysics (see also below). It also shows that deconstruction is not something that Derrida does or that other philosophers can do after him. Deconstruction is rather something that 'occurs'. Or, in Derrida's own words: '"[D]econstructions", which I prefer to say in the plural ... is one of the possible names to designate ... what occurs [*ce qui arrive*], or cannot manage to occur [*ce qui n'arrive pas à arriver*], namely a certain dislocation, which in effect reiterates itself regularly—and wherever there is something rather than nothing' (Derrida and Ewald, 2001, p. 67). This not only helps to explain why deconstruction is not a method and cannot be transformed into one. It also shows that, in a sense, all deconstruction is 'auto-deconstruction' (see Derrida, 1997, p. 9)—deconstruction 'occurs', whether we want it or not. But that doesn't mean that there is nothing to do in relation to deconstruction. While it's not up to us to let deconstruction happen or prevent it from happening, what we can do—and what Derrida has done many times in his writings, for example, in relation to notions like presence, meaning, the gift, democracy, friendship and justice—is to show, to reveal, or, as Bennington (2000, p. 11) has suggested, to *witness* the occurrence of deconstruction or, to be more precise, to witness *metaphysics-in-deconstruction*. Witnessing the occurrence of deconstruction means to bear witness to events of which the condition of possibility is at the very same time the condition of impossibility.

Why would it be important to witness metaphysics-in-deconstruction? The most straightforward answer to this question is that we should do this in order to bear witness to what is made *in*visible by a particular presence but is nonetheless necessary to make this presence possible. It is to do justice to what is excluded by what is present. It is to do justice to the 'other' of presence (see Biesta, 2001)—which is one reason why Derrida has claimed that 'deconstruction *is* justice' (Derrida, 1992, p. 35; see also Biesta, 2003). This already suggests that the point of deconstruction is not negative or destructive but first and foremost *affirmative* (see Derrida, 1997, p. 5). It is an affirmation of what is excluded and forgotten; an affirmation of what is *other* (see also Gasché, 1994). Another way of putting this is to say that deconstruction wants to open up the metaphysics of presence—or, for that matter any system—in the name of what cannot be thought of in terms of the system and yet makes the system possible. This means, however, that the point of deconstruction is not simply to affirm what is known to be excluded by the system. What is at stake in witnessing metaphysics-in-deconstruction is an affirmation of what is wholly other, of what is unforeseeable from the present. It is, as Derrida puts it, an affirmation of an otherness that is always to come, as an event that 'as event, exceeds calculation, rules, programs, anticipations' (Derrida, 1992, p. 27). In this sense it is not simply an affirmation of who or what is other, but rather of the *otherness* of who or what is other. Deconstruction is an opening and an openness towards an *unforeseeable* in-coming (*l'invention*; invention) of the other, which is why Caputo has suggested that we might characterise deconstruction as a form of 'inventionalism' (see Caputo, 1997, p. 42). In some places Derrida refers to this as 'the impossible'. For Derrida 'the impossible' is not what is *im*possible but what cannot be foreseen as a possibility (see also Biesta, 2001).

It is important to see that all this does *not* amount to an attempt to overcome, to do away with or to destroy metaphysics. Whereas Derrida wants to put the metaphysical 'gesture' of Western philosophy into question, he states that his approach is different from Nietzsche's 'demolition' of metaphysics or Heidegger's 'destruction' (*Destruktion* or *Abbau*) (see Derrida, 1991, pp. 270–1). Nietzsche, Heidegger, and all the other 'destructive discourses' in Western thought wanted to make a total break with the metaphysical tradition. They wanted to end and to overcome metaphysics. Derrida believes, however, that such a total rupture is not a real possibility because if we were to leave metaphysics behind, we would have nothing to stand on and no tool to work with: 'There is no sense in doing without the concepts of metaphysics in order to shake metaphysics. We . . . can pronounce not a single destructive proposition which has not already had to slip into the form, the logic, and the implicit postulations of precisely what it seeks to contest' (Derrida, 1978, p. 280). While Derrida wants to 'shake' metaphysics, he acknowledges that this cannot be done from some neutral and innocent place 'outside' of metaphysics. He acknowledges that we cannot step outside of the tradition, since that would leave us without any tools, without even a language to investigate, criticise and 'shake' metaphysics—it would even leave us without a place to stand. What is more to the point, therefore, is to say—in simple words—that Derrida wants to shake metaphysics by showing that it is itself always already 'shaking', by showing, in other words, the impossibility of any of its attempts to fix or immobilise being through the presentation of a self-sufficient, self-identical presence. This is what witnessing metaphysics-in-deconstruction is about. The act of witnessing can, however, be performed only from the 'inside'—or at least *not* from some kind of neutral, uncontaminated position outside of the system. In this respect Derrida clearly rejects the traditional philosophical 'position' of the philosopher as the outside-spectator, the one who oversees the universe without being part of it. This is precisely why Derrida has identified the question as to 'from what site or non-site (*non-lieu*) philosophy [can] as such appear to itself as other than itself, so that it can interrogate and reflect upon itself in an original manner' (Derrida, 1984, p. 108) as central for his 'project'.

DECONSTRUCTION IN EDUCATION—EDUCATION-IN-DECONSTRUCTION

Are there signs of deconstruction occurring in education and of education-in-deconstruction? And if there are, why would it matter to bear witness to such signs? Let me begin with the first question and relate this to some of my own writings on education.

One theme I have pursued through a number of publications is that of the role of communication in educational processes and practices. The question I have asked in relation to this is how education is possible (see, for example, Vanderstraeten and Biesta, 2001; 2006; see also Biesta, 2004; Osberg and Biesta, 2008; Osberg, Biesta and Cilliers, 2008). In one respect the answer to this question is simple in that we can say that education is made possible through communication—most notably the communication between teachers and students, although it can be argued that textbooks, curricula and school buildings, to name but a few educational artefacts, also try to communicate something to students. A common way to theorise communication is through the so-called sender–receiver model. Here communication is conceived as the transmission of information from one place (the sender) to another place (the receiver) through a medium or channel. It includes processes of encoding on the side of the sender in order to put the information in such a form that it can go through the medium or channel. It involves processes of decoding on the side of the receiver in order to transform the encoded information back into its original state.

While the sender–receiver model might be an adequate way to describe the transportation of bits of information from one location to another—it's very useful, for example, to describe how information from a television camera ends up on the television screen at home—I have argued that it is an inadequate model for understanding human communication. The main reason for this is that human communication is not about the transportation of *information* but about the exchange of *meaning*. In the sender–receiver model 'decoding' is seen as just a technical matter: that of taking away the 'packaging' that was needed to send the information safely from one location such as the TV studio to another location such as the home. What is omitted in this account, however, is not only what is happening in front of the camera but also, and more importantly, the fact that for the meaning of what is happening in front of the camera to 'arrive' at the other end, someone actually needs to watch the screen and make sense of what is being seen. What we find at the 'end' of human communication, therefore, are processes of interpretation and sense-making rather than simple unpacking and retrieving.

This reveals that there is a fundamental flaw in the sender-receiver model, at least if it is being used as a model to understand human communication, as it is based on the assumption that the meaning of information is attached to the medium that carries the information—that is, that the meaning of a book is in the book, that the meaning of a lecture is in the words spoken, that the meaning of a curriculum is in the curriculum, and so on—so that identity of meaning between sender and receiver is just a technical matter, just an issue of *transportation*. As soon as it is acknowledged, however, that meaning is *not* something that we passively receive but that we actively (though not necessarily always consciously) ascribe—we give meaning *to*, we make sense *of*—it becomes clear that the sender–receiver model omits the most crucial part of human communication; namely, that of the interpretation of the 'message' (which then ceases to be just a message) on the side of the 'receiver' (who then ceases to be just a receiver).

If we look at educational communication from this angle we can already begin to see that what makes such communication possible—interpretation— at the very same time threatens to make communication impossible. The reason for this is that the interpretations on the side of the 'receiver' *are* never completely determined by the intentions of the 'sender' and also *can* never be completely determined by the intentions of the 'sender' for the very reason that even if the 'sender' were to articulate his or her intentions explicitly, these would always need to be interpreted by the 'receiver' as well.[4] Educational communication—but for that matter any form of human communication—is therefore not a matter of give and take, but more a matter of give and mis- take. It is here that we can begin to see deconstruction occurring in education in that the condition of possibility of educational communication appears to be at the very same time its condition of *im*possibility. This is not to suggest that educational communication is *not* possible; what it rather highlights is *how* educational communication is possible—namely, on the basis of a strange, deconstructive 'logic'.

If this is so, why, then, might it be important to highlight the occurrence of deconstruction in education? Why might it be important to witness the event of education-in-deconstruction? Let me now turn to this question.

OPENINGS, CLOSURES, AND IN(TER)VENTIONS

The deconstructive nature of educational communication suggests that there is a certain 'slippage' in the processes of education, that there is an imperfection or weakness, so we might say, a certain 'opening' that occurs each time we engage in education. From one angle this is pretty irritating. If we want to teach our students that 2 and 2 makes 4, if we want them to learn how to drive a car, how to weld, how to administer anaesthesia, if we want them to understand how the convention of the rights of the child came into existence, what racism is and why it is wrong, what democracy is and why it is good, what evolution theory and creationism are about, or why deconstruc- tion is not a method and cannot be transformed into one, our aim is to get it 'right' and, more importantly, our aim is for our students to get it 'right'.[5] Teachers have a special 'trick' for getting it right. It is not called effective teaching but *assessment* (see Biesta, 2008). Assessment is the mechanism that constantly tries to close the gap between teaching and learning. It does this by saying 'this is right' and 'this is wrong'—and, more often, by saying 'you are right' and 'you are wrong'. In a sense it is as simple as that. But because the slippage is there all the time, achieving closure in education requires an enormous amount of effort. Looking at the financial and human resources societies put into this 'project', one can begin to get a sense of the force of this little opening that occurs 'wherever there is something rather than nothing'

(Derrida and Ewald, 2001, p. 67).[6] Of course, societies invest in this project because they believe that they have it right and because they believe that it is important for the next generation to get it right as well—which is precisely where Dewey started his discussion of education in *Democracy and Education* (Dewey, 1966).

To witness deconstruction in education is thus first of all helpful in order to understand why education as a 'project' requires so much effort. But the point of witnessing deconstruction is not about identifying its occurrence in order then to effectively tame it. There is, as I have shown, something more at stake, which is the fact that this little opening called 'deconstruction' can also be an entrance for the in-coming of something unforeseen. Derrida connects these points very helpfully in a discussion of J. L. Austin's speech act theory (see Derrida, 1988). Austin is concerned with the question how performative speech acts—speech acts that try to 'do' something rather than that they are intended to convey meaning—can work successfully. Austin acknowledges that performative speech acts always run the risk of failure. Austin, however, sees such failures as accidents, as events that our outside of 'normal' human interaction. This is why he puts a lot of effort into specifying the conditions under which performative speech acts can work—conditions, so we might say, that must be met before we can engage successfully in performative speech acts (see Derrida, 1988, pp. 14–5). Derrida, on the other hand, suggests that if the potential failure of performative speech acts is *always* a possibility, then we should perhaps see this 'necessary possibility' of failure as constitutive of rather than as the exception of performative speech acts. Derrida takes up this issue in the context of a wider discussion about the conditions of possibility of communication more generally, particularly in relation to the question of the 'context' of communication (p. 2).[7]

The reason for suggesting that the risk of misunderstanding should be seen as constitutive of communication rather than as something external to it stems from Derrida's observation that the only way in which we can guarantee 'perfect' communication—that is, communication in which there is an identity between what the speaker intended to convey and what the listener 'receives'—is when the context in which such communications disseminate is exhaustively determined (p. 18). Derrida argues, however, that this can never be an empirical reality because in order for communication to be possible there needs to be interpretation—that is, 'receivers' need to make sense of what is being communicated. Derrida thus argues that communication is, in this regard, a fundamentally open process and to claim otherwise—as he sees Austin trying to do by taming the unpredictability of communication—is maintaining an 'idealized image' and 'ethical and teleological determination' of the context in which communication occurs (p. 17). The general risk or failure therefore does not surround language 'like a kind of *ditch* or external place of perdition which speech ... can escape by remaining "at home", by and in itself'. On the contrary, this risk is 'its internal and positive condition of possibility' (ibid.).

The plausibility of Derrida's argument becomes clear when we imagine a situation in which language would be *without* risk. In such a situation communication would have become a strictly mechanical, a strictly calculable and predictable process. Under such conditions it would actually be meaningless to intervene in social interaction by means of speech acts. In such a mechanistic universe an utterance such as 'I promise' would add nothing to the interaction, because all the possible consequences of any action would already be determined and would already be strictly transparent for all other actors, whose own reactions would already be determined as well. The fact that speech acts can always and structurally fail therefore suggests that human communication is *not* mechanistic but that it is an *event*.

The importance of these considerations does not so much lie in Derrida's account of the fact that communication relies on interpretation and therefore can always go 'wrong.' It rather relies in his insight that if communication would go 'right'—that is, if the connection between input and output, between utterance and response, between teaching and learning, would be perfect—we would have ended up in a completely *deterministic* universe in which there is actually no reason for communication as utterances and responses would simply be mechanically connected. This is first of all a universe in which there is nothing to learn. Yet it is also a universe in which there is no possibility for anything new to emerge on the scene. It's a universe in which invention, in-coming, is no longer a possibility. If we take away the risk involved in communication—and perhaps Derrida would say: if we were able to take away the risk involved in communication—we therefore also take away the opportunity for the in-coming of the other as other. Derrida's insistence on the necessary role of misunderstanding in communication should therefore not be read as a plea for a release from the rules and constraints of interpretation and understanding—a kind of 'hermeneutics free-for-all' (Norris, 1987, p. 139)—but as motivated by a concern for the impossible possibility of the invention, the in-coming of the other. The 'point,' in other words, is an ethical and political one but it is, therefore, also an educational one. Let me briefly explain.

Teachers sometimes jokingly say that their job would be so much easier—and could be so much more effective—if they could do it without students. But what may seem the administrator's heaven should be the educator's nightmare *if*, that is, the interest of education is not exclusively in the reproduction of what exists—in the insertion of 'newcomers' into existing social, cultural, political, religious, economic, cognitive and other orders—but is also an interest in the 'coming into the world' of something new, of 'new beginnings' and 'new beginners' to use Hannah Arendt's terminology.[8] The simple question, then, is whether we value such inventions—which always announce themselves as interventions (see Fryer, 2004)—or not. The simple question is whether we think that education should *only* be a big reproduction machine, or whether we think that education should *also* express an interest in what we might perhaps best refer to as human *freedom* (see also Biesta, 2007).

If the latter is the case, then it might matter that we witness the occurrence of deconstruction in education, as this may point us towards openings that can be a potential entrance for the event of freedom.

DOING AND UNDOING PHILOSOPHY OF EDUCATION

In the preceding pages I have engaged in a form of writing on, in and to a certain extent against education that takes inspiration from the work of Derrida. I have tried to demonstrate that such writing is not about the application of a method called 'deconstruction' to educational issues. The most important reason for this lies in the simple fact that deconstruction is not a method and cannot be transformed into one. Deconstruction, to repeat Derrida's point one more time, is rather 'one of the possible names to designate ... what occurs [ce qui arrive], or cannot manage to occur [ce qui n'arrive pas à arriver], namely a certain dislocation, which in effect reiterates itself regularly—and wherever there is something rather than nothing' (Derrida and Ewald, 2001, p. 67). This means, as I have argued, that if we want to use a deconstructive 'register' in our writing we should not aim to deconstruct anything, but should rather engage in witnessing the *event* of deconstruction. I have not only tried to make clear what it might mean to do this, but have also made a case for why I think that witnessing the event of deconstruction in education—that is, trying to point at those moments where conditions of possibility and impossibility 'cross' each other and in their crossing provide a deconstructive opening—matters educationally. Here, my main point has been to argue that a deconstructive opening can become a deconstructive entrance, an entrance for the incoming of something new, something unforeseen—or, in more 'personal' terms, someone new, someone unforeseen. I have articulated the interest in such inventions as a 'genuine' or 'proper' educational interest, although I wish to add that to name this interest as an educational interest is not to suggest that it has always been and will always be an educational interest. It is an interest with a very particular and very specific history (see Biesta 2006; 2007), which means that one of the questions it raises is whether we want to identify ourselves with and take a certain responsibility for this history or not.

Whereas Derrida's writing therefore does not offer philosophers of education a method, it definitely has something to offer and in my own work I have tried to take up this offer and run with it, so to speak. But would those writings count as philosophy of education? Let me, in conclusion, make two observations about this in order to (dis)locate the discussion in this chapter within the context of 'philosophy of education'.

The first has to do with the question of philosophy in the idea of philosophy of education. As I have mentioned at the very beginning of the chapter, Derrida's own work is not simply a continuation of a particular tradition of philosophy but is a form of philosophical writing or writing philosophy that at the very same time raises deep and important—and in a sense unsettling—questions about the very possibility of 'doing' philosophy. Whereas, on the one hand, Derrida defends the unconditional right of philosophy to ask critical questions (see, for example, Derrida, 1994), he also, on the other, turns this right onto philosophy itself by asking from what site or non-site philosophy can appear to itself as other than itself 'so that it can interrogate and reflect upon itself in an original manner' (Derrida, 1984, p. 108). It is my view that in this 'move' Derrida transforms philosophy's right to ask critical questions into a responsibility for the affirmation of the impossible, unforeseeable and incalculable event of the in-coming of the other. This transformation puts philosophers in quite a different position, not only in relation to themselves and their traditions and activities, but also, when they take the guise of philosophers of education, in relation to education. In this respect we might say, therefore, that an engagement with Derrida's writings is more than just the adoption of a particular philosophical stance in one's activities as a philosopher of education. It also undoes and unsettles a little what philosophy of education is or might be. It is important to note that this unsettling does not take place at a cognitive level—after all, that kind of unsettling has always been the business of philosophy—but at an ethico-political level. Derrida's writing comes with a responsibility, so to say—a responsibility that I would be happy to characterise (and actually have characterised in my work) as an *educational* responsibility.

This brings me to my second observation that stems from the question how we might be able to identify such a responsibility as an *educational* responsibility. The problem here has to do with the very idea of 'philosophy of education'. 'Philosophy of education' is not only a phrase consisting of three English words—which means that we should not assume that anything that tries to translate itself into these three words can actually be translated that simply.[9] The idea of 'philosophy of education' belongs to a very particular, Anglo-American construction of the field of educational studies, one in which this field is seen as that of the interdisciplinary study of educational phenomena (see, for example, Tibble, 1966). Philosophy here takes the position of one of the 'foundational disciplines' for the study of education, together—at least traditionally—with history, psychology and sociology. The problem with this configuration is not that these disciplines—and others that have been added since—have nothing important to say about education. The problem rather is that when they speak about education they tend to do so with their disciplinary voice. Hence sociology of education asks sociological questions, psychology of education psychological questions, history of education historical questions and philosophy of education philosophical questions. But if this is so, then one important question emerges: Who asks the educational questions? Unless we are to believe John Dewey who simply (and imperialistically) claimed that educational questions are by definition philosophical questions and vice versa—which, as a good deconstructionist would point out, already relies on the very distinction between philosophy and education that it wants to overcome, I have tried to show in this chapter that in order to see the educational significance of what follows from deconstruction we need to do more than just apply Derrida's 'philosophy' to the 'field' of education. We also need to have a sense of where and why we might find this field. In this way Derrida also helps us to see the occurrence of deconstruction in the idea of 'philosophy of education'—which means that doing philosophy of education 'after' Derrida also requires some undoing of the very idea.

NOTES

1. With the exception, perhaps, of the recipe for 'deconstructed banoffee pie' (see http://www.channel4.com/food/recipes/occasions/dinner-parties/come-dine-with-me/series-6/deconstructed-banoffee-pie_p_1.html).
2. After all, there is as such nothing wrong with pinning things down as long as we do not forget why we did it in the first place. Or, in a language that stays closer to Derrida: there is nothing wrong with laws as long as we do not assume that they can fully embody justice—there may always be 'more' or 'different' justice just around the corner (see Derrida, 1992).
3. For such an ethico-political reading of Derrida's work in the context of education see the contributions in Biesta and Egéa-Kuehne (2001); see also Peters and Biesta (2009).
4. This point goes back to a discussion within hermeneutics about the question whether the intentions of the author—or in this case the sender—can serve as the arbiter for the correctness or truth of the interpretation. Gadamer (1994) would object to such an objectivist ambition of hermeneutics, arguing that the open character of interpretation means that the most we can achieve is an ongoing 'fusion of horizons'. Derrida, as I will indicate below, radicalises this insight by questioning whether communication does indeed start from the self-transparent intentions of an author (see also Derrida, 1976; 1988).
5. I believe that it is important to acknowledge that 'getting it right' is part of what education is for. The only important point not to forget, however, is that 'getting it right' is only *part* of what education is about, so that, without connection to other functions and purposes of education 'getting it right' becomes as problematic as any other one-sided view (see Biesta, 2009).
6. In this regard there is a strong similarity between the practice of education and the practice of government, as government has to deal with the same slippage as education has, and tends to make efforts of a similar scale to 'tame' this slippage.
7. The reason why Derrida moves from a discussion of performative speech acts to wider questions about understanding and misunderstanding partly has to do with his claim that whereas Austin sees a sharp distinction between the two, his approach actually ends up in a situation where it is not possible to maintain this distinction, so that in Austin 'performative communication becomes once more the communication of an intentional meaning' (Derrida 1988, p. 14; see also p. 16 and p. 19).
8. In my book *Beyond Learning* I have made a detailed case for seeing 'coming into the world' as a central educational category and concept (Biesta, 2006).
9. This becomes even more of a problem when acts of 'counter-translation' occur and *Bildungstheorie* becomes renamed as *Philosophie der Erziehung*—for example.

REFERENCES

Bennington, G. (1993) Derridabase, in: G. Bennington and J. Derrida, *Jacques Derrida*, G. Bennington, trans. (Chicago, The University of Chicago Press).

Bennington, G. (2000) *Interrupting Derrida* (London, Routledge).

Biesta, G. J. J. (2001) 'Preparing for the Incalculable': Deconstruction, Justice and the Question of Education, in: G. J. J. Biesta and D. Egéa-Kuehne (eds) *Derrida & Education* (London, Routledge), pp. 32–54.

Biesta, G. J. J. (2003) Jacques Derrida: Deconstruction = Justice, in: M. Peters, M. Olssen and C. Lankshear (eds) *Futures of Critical Theory: Dreams of Difference* (Lanham, MD, Rowman and Littlefield), pp. 141–54.

Biesta, G. J. J. (2004) 'Mind the Gap!' Communication and the Educational Relation, in: C. Bingham and A. M. Sidorkin (eds) *No Education Without Relation* (New York, Peter Lang), pp. 11–22.

Biesta, G. J. J. (2006) *Beyond Learning: Democratic Education for a Human Future* (Boulder, CO, Paradigm).

Biesta, G. J. J (2007) Who is Afraid of Education?, *University of Tokyo Center for Philosophy Bulletin*, 10, pp. 25–31.

Biesta, G. J. J. (2008) Five Theses on Complexity Reduction and its Politics. A paper presented at the Annual Meeting of the American Educational Research Association, New York.

Biesta, G. J. J. (2009) Good Education in an Age of Measurement, *Educational Assessment, Evaluation and Accountability*, 21.1, pp. 33–46.

Biesta, G. J. J. and Egéa-Kuehne, D. (eds) (2001) *Derrida & Education* (London, Routledge).

Biesta, G. J. J. and Stams, G. J. J. M. (2001) Critical Thinking and the Question of Critique: Some Lessons from Deconstruction, *Studies in Philosophy and Education*, 20.1, pp. 57–74.

Caputo, J. D. (ed.) (1997) *Deconstruction in a Nutshell. A Conversation with Jacques Derrida* (New York, Fordham University Press).

Derrida, J. and Ewald, F. (2001) 'A Certain "Madness" Must Watch Over Thinking': Jacques Derrida's interview with François Ewald; D. Egéa-Kuehne, trans, in: G. J. J. Biesta and D. Egéa-Kuehne (eds) *Derrida & Education* (London, Routledge), pp. 55–76.

Derrida, J. (1967a) *De la grammatologie*. Collection Critique (Paris, Minuit).

Derrida, J. (1967b) *L'écriture et la différence* (Paris, Seuil).

Derrida, J. (1967c) *La voix et le phénomène: Introduction au problème du signe dans la phénoménologie de Husserl* (Paris, Presses Universitaires de France).

Derrida, J. (1973) *Speech and Phenomena, and Other Essays on Husserl's Theory of Signs*, D. B. Allison, trans. (Evanston, IL, Northwestern University Press).

Derrida, J. (1976) *Of Grammatology*, G. C. Spivak, trans. (Baltimore, MD, The Johns Hopkins University Press).

Derrida, J. (1978) *Writing and Difference* (Chicago, The University of Chicago Press).

Derrida, J. (1982) *Margins of Philosophy*, A. Bass, trans. (Chicago, University of Chicago Press) [*Marges de la philosophie* (Paris, Minuit, 1972)].

Derrida, J. (1984) Deconstruction and the Other: An Interview with Jacques Derrida, in: R. Kearney, *Dialogues with Contemporary Continental Thinkers* (Manchester, Manchester University Press), pp. 105–26.

Derrida, J. (1988) *Limited Inc.* (Evanston, IL, Northwestern University Press).

Derrida, J. (1991) Letter to a Japanese Friend, in: P. Kamuf (ed.) *A Derrida Reader: Between the Blinds* (New York, Columbia University Press), pp. 270–76.

Derrida, J. (1992) Force of Law: The 'Mystical Foundation of Authority', in: D. Cornell, M. Rosenfeld and D. Carlson (eds) *Deconstruction and the Possibility of Justice* (London, Routledge), pp. 3–67.

Derrida, J. (1994) Of the Humanities and the Philosophical Discipline: The Right to Philosophy from the Cosmopolitical Point of View, *Surfaces*, IV, 310 Folio 1.

Derrida, J. (1995) *Points . . . Interviews, 1994* (Stanford, CA).

Derrida, J. (1997) The Villanova Roundtable: A Conversation with Jacques Derrida, in: J. D. Caputo (ed.) *Deconstruction in a Nutshell: A Conversation with Jacques Derrida* (New York, Fordham University Press), pp. 3–28.

Dewey, J. (1966) [1916] *Democracy and Education* (New York, The Free Press).

Fryer, D. R. (2004) *The Intervention of the Other: Ethical Subjectivity in Levinas and Lacan* (New York).

Gadamer, H.-G. (1994) *Truth and Method* (New York, Continuum).

Gasché, R. (1994) *Inventions of Difference: On Jacques Derrida* (Cambridge, MA, Harvard University Press).

Lucy, N. (2004) *A Derrida Dictionary* (Oxford, Blackwell).

Norris, C. (1987) *Derrida* (Cambridge, MA, Harvard University Press).

Osberg, D. C. and Biesta, G. J. J. (2008) The Emergent Curriculum: Navigating a Complex Course Between Unguided Learning and Planned Enculturation, *Journal of Curriculum Studies*, 40.3, pp. 313–28.

Osberg, D. C., Biesta, G. J. J. and Cilliers, P. (2008) From Representation to Emergence: Complexity's Challenge to the Epistemology of Schooling, *Educational Philosophy and Theory*, 40.1, pp. 213–27.

Peters, M. A. and Biesta, G. J. J. (2009) *Derrida, Deconstruction and the Politics of Pedagogy* (New York, Peter Lang).

Tibble, J. W. (1966) *The Study of Education* (London, Routledge & Kegan Paul).

Vanderstraeten, R. and Biesta, G. J. J. (2001) How is Education Possible?, *Educational Philosophy and Theory*, 33.1, pp. 7–21.

Vanderstraeten, R. and Biesta, G. J. J. (2006) How is Education Possible? A Pragmatist Account of Communication and the Social Organisation of Education, *British Journal of Educational Studies*, 54.2, pp. 160–74.

7

Under the Name of Method: On Jacques Rancière's Presumptive Tautology

CHARLES BINGHAM

The first chapter of John Dewey's *Experience and Education*, entitled 'Traditional vs. Progressive Education', was published under circumstances that perhaps presaged rather more than Dewey could have expected. Describing the traditional forms of schooling that his progressive education would replace, Dewey noted, 'The subject matter of education consists of bodies of information and of skills that have been worked out in the past; therefore, the chief business of the school is to transmit them to the new generation' (Dewey, 1998, p. 2). Seventy years have passed, and it is hard to overlook the similarities between today's educational 'improvements' and the sorts of methods that Dewey railed against. With accountability measures ruling the day in Anglo educational institutions, K-12 education is experiencing what might best be described as a return to rote, drill and test. Such programmes cannot help but treat knowledge as a thing of the past, a thing that is set-in-stone and thus testable. When teachers teach to a predetermined test, it is inevitable that students prepare for knowledge that *was there before*. Traditionalism has indeed returned with a vengeance, this time in the form of accountability.

Three decades after that first chapter in Dewey's *Experience and Education*, Paulo Freire would publish his own critique of traditional education, this one considerably different from Dewey's in most ways. Whereas Dewey's critique of the old methods was based on an epistemological critique of traditionalism's transmission of knowledge and skills, Freire understood traditional education, or 'banking education' as he would call it, as an imposition of the oppressor over the oppressed. As Freire notes, 'The capability of banking education to minimise or annul the students' creative power and to stimulate their credulity serves the interests of the oppressors, who care neither to have the world revealed nor to see it transformed' (Freire, 1998, p. 54). For Freire, traditional education is a matter of ideological imposition. Traditional education passes down knowledge that has been worked out in the past and that, furthermore, conceals the ideological underpinnings of an oppressive regime. Students are taught knowledge that is not only fixed and regurgitated but that bears with it the hoodwinking ability to paint over the epistemological tactics of elites over subordinates. So while Dewey assails traditional education because it is wrong-headed *per se*, Freire assails it because it is a wrong-headed form of domination, one that keeps the oppressed unaware of the extent to which they are dominated by the oppressor. In fact, Paulo Freire would not be as surprised as John Dewey about the tenacity of traditionalism. Today's accountability measures in schools are, from a Freirean perspective, just one of the Hydra's many heads. Oppression knows no absolute form but morphs at will to sustain the master/slave dialectic upon which Freire bases his educational analysis.

PROGRESSIVIST AND CRITICAL OBJECTIONS TO TRADITIONALISM: EPISTEMOLOGY, AUTHORITY AND SPECTATORSHIP

Epistemology

Indeed, Dewey and Paulo Freire are exemplars of the progressive and critical critiques of traditional education. And I begin this essay by detailing three major themes shared by these important critiques: epistemology, authority and spectatorship. Dewey's first objection to traditional education, as has been intimated above, is an adherence to all ideas past. 'The material to be learned', writes Dewey of traditional education, 'was settled upon outside the present life-experience of the learner. In consequence, it had to do with the past; it was such as had proved useful to men in past ages' (Dewey, 1998, p. 92). There is, according to Dewey, an epistemological error being made in the traditional classroom. Human beings do not gain knowledge in a passive, abstract manner, as the traditional model would have it. Instead, Dewey advocates a different epistemological orientation, diametrically opposed to the first: 'There is, on one side, a body of truth, ready-made, and, on the other, a ready-made mind equipped with a faculty of knowing—if it only wills to exercise it, which it is often strangely loath to do' (Dewey, 1916, p. 335). Whereas traditionalists place the emphasis on the object of knowledge, progressive education will place its emphasis on the subject of knowing.

Paulo Freire takes Dewey's critique of traditional epistemology and explains the teacher's role in promulgating such an orientation toward knowledge. He explains the tendency of the traditional (or, 'banking') educator to prepare his or her material beforehand so that the knowledge to be discussed in the classroom has the appearance of being fixed in time, already decided upon. Freire points out the *ruse* of this particular epistemological approach. The teacher must go out of his or her way to create the illusion that knowledge has been fixed in the past:

> The banking concept (with its tendency to dichotomize everything)
> distinguishes two stages in the action of the educator. During the first, he
> cognizes a cognizable object while he prepares his lessons in his study or his
> laboratory; during the second, he expounds to his students about that

object. The students are not called upon to know, but to memorize the contents narrated by the teacher. (Freire, 1998, p. 61)

As the teacher prepares his or her lessons beforehand, this very preparation lends credence to traditional epistemological assumptions. The teacher hides the fact that knowledge does not actually come ready-made and passed down, but from the here-and-now, even as traditional educators attempt to act as if it doesn't.

From these critiques launched by Dewey and Freire, there are distinct educational measures to be taken in order to combat such a rear-facing epistemology. In Dewey's case, an emphasis on experience serves to push learning forward rather than backward. In *Experience and Education*, Dewey explains the importance of a progressive orientation toward experience in classrooms: 'The lesson for progressive education is that it requires in an urgent degree, a degree more pressing than was incumbent upon former innovators, a philosophy of education based upon a philosophy of experience' (Dewey, 1998, p. 19). Subject matter needs to be organised by the teacher in such a way that it will facilitate experiential, rather than cerebral, learning. Freire, on the other hand, emphasises a dialogic answer. Anti-banking education will engage student and teacher in dialogue, such dialogue demonstrating to the student the temporality and co-construction of knowledge. Through dialogue, there will be no more pretending that knowledge comes ready-made from times gone by: 'the practice of problem-posing education entails at the outset that the teacher-student contradiction to [sic] be resolved. Dialogic relations—indispensable to the capacity of cognitive actors to cooperate in perceiving the same cognizable object—are otherwise impossible' (Freire, 1998, pp. 60–1).

Authority

As might be expected, the progressive and critical critiques of traditional education have much to say on the role of authority in education. To put these two orientations toward authority in general terms, one can say that while progressivists eschew traditional authority, criticalists embrace traditional authority but only if it can be employed as a means to foster social justice. For Dewey, the authority of tradition has been used to impinge upon the freedom of individuals. Thus, Dewey makes the case that progressive education must embrace a different form of authority:

> We need an authority that, unlike the older forms in which it operated, is capable of directing and utilizing change and we need a kind of individual freedom unlike that which the unconstrained economic liberty of individuals has produced and justified; we need, that is, a kind of individual freedom that is general and shared and that has the backing and guidance of socially organized intelligent control. (Dewey, 1991, p. 137)

Embedded in these words is Dewey's educational remedy for the traditional imposition of authority. What Dewey is *not* recommending, and this he is at pains to clarify at various times, is a simple abdication of authority on the part of the progressive educator. Instead, Dewey insists that the progressive educator must enact authority in particular ways, ways that encourage change, freedom, experience and community. The progressive educator, as opposed to the traditional, will enact authority against the conservation of the past rather than for it.

Freire's response to traditional authority arises from his psychic understanding of the relationship between oppressor and oppressed. He argues that in society, in schools, and in families, those in power all too often act in authoritarian ways. In so acting, circuits of domination and submission are set up between adults and children, between teachers and students, between leaders and citizens. In such circuits, the person who dominates is trapped in his or her role, just as the person-dominated is trapped into submission: 'Well-intentioned professionals (those who use "invasion" not as deliberate ideology but as the expression of their own upbringing) ... feel the need to renounce invasion, but patterns of domination are so entrenched within them that this renunciation would become a threat to their own identities' (Freire, 1998, p. 137). The Freirean pedagogue must resolve this whirligig of domination and submission by creating the classroom circumstances wherein 'the teacher is no longer merely–the-one-who-teaches, but one who is himself taught in dialogue with the students ... In this process, arguments based on "authority" are no longer valid' (p. 161).

Spectatorship

Another major concern for both Dewey and Freire is the practice of spectatorship in traditional education. Freire's objection to traditional spectatorship is a consequence of his Marxist-inspired loathing of human alienation. For Freire, traditional education creates a drama wherein students watch and teachers act. As Freire notes,

> The conflict lies in the choice between being wholly themselves or being divided; between ejecting the oppressor within or not ejecting them; between human solidarity or alienation; between following prescriptions or having choices; between being spectators or actors; between acting or having the illusion of acting through the action of the oppressors. (Freire, 1998, p. 30)

Freire insists on a sharp distinction between those who do and those who simply watch. The former are able to feel the consequences of their work while the latter can only imagine what it means to do, rather than to watch. The latter—the oppressed, the student of traditional education—do not fully fathom what it means to *do* the things that the teacher does. If the traditional teacher thinks for him or herself, the student of traditional education has the illusion of thinking through the thought of the teacher. The role of the Freirean educator is, of course, to engage the student in true action rather than the alienation of acting through an other. By the method of 'problem-posing' education, the Freirean teacher will create circumstances in which the student is no longer just a spectator. Instead, student and teacher will co-construct knowledge through dialogue. Such dialogue, facilitated by the teacher, will enable students to quit being watchers and start being actors.

As in the case of their respective critiques of rear-facing epistemology and traditional authority, John Dewey is critical of spectatorship in traditional education, but in a way that is less political than Freire's programme. For Dewey, spectatorship is to be eschewed not because it supports the oppression of certain groups of people, but because it is not pragmatic. It does not form a basis for authentic experience and does not get a person anywhere. Dewey writes:

> In schools, those under instruction are too customarily looked upon as acquiring knowledge as theoretical spectators, minds which appropriate knowledge by direct energy of intellect. The very word pupil has almost come to mean one who is engaged not in having fruitful experiences but in absorbing knowledge directly. Something which is called mind or consciousness is severed from the physical organs of activity. (Dewey, 1916, p. 140)

For Dewey—and this is once again an epistemological difference that he has with traditional education—the habit of theoretical spectatorship is not a habit grounded in experience. It is a habit abstracted from experience and thus not educative in the same way that experiential learning is. Dewey's recommendation for the teacher is that he or she make learning real rather than theoretical. Let the teacher create circumstances where the pupil's consciousness will not be severed from the physical organs of activity, where knowledge will be appropriated through action rather than passivity.

It is possible to go on at length about the many critiques of traditional education emanating from progressive and critical educational theory. Indeed there are many more parallel lines of assault to be found in addition to the three mentioned above. In all, the progressive and critical accounts of education offer a cohesive account of the traditional practices to which they offer themselves as antidotes. Traditionalists are past-oriented. They rely too much on conservative authority. They promote a drama of spectatorship on the part of the student, and activity on the part of the teacher. Other attributes might be added to this traditional programme if one were to give a fuller picture of the traditionalism to which both Dewey and Freire object. For example: Traditional educators objectify knowledge. They substitute discipline for intellectual rigor. They encourage tradition over personal freedom. Et cetera. But let it suffice here to have detailed just three attributes of traditional education: As a past-oriented, authoritative, dramatic actor, the traditional teacher beckons the censure of progressives and criticalists.

COMPLICITY WITH TRADITIONALISM

However, as both progressivists and criticalists counter traditional education, something is glossed over. In spite of the best efforts of progressive and critical educational theory to denounce traditional education, both remain faithful to the guiding *pedagogical* assumption of traditionalism. In spite of the different pedagogical projects announced by progressivism and critical theory, teaching remains. And teaching itself remains rather traditional no matter how much one attempts progress or critique. Progressive and critical education remain faithful to this essence of teaching, this model of the less-than-sage being guided by the more-advanced. Even if one puts aside the traditional favouring of the past, of authority, or of spectatorship—even if one puts aside these or other attendant qualities imputed to traditional education—one is still left with the crux of the problem, that crux being *teaching*.

Teaching is the employment of one person to give something to someone else. The traditional programme of education is not, after all, particularly notable for its reliance on the past, on authority, or on spectatorship *per se*. These themes can be maintained without being taught. Indeed, as both Dewey and Freire repeatedly note, these matters of the past, of authority, of spectatorship and so on, are matters that plague society in general. They are matters that curtail the agency and freedom of people whether or not people attend schools. What is unique and problematic in traditional education is an embracing of pedagogy to bolster its particular biases. And for all their critique of traditional education's biases, neither progressive educators nor critical educators are able to give up on the only thing that makes a traditional educator anything different from any other traditionally-minded person. The critique of traditional education maintains the guiding assumption that teaching itself is not to be questioned. At a most basic level, traditionalism is not what is at stake in these critiques. What is at stake is the *teaching* of traditionalism. But teaching will not be abandoned.

Take the case of Dewey's educational programme. Progressive teaching is touted as an antidote to traditional teaching. It is assumed that progressive teaching methods will foster a timely epistemology, a freedom-oriented authority, and a participatory student body. What is not mentioned is that teaching itself, even in its new, progressive iteration, carries the weight of past knowledge. Teaching threatens individual freedom and tends to encourage spectatorship. It does so through the momentum of past teaching practices, and by the vicissitudes encountered when an elder-who-knows attempts to shuttle a young scholar somewhere he or she has not been before. The problem with traditional teaching is no different from the problem of teaching itself, but progressivism refuses to step outside of teaching's magic circle. Instead, progressivism offers yet another version of teaching. It offers a form of teaching that must be impossibly vigilant. It must be vigilant enough to reverse the teaching problems that it has inherited as a matter of teaching itself. It must by hyper-vigilant through new advances in psychology, and through the pseudo-science of teacher effectiveness. It must be hyper-vigilant in order to lift teaching out of its teaching-ness. Hence the impossibility of progressivism.

A similar observation can be made of critical education, although the latter offers a different solution. Critical theory brings to the teacher, and then to the student, an awareness of education's ideological biases. It instils awareness not through progress, but through insight. The student is brought to an awareness of the oppressive underpinnings of education. That is to say, the student will be shown *by a teacher* that teaching is full of oppression. 'Minds and bodies must not be oppressed in my classroom as they are in the world at large,' the critical teacher avers. He or she brings students to an awareness of the real world hidden behind the world of the teacher. The critical educator convinces students not to be convinced. Hence the ideological and pedagogical bind of critical education. Critical education, like progressive education, fights teaching with teaching. It, too, will not step outside of teaching's magic circle. One must see the truth that truth is hidden, and one must be taught not to trust teaching. The ideological teaching of critical theory, like the enlightened teaching of progressive education, fights fire with fire.

UNDER THE NAME OF RANCIÈRE

At this point in the argument it would be most natural to progress in an orderly fashion toward a reasonable alternative to both progressivism and criticalism. Having noted that neither actually escapes the fundamental teaching predicament that characterises traditional education, it is logical, after offering the body of an argument against progressivism and criticalism, to formulate a positive organising principle, one that yields direction and perhaps educational recommendations. But irresponsible as it may seem, my argument will remain without any educational conclusion, save for the educational conclusions that might be drawn from a different, more metacognitive, analysis. Instead of providing an alternative to progressivism and criticalism, I want to discuss the way that I constructed the above argument, on the method used to construct it. Method itself will be the subject of the rest of this essay's investigation. In this way, I will *not* follow the example of the teacher whom Freire criticises for separating pedagogy into stages. To repeat: The teacher 'cognizes a cognizable object while he prepares his lessons in his study or his laboratory; during the second, he expounds to his students about that object' (Freire, 1998, p. 61). I will instead admit to the process of preparation. And in particular, I will admit to borrowing a method from Jacques Rancière, the argument above being methodologically similar to a method employed by Rancière in various works.

The above work, then, employs a method. I call this method 'presumptive tautology'. Following this method, the author—in this case I, though I have admitted borrowing the method from Rancière—looks for two theoretical responses to a certain longstanding problem. One finds the differences in opinion, in logic and in practice that accompany these two responses to one and the same problem. One is careful to draw out these differences in all their particularities. Once again, these differences will be in response to a long-standing problem: certainly not a 'straw man' of a problem, rather a specific philosophical theme that has come under fire in concrete and distinct ways through the two articulated responses. Then, once these two positions have been elucidated, one proceeds to compare these responses to the problem itself, the theoretical position under assault. After close scrutiny, as well as a certain interpretive confidence, one finds at least one element of the position under critique that has not been abandoned by either one of the theories proposed to counter it. One shows, furthermore—again a certain interpretive confidence is needed—that the element in common to all three is none other than a matter central to the initial position. That is to say, both responses carry in them a seed of the problem itself. Each theoretical position, in spite of being critical of the long-standing problem, cannot extricate itself from the very problematic it is trying to escape. One catches the two responses unawares, neither having admitted its own complicity.

In the argument above, the longstanding problem was that of traditional education's shortcomings. The theoretical responses were those of progressivism and traditionalism as represented in the works of John Dewey and Paulo Freire. Both Dewey and Freire had set themselves against traditional education, Dewey calling the target of his critique by that name, Freire using the phrase 'banking education', which I took to mean the same. I ultimately settled on the identical presumption shared by Dewey, Freire and traditionalists—namely, the unquestionable benefit to teaching itself.

This sort of method can be discerned in more than one of Jacques Rancière's works, and it is in these works that I learned the method. In *The Future of an Image*, Rancière uses this method to indicate the underlying assumption embraced by those who *claim* to take different positions on the nature of the artistic image (Rancière, 2007). In a paper entitled, 'The Emancipated Spectator', he uses the method to dissect the similar assumptions about theatrical spectatorship embraced by Plato and also by Plato's modern detractors, Bertolt Brecht and Antonin Artaud (Rancière, 2004b). In a 2004 lecture on his book *The Ignorant Schoolmaster*, Rancière uses this method to show that educational sociologists such as Bourdieu and Passeron, as well as their republicanist counterparts, share the same orientation toward equality in spite of their professed ideological opposition

(2004a). They both see equality as being a goal rather than a given. Rancière uses the presumptive tautology in these and other instances to move his arguments along.

A METHOD THAT BELONGS TO WHOM?

But whose method is this really? The person behind this method is Jacques Rancière but, to my knowledge, Rancière never announced that the presumptive tautology was one of his methods. He uses the method, if it can be so called, in more than one of his writings. But does this method really belong to Rancière if Rancière does not name it *qua* method in his work? If I have named the method—for Rancière certainly does not give this method the name that I have—does the method have my name, or does it have the name of Jacques Rancière? If it is named mine, does it belong to me or, if named Rancière's, does it belong to him? Or, is it possible to assert that this method does not belong to someone, but that the method nevertheless works under the name of Rancière, or perhaps under the name of Bingham, in the more literal sense that Winnie-the-Pooh lived under the name of Sanders because 'Sanders' was written over the door of his house? What I want to pose here is a question as to whether a method can ever belong to someone, or, more precisely, what the rapport might be between a method and the person whose name the method bears. The rest of this essay will be devoted to an inquiry on the Rancièrean method that I have used, and more specifically to the implications of method's debt to a name.

Properly speaking, a method should never belong to anyone. It should never reside under the name of someone in any metaphorical sense, as opposed to the literal sense mentioned above. Why? Because a method is that great invention of the Enlightenment move toward a dissociation between the subjective ambiguity of personal inquiry and the objective specificity of scientific inquiry that relies not on the name of the scientist but on the authority of science itself. So, on one hand, it makes no sense at all to claim that a method refers back to some person. Methodology, if it is true to its Enlightenment roots, should not need a person. It should be able to stand on its own, and indeed, should cease to be a method if it does not stand on its own.

But, on the other hand, there is a certain use in admitting that people do initiate methods or that there are methods that can be traced to names. If there is anything that can be called philosophical method, then such method is most often linked to a name. When one thinks of hermeneutic method, one thinks of Hans-Georg Gadamer or Paul Ricoeur, among others. When one thinks of deconstructive method, one thinks of Jacques Derrida. When one thinks of phenomenological method, one thinks of Edmund Husserl and so on. Whether method is linked to a name literally, like Pooh is linked to Sanders, or metaphorically, as the work of Jacques Rancière is linked to his own name, is, I propose, a matter that sets one on the way to an analysis of the question posed above, namely: can a method every really belong to a name? And, if it does, what is the relation between such method and its namesake?

Before pushing further with this question, though, it is useful to probe a bit more into Rancière's particular method, the one I have dubbed the 'presumptive tautology'. Such probing proves to be germane to the question of the method's name. I have claimed to use Rancière's method. Or, I have claimed to use a method that I detect in the work of Rancière. Whatever. Indeed, the task I set for myself, through the writing of this essay, was to use Rancière's method in a way that was honest to his own use of it. To that end, I wrote the initial argument of this chapter. Having succeeded, I believe, in using this Rancièrean method, I began to notice something else, namely that mine was not quite the argument I thought it was. It did not quite stand up on its own. I realised that the method I had just used was not quite the method I thought it was. It was not only one method among others. I noticed that this method itself has traces of Rancière's thought that cannot be so easily articulated under the literal name of 'Rancière's presumptive tautology' that I had given it. It is a method that garners its methodological acuity from a set of theoretical suppositions that are none other than Rancière's own suppositions. But these suppositions cannot be captured in the methodological logic of the presumptive tautology as I have described it above. These suppositions are actually informed by the trajectory of much of Rancière's philosophical work. I shall try to explain this.

It might seem at first glance that the method of the presumptive tautology entails a fairly straightforward procedure: Search for an incriminating link, one that connects potential solutions back to the problem itself. It would seem that, if there is such a link intrinsic to the two solutions and to the problem itself, then an analysis employing the presumptive tautology is suitable for application. On further investigation, though, it becomes clear that Rancière's own links, the ones he establishes in his own uses of the presumptive tautology, actually do not depend on any *obvious* commonality between the given framework and its opposing theories. In the case of Rancière's examination of the 'republican' and 'sociological' alternatives to educational 'failure' in the later 20th century, for example, he proposes an anachronistic commonality that only the now-obscure 19th century pedagogue, Joseph Jacotot, was aware of: that equality has been treated, by both 'republicans' and 'sociologists', as an end to be achieved rather than as a given (Rancière, 2004a). In this case, as is generally the case when Rancière uses the presumptive tautology, Rancière does not choose a theme that is common to two theoretical positions in any obvious way. Instead, the obviousness of the common theme is made clear by Rancière's own work.

Rancière's work thus shores up his method. One of his central philosophical themes is at work in this method. This particular method is informed by an adherence to reconfiguring 'the distribution of the sensible'.

For, when two theoretical responses to a long-standing problem can be revealed to share a common foothold, then one of two means must have been used to reveal that foothold: either, the common ground was already there and just needed to be teased out; or, as I have intimated is commonly the case with Rancière's use of the presumptive tautology, an unexpected presumption is underscored, one that is not necessarily there to begin with but is instead translated afresh out of the two responses. This sort of translation is precisely what Rancière advocates as an emancipatory political and artistic goal when he advocates that thinkers change the world's understanding of things. This changing, this 're-distribution of the sensible', is described in numerous works by Rancière, a typical description being the following from his book *Disagreement*: 'Politics is a matter of subjects or, rather, modes of subjectification. By *subjectification* I mean the production through a series of actions of a body and a capacity for enunciation not previously identifiable within a given field of experience, whose identification is thus part of the reconfiguration of the field of experience' (Rancière, 1999, p. 35). So it seems that this particular method does have a person behind it. The method of presumptive tautology does not stand alone. It must be linked back not only to the literal name of Rancière, but back to Rancière's metaphorical name as well. That is to say, it is not only Rancière's method in the sense that the method should be found under his name. It is also Rancière's method in the metaphorical sense that who he is as a philosopher, who he is as a person who thinks about certain things in certain ways, that is to say, what his name *stands for* more generally—this larger sense of his name must also be included in a proper understanding of the presumptive tautology. To return to the question posed earlier, a method can belong to someone specific in this metaphorical sense. This particular method is difficult to understand completely without looking at the thinking that orients it. But is it, then, still a method? As I have noted, in the strictest sense of the Enlightenment notion of method, a method that belongs to someone is no method. So in this strict Enlightenment sense, the presumptive tautology is no method.

PHILOSOPHICAL METHOD, THE LITERAL AND METAPHORICAL

However, as noted, there is a caveat to bear in mind when it comes to philosophical method. 'Philosophical method', which is perhaps, in this strict sense, a contradiction in terms, usually does have a founder. It is the name of this founder, both literal and metaphorical, that I want to underscore and interpret by way of concluding this essay. Take the literal first: It is possible, and, I fear, too often done, that those who use a particular philosophical method take the founder's name too literally. For example, 'under the name of Gadamer', researchers, theorists and, sometimes, even philosophers employ the hermeneutic method to study a given problem. In such cases the method of hermeneutics is attached to one who has named it, but such a name has no other role than being a name. It is, literally, a name. It is a bad metaphor, one that does not stand for more than itself. Interestingly, though, such literal use of a method's name helps to keep up appearances of method-ness in the strict Enlightenment sense. When the name is just a name, there is no need to worry about intrinsic links between the work of an author and the method under his or her name. Naming a philosophical method literally gives method a certain philosophical appearance even while its use can remain methodical in the strict Enlightenment sense of the term. It is possible to use the method of Gadamer, for example, 'under the name of Gadamer', without seeking any interpretive resonances between one's use of hermeneutic method and the actual provocation of Gadamer's thought. This happens all the time, especially in research in the social sciences.

But it is also possible to take the namesake of a method metaphorically. In such cases, philosophical method does what philosophical method should do. Indeed this is what philosophers do. We name names, and we take those names metaphorically. And in naming those names, a philosopher does not do without method. Instead, he or she does with method, and does with method exactly what should be done. When one attributes a name to a method, there are two aspects of the name's metaphor that are philosophi-cally significant. The first one has already been mentioned: the method's place in its surroundings, its place in the overall oeuvre of the person named. An example of this is what I have briefly done with the method of presumptive tautology in its relation to Rancière's 'redistribution of the sensible'.

The second metaphorical aspect is the name's meaning in relation to the thought of the one who is using the method. This is to say, the meaning of one person's method once it has been changed by another person's particular way of using that method. In my case, for example, there is not only my use of Rancière's method, but there is also a sense in which my use of Rancière's method can never be precisely the same as another person's use of the 'same' method. Thus, Rancière's name is metaphorical in the second sense that it stands for 'my Rancière'. 'My Rancière's method' has meanings that must be interpreted in the context of my own thinking just as 'Rancière's method' has meanings that must be interpreted in the context of his own thinking. This second metaphorical aspect is thus a partial answer to the question posed earlier about whether a method named by me, but gleaned from the work of Rancière, will have his name or mine. It will have both. It will be Rancière's presumptive tautology, but, metaphorically, it will also be Bingham's Rancière's presumptive tautology.

METHOD'S NAME

And let us apply this metaphorical analysis to the name of method itself. The name of method can be taken literally or metaphorically. What I am advocating in this essay, and it does turn out that I am advocating something, is that one take the name of method metaphorically as well as literally. I am advocating that when something goes 'under the name of method', that the name method be taken as just that, a name, but also that it be taken as more than a name. Method, in its strict Enlightenment meaning, and this, too, is its literal sense, is that which guides one through a set of steps in order to conduct fruitful inquiry. In this literal sense, method is not supposed to belong to anybody. There is nothing wrong with this literal sense. Or at least, there is nothing wrong with this literal sense *existing* since its existence, indeed, provides the denotative correlative for a more nuanced, metaphorical analysis. A metaphor is not a metaphor unless there is both denotation *and* connotation. For method to be a metaphorically nuanced matter, there must also be an anchor point, however strict and Enlightenment-oriented, as to what method is in the first place.

But method should be taken as more than a name. 'Under the name of method' resides the potential that I have been trying illustrate in my own use of Rancière. From naïve application of a model, to self-aware translation of one methodological paradigm into circumstances unforeseen and fruitful, to probing conjectures on the philosophical commitments of a method, to creative inauguration of methods yet to come—in all these uses of method, the metaphorical name of method, the multiple meanings that can be associated with method, create the circumstances for methods that are more than methods. And none of these methods are worth leaving behind. Indeed, even as I began this essay, even as I simply used a Rancièrean method to analyse the progressive and critical responses to traditionalism—even if this was a simple, and perhaps literal, use of the name 'method'—such a simple use enabled me to become aware of unforeseen aspects of progressivism, criticalism, and traditionalism. Thus it may be the case—at least it was, I hope, the case for my own use of Rancière's method—that a philosophically nuanced, metaphorical attention to method also includes a literal use of method that is, even with its strict Enlightenment qualities, quite provocative. The literal aspect of method is essential to the metaphor not only because it provides a denotative correlative but because it may provide the beginnings of metaphorical method's excess of meaning.

Self-aware translation of one methodological paradigm into circumstances unforeseen and fruitful, probing conjectures on the philosophical commit-ments to method, creative inauguration of methods yet to come—these are all metaphorical aspects of method, and I would like to focus primarily on the last. As I have noted, one of the ways that a method's name acts metaphorically is by the transformation of one person's method into an interpretation of that method, an interpretation that engages the name of an other. This, it seems to me, is the most important metaphorical use of method: When a method stands for more than itself, it so stands most significantly through the interpretation of an other. When A uses the method of B, it cannot be said that it is still B's method. The method has become more than B's. It has become B's-subject-to-the-interpretation-of-A. Or, as I have noted in terms of my own argument, Rancière's method has become Rancière's method subject to the interpretation of Bingham. When method becomes metaphorical, it does so in this possession-of-one's-possession fashion.

This is the method of method. It is a relation between method itself, the name of the person who has come up with method, and then the name of the person who uses method. It is when method treats method as metaphor. It assumes that method is larger than itself, that the person who uses method will inevitably put a creative stamp on the method used. In this way, the metaphoric, philosophical method of naming names puts a methodological twist on the strict method of Enlightenment. The metaphoric method of naming names has its own strict method. It must name names, to begin with. But if it were just to name names, then its strictness is no different from the strictness of Enlightenment method. For when one names names, it is easy to stay at the literal level, that is, to stay at the literal level of being 'under the name of' some method. The strict method of metaphor, as opposed to Enlightenment method, requires method to do more. It requires method to name the names of those who name names. This is its strictness. In this way method honours the name of method and treats its own name metaphorically.

CONCLUSION

This chapter has taken a few turns. From a problematising of John Dewey and Paulo Freire, to a method of Jacques Rancière dubbed the 'presumptive tautology', situated, as it is, in the context of his larger philosophical project, to a more general discussion on philosophical method *per se*. Now by way of conclusion, and at the risk of taking one more turn, this time back once again to matters of education, I want to show resonance between Rancière's primary piece of educational writing, *The Ignorant Schoolmaster*, and this problem of method's name. The resonance can first be seen in the very idea of a jacotist/Rancièrean pedagogy, a pedagogy that itself claims not to be a method, and thus perhaps to lack a name as well. As Rancière reminds us, there is no 'jacotist' pedagogy: 'If I thought it good to revive this forgotten discourse, it is not, to repeat, in order to propose some new pedagogy. There is no jacotist pedagogy. Nor is there a jacotist anti-pedagogy, in the sense that this word is ordinarily used' (Rancière, 2004a). Yet Rancière claims this even as he goes to great lengths to explain what can only be described as a jacotist 'method' of emancipation in education. What are we to make of a text like *The Ignorant Schoolmaster* that methodically details a method that is supposed to be no method? Under whose name does it reside?[1]

The answer to this question can be framed in terms of the methaphorics of method's name, and in particular, the name of *educational* method. With regard to educational method, Rancière has precisely enacted a version of the metaphorising I have tried to describe above. Rancière has detailed the method of Joseph Jacotot. About this, let us not be unclear: It is easy to discern an educational method in *The Ignorant Schoolmaster*, this, in spite of Rancière's protests, and in spite of the protests of Joseph Jacotot himself. As readers of *The Ignorant Schoolmaster*, we can easily take the position of Jacotot's followers who, in spite of Jacotot's protests, 'sought to lead the students of universal teaching to intellectual emancipation' (Rancière, 1991, p. 135). All the while, Jacotot 'refused all progressive and pedagogical translation of emancipatory equality' (p. 134). There is indeed a jacotist method to be found, but it is a method whose name Rancière does his best to translate into metaphor. He carries out this translation through the protests I have just mentioned. But these disavowals are too facile not to be ignored.

First, then, there are disavowals by both Rancière and Jacotot. But this translation is not primarily through disavowals of Jacotot's anti-method method. It rather comes about through a dramatisation of the fall of Jacotot's universal teaching by means of its own methodising. The fall comes as Rancière affirms, dramatically rather than conceptually, that universal teaching will never catch on, that is, it will never actually succeed as method even if it is taken as a method: 'Let's affirm, then, that universal teaching *will never take*, it will not be established in society. But *it will not perish*, because it is the natural method of the human mind, that of all people who look for their path themselves' (p. 105). Indeed, the fall of Jacotot is more significant than any discernable jacotist method. The fall is a dramatisation of the death of a method whose name is not metaphorised. Jacotot's method could not stand the test of time precisely because others treated it as method. In Jacotot's name, there was too much certainty, even if it was a certainty of his madness: 'On this point he agreed with the disciples who hid his name under the label "natural method": no one in Europe was strong enough to bear that name, the name of the madman' (p. 134). When method's name is taken too seriously, and more precisely, when method's name is taken too seriously in an educational context, this is itself the death of an educational method.

Then we have the book itself. We have *The Ignorant Schoolmaster* right in front of us. We are the readers of an educational method that claims not to be a method. And as one reads this book, there is the distinct feeling that whatever is claimed or disavowed by either Jacotot or Rancière is claimed or disavowed by some admixture of the two. As Rancière's voice narrates Jacotot, then quotes Jacotot, then slips largely into being the same voice as Jacotot, it is not at all clear whom we are reading. Is it Rancière? Is it Jacotot? Is it Rancière's Jacotot in a similar sense to the Bingham's Rancière that I described above.[2] Stylistically, then, Rancière turns jacotist method into a metaphor. He establishes a transformation of one person's method into an interpretation of that method, an interpretation that engages the name of an other.

Even more interesting, though, from an educator's point of view, are the teachings of this book that claims not to teach. If we are sympathetic to Jacotot's name and to his teachings, we have in front of us a book, an educational path, to follow, but the path has been shown to be unfollowable through Rancière's staging, through to the path's end. We are thus sympathetic not to Jacotot's name, but to its metaphor, not to Rancière's name, but to its metaphor. The book leaves us with a method whose name can only be a metaphor, and this book is educative precisely in the sense that it forces its reader to translate its contents into his or her experience without any certainty as to how its contents are to be translated. That is to say, the book is to be read without a teaching. This book is, as Rancière will put it elsewhere, akin to the idiom of the artist, as well as the researcher: 'The effect of the idiom cannot be anticipated. It calls for spectators who are active interpreters, who render their own translation, who appropriate the story for themselves, and who ultimately make their own story out of it. An emancipated community is in fact a community of storytellers and translators' (2004b). Faced with a book whose effect cannot be anticipated because its method cannot be generalised, one is left to one's own experience of the book's words. One is taught, but only in metaphor.

NOTES

1. For an account of how Paulo Freire and Jacques Rancière might somehow share the same metaphorical name, see Tyson (2009).
2. As Kristin Ross points out in her introduction to *The Ignorant Schoolmaster*, 'The reader, in other words, is not quite sure where the voice of Jacotot stops and Rancière's begins. Rancière slips into Jacotot's text, winding around or worming in; his commentary contextualizes, rehearses, reiterates, dramatizes, elaborates, *continues* Jacotot' (Ross, 1991, p. xxii).

REFERENCES

Dewey, J. (1916) *Democracy and Education* (New York, The Free Press/Macmillan).
Dewey, J. (1991) [1936] Authority and Social Change, in: J. A. Boydston (ed.) *John Dewey: The Later Works*, Vol. 13 (Carbondale, Southern Illinois University Press).
Dewey, J. (1998) [1938] *Experience and Education: The 60th Anniversary Edition* (West Lafayette, IN, Kappa Delta Pi).
Freire, P. (1998) [1970] *Pedagogy of the Oppressed* (New York, Continuum).
Rancière, J. (1991) *The Ignorant Schoolmaster: Five Lessons in Intellectual Emancipation* (Stanford, CA, Stanford University Press).
Rancière, J. (1999) *Disagreement: Politics and Philosophy* (Minneapolis, University of Minnesota Press).
Rancière, J. (2004a) Sur *Le Maître Ignorant*. Online at http://multitudes.samizdat.net/article1714.html (accessed 20 April 2009).
Rancière, J. (2004b) The Emancipated Spectator. Online at http://voidmanufacturing.wordpress.com/2008/08/29/jacques-ranciere-the-emancipated-spectator/ (accessed 20 April 2009).
Rancière, J. (2007) *The Future of the Image* (London, Verso).
Ross, K. (1991) Translator's Introduction, in: J. Rancière, *The Ignorant Schoolmaster: Five Lessons in Intellectual Emancipation* (Stanford, CA, Stanford University Press).
Tyson, E. (2009) Education in the Realm of the Senses: Understanding Paulo Freire's Aesthetic Unconscious through Jacques Rancière, *Journal of Philosophy of Education*, 43.2, p. 285.

8

Distance and Defamiliarisation: Translation as Philosophical Method

CLAUDIA RUITENBERG

> The difficulty of a translation is never merely a technical issue but concerns the relation of human beings to the essence of the word and to the worthiness of language. Tell me what you think of translation, and I will tell you who you are.
>
> (Heidegger, 1996, p. 63)[1]

INTERLINGUISTIC TRANSLATION

In recent work I have grappled with the phrase 'ways of knowing' (Ruitenberg, 2008). My investigation started with puzzlement over the phrase 'ways of knowing', which seems to imply the possibility of knowing as an act or activity that can be conducted in different ways. Since I could find no fault with Richard Robinson's assertions that 'knowledge is never an act, or any kind of event' and that '"the act of knowing" does not occur' (Robinson, 1971, p. 17), I sought a different explanation for the frequent use of the phrase 'ways of knowing'. I concluded that the epistemological-sounding phrase 'ways of knowing' is often used as a trope for contiguous claims about ontological and metaphysical assumptions that are part of larger worldviews.

A possibility I did not explore during that initial investigation is that at least part of the ambiguity in the phrase 'ways of knowing' is caused by the use of the phrase without object, as if knowledge could ever be without object and as if 'knowing' could be an intransitive verb. The examples of uses of the phrase 'ways of knowing' that I cited all focused attention on the *subjects* rather than the *objects* of knowledge: they spoke frequently about '*women's* ways of knowing', '*Indigenous* ways of knowing' or '*African* ways of knowing' but rarely about 'ways of knowing *X*' or 'ways of knowing *Y*'.

Paul Hirst turned his attention to the relation between different types of knowledge or 'ways of knowing' and different objects of knowledge. In commenting on the work of Philip Phenix, Hirst distinguished three categories of objects of knowledge, and the types of knowledge associated with these objects: 'knowledge with the direct object', 'knowledge-that' (propositional knowledge) and 'knowledge-how' (procedural knowledge)

(Hirst, 1975, p. 57). He was, however, sceptical about both the separate and epistemic status of 'knowledge with the direct object':

> Clearly much of what this covers is 'knowledge that' about the objects or persons concerned. To this, however, is usually added a claim to have direct experience of the person or object, and many writers speak here of having existential knowledge, a form of experience which is not itself expressible in statements of propositions. Phenix clearly considers 'knowledge with the direct object' to be a distinct type of knowledge primarily because of these existential aspects. It is, however, very debatable whether it should be so regarded, and particularly so if knowledge is to be kept clear of all other states of mind. ... What one knows in the existential form of 'knowledge with the direct object' is thus characterisable as 'knowledge-that' concerning the object on which supervenes an occurrent state of awareness which is of a quite different character. Knowledge of the first kind, I therefore suggest, is reducible to 'knowledge-that'. (pp. 57–8)

According to Hirst, it is perfectly coherent in everyday language to say that one knows one's brother, that one knows the island on which one lives, or that one knows wine, but in a philosophical sense such statements are confusions between 'knowledge-that' and feelings or other 'states of awareness' such as affection or pride. Following Hirst's analysis, 'ways of knowing' can logically only be understood as 'ways of knowing that' and 'ways of knowing how'. So what does someone claim when she claims that there are several different 'ways of knowing'? Does she claim that there are several different ways of knowing that or different ways of knowing how or both?

The area of propositional knowledge is perhaps the easiest to address, for it is simply not linguistically or conceptually possible to claim that one can know that it is raining in several different ways. One either knows that it is raining, or one does not. One may have *come to know* about the rain in different ways, for example by standing outside and getting rained on, or by sitting inside and looking out through a window, but this, as I have explained elsewhere, is a matter of different ways of *learning* that it is raining, not of different ways of *knowing* it.

The matter is more difficult when it regards procedural knowledge: could one coherently claim that there are different ways of knowing how to ride a bike, or different ways of knowing how to make an omelette? The immediate impulse to paraphrase the question whether one can *know in different ways* how to make an omelette, as whether one can know *different ways of making* an omelette, and the confusion that results from trying to distinguish these two questions, suggests that procedural knowledge might not be a good object of 'ways of knowing'. At a breakfast meeting with an academic colleague, however, he suggested that, surely, there must be a difference between his way of knowing how to make an omelette, something he does only occasionally, and—here he pointed to the chef at the omelette station of the breakfast bar—the chef's way of knowing how to make an omelette, assuming that he does so several times a day, several days a week. Thus, it indeed seems possible to refer to multiple 'ways of knowing how', although it seems to me that there are much better ways of characterising the difference between my colleague's and the chef's knowledge of omelette-making. It is clear that the chef has more *experience* making omelettes, for example, and that he has *learned* how to make an omelette in different circumstances. Although this carries beyond the scope of this essay, it would be worth examining further if and how the possibility of different 'ways of knowing how' might be relevant to the broader investigation into the use of the phrase 'ways of knowing' by groups who claim a marginalised epistemic status.

I wish to return, however, to Hirst's claim that 'knowledge with the direct object' is not a distinct type of knowledge. I am troubled by Hirst's certainty, because he operates in English, in which there is just one verb, 'to know', whereas there are two verbs in Dutch (my mother tongue), as well as in German and French. The French use *savoir* for propositional and procedural knowledge: 'She knows that it is raining' would be '*Elle sait qu'il pleut*' and 'He knows how to write' would be '*Il sait écrire*'. The verb *connaître* is reserved for being acquainted with a person, object or phenomenon: 'She knows her brother well' would be '*Elle connaît bien son frère*', and 'I don't know much about trees' would be '*Je ne connais pas bien les arbres*'. The German distinction between *wissen* and *kennen* (and the Dutch distinction between *weten* and *kennen*) operate along similar lines as the distinction between *savoir* and *connaître*.[2]

David Edgerton, in reference to John Pickstone's 'Ways of Knowing: Towards a Historical Sociology of Science, Technology and Medicine' (1993), writes:

> L'identification moderne du savoir de pointe aux savoirs en général ne fait pas seulement violence aux savoirs passés mais aussi aux savoirs actuels. Nous ignorons aussi en quoi les sciences et les techniques sont et ont été *des manières de savoir*, et pas seulement des manières de créer du savoir neuf ou des choses. [The modern identification of advanced knowledge with knowledge in general does violence not only to past knowledge but also to present knowledge. We ignore also how science and technology are and have been *ways of knowing* and not only ways of creating new knowledge or things.] (Edgerton, 1998, p. 833, emphasis added)

Edgerton translates 'ways of knowing' straightforwardly with *manières de savoir*, without giving consideration to the conceptual difficulties of this phrase. Christelle Rigal, at a book presentation of Pickstone's *Ways of Knowing: A New History of Science, Technology and Medicine* (2000) at the University of Paris Diderot, chose not to translate the English phrase 'ways of knowing' into French. She notes:

... plutôt que de traduire « Ways of knowing » par « façons/manières de savoir » —expression peu élégante—ou par « styles d'élaboration des connaissances » —traduction probablement trop réductrice—j'ai préféré conserver l'expression originale, sous la forme abrégée de WOK. [rather than translating 'Ways of knowing' with 'façons/manières de savoir'—a not very elegant expression—or with 'styles d'élaboration des connaissances'— a translation that is probably too reductive—I have chosen to keep the original expression, in its abbreviated form WOK.] (Rigal, 2006, p. 1)

In considering possible candidates for a translation she does not, in the end, adopt, she lists *façons de savoir, manières de savoir* and *styles d'élaboration des connaissances*. The phrases *façons de savoir* and *manières de savoir* are the more obvious and literal French translations of 'ways of knowing', although she calls them 'not very elegant', possibly because they sound foreign and translated. Her last suggestion could be translated more literally into English as 'styles of knowledge development', a phrase that may seem, at first glance, far removed from 'ways of knowing' but that is connected to the use of 'ways of knowing' as shorthand for 'ways of coming to know'.

I suspect that Edgerton and Rigal suggest *manières de savoir* rather than *manières de connaître* because of the particular areas of knowledge that are the focus of Pickstone's book: science, technology and medicine. *Manières de connaître* are not about technical skills and scientific facts, but about more intimate 'ways of knowing': knowing something like the back of one's hand, for example, or, in French, like one's pocket: *connaître quelque chose comme sa poche.*[3] Hirst's assertion that *connaître* is not a distinct type of knowledge seems too bold, not least because of his suggestion that knowledge and other 'states of awareness' such as feelings can and should be kept separate. When discussing my investigation into 'ways of knowing' with philosopher of education Barbara Houston, she suggested that it might be possible to claim that there are different ways of knowing *anger*. This suggestion extends to many other emotions: knowing joy, knowing sadness, knowing fear and so on. What we did not discuss at the time was that 'knowing' in the phrase 'ways of knowing anger' is 'knowing' in the sense of *connaître (kennen)*, not *savoir (wissen)*. Knowing an emotion is not propositional or procedural knowledge, but a matter of being acquainted with the emotion. This is illustrated quite well by the title of the 1954 novel *Bonjour Tristesse (Hello, Sadness)* by Françoise Sagan and the lyrics 'Hello darkness, my old friend, I've come to talk with you again' in the Simon and Garfunkel song *The Sound of Silence*. Of course here, too, one can and should distinguish 'coming to know' anger, sadness or darkness from 'knowing' these emotions, but it seems to me that in the context of emotions ways of knowing-in-the-sense-of-*connaître* are indeed possible.

Although this use is now uncommon, the English verb 'to know' has in the past also been used to mean to be sexually acquainted with, which is reflected in the expression 'knowing in the biblical sense'. In English this use is perhaps known from some of the plays of William Shakespeare, such as the comedy *All's Well That Ends Well*, in which Diana says to the King of France, 'By Jove, if ever I knew man, 't was you' (V. iii. 286), or *Measure for Measure*, in which Mariana says to the Duke, 'That is Angelo, who thinks, he knows, that he ne'er knew my body, but knows, he thinks, that he knows Isabel's' (V. i. 199–200). In this context, too, different ways of knowing-in-the-sense-of-*connaître* seem quite possible: the King of France's way of knowing Diana, after all, may be different from another suitor's way of knowing Diana.

This lengthy exploration of translations of the phrase 'ways of knowing' serves to illustrate the use of translation as a method in philosophical thinking and writing. Where my previous investigation into the phrase 'ways of knowing' had led me to conclude that the phrase served certain political purposes but was always linguistically problematic, translating the phrase into French and German enabled a new approach to the concept. Although neither is a language which I understand, speak or write fluently, the displacement of the object of investigation into a new, less familiar context provided me with the requisite distance for a fresh perspective. Regardless of whether the authors who use the phrase 'ways of knowing' do so in the sense of *connaître*, I can see that knowing-in-the-sense-of-*connaître* may indeed occur in different ways, and this raises new questions for educational contexts. For example, students in my class may have different ways of knowing (*connaître*) racism; some may have been the objects of racist oppression and know racism in a way that has seeped into their bodies, while others know racism more distantly as something that they have heard and read about but have not experienced viscerally. If these different ways of knowing racism are present in the class, they will affect any discussions about racism and anti-racist education we have.

DISTANCE AND DEFAMILIARISATION

Alfred Langewand writes that 'the activity of translating is an eminently hermeneutic activity' (Langewand, 2001, p. 145). A translation is, inevitably, an interpretation, and may indeed be an activity that seeks to make sense of a text. In this interpretation of translation as interpretive activity the emphasis is on seeking meaning and understanding, even if there is no certainty about the correctness of that understanding. However, translation as philosophical operation seeks to disrupt commonsense meaning and understanding: by displacing language, it can arrest thinking about a text in a way that assumes the language is understood. That has been the purpose of my displacement of the phrase 'ways of knowing' into languages other than English: to disrupt the unquestioned understanding with which this phrase has been made to operate in various texts. Translation in this sense serves the purpose of disrupting the complacent belief that one understands one's own thoughts and the language in which one formulates one's thoughts. It can illustrate that ideas and concepts that seemed familiar and commonsensical carry foreign and unfamiliar traces that call into question their current obviousness. In the words of Jonathan Rée:

> Philosophical thinking … is in constant flight from cozy nests of reliable belief: perpetually in quest of a sense of strangeness, especially the strangeness of ordinary thought. And one of the indispensable conditions for philosophy is a capacity for linguistic insecurity—for taking a certain distance from one's customary everyday words … Thinking only becomes philosophical when familiar words grow strange. (Rée, 2001, pp. 246, 252)

Angélica Maia shows how productive it can be to force educational theorists to take distance from words that have become customary. She considers the Portuguese term *conscientização* as used by Paulo Freire and its common translations into English as 'consciousness raising' and 'conscientization'. Maia points out that when Freire chose the Portuguese noun *conscientização* (derived from the verb *conscientizar*, meaning 'to make oneself or someone else aware of something') 'he … took advantage of the fact that *ação* is also the word used in Portuguese for action. In this context, *conscientização* can also be seen as a combination of *conscientizar* (make or become aware) and *ação* (action) in one single word' (Maia, 2009). The English 'conscientization' does not highlight the action-component of the concept that is so important in Freire's work: 'The term *conscientização* refers to learning to perceive social, political and economic contradictions, *and to take action against the oppressive elements of reality*' (Ramos in Freire, 2000, p. 35, n. 1, emphasis added). Therefore, at the most literal level, *conscientização* might be more 'strangely' and more productively translated by the English neologism 'conscientizaction'.

Walter Benjamin writes that 'the basic error of the translator is that he preserves the state in which his own language happens to be instead of allowing his language to be powerfully affected by the foreign tongue' (Benjamin, 1969, p. 81). He is referring here to the conscientious translator who seeks to produce a text in his own language that does not reveal that it is a translation, for, as Rée reminds us, it is all too easy to ridicule the work of a translator for '*sounding like a translation*' (Rée, 2001, p. 223). The situation is very different for the use of translation in philosophy that I am advocating: in translation as philosophical method the translator does not commit the 'error of the translator' and indeed seeks to have her or his language powerfully affected by the foreign tongue. Rather than seeking the 'proper' translation of 'knowing', I sought to have *connaître* and *savoir* disrupt the English language in which the rest of my inquiry was being conducted.

TRANSLATION AND THE HUMAN CONDITION

Even if we are not using a translated text in the interlinguistic sense, each text we are using is still translated, in the Derridean sense that all language is 'from somewhere else' (Derrida, 2001a, p. 38). All language we use, even if we refer to it as our mother tongue, is 'always already' full of translations, as the use of language consists in its movement from one context to another and this movement is translation.[4] Derrida writes: 'I have only one language and it is not mine; my "own" language is, for me, a language that cannot be assimilated. My language, the only one I hear myself speak and agree to speak, is the language of the other' (Derrida, 1998, p. 25). Tracing the various moments of translation by which words, concepts, ideas and categories have arrived at our doorstep is, therefore, one of the methods philosophers may choose to include in their repertoire. Such etymological tracing, it should be emphasised, is *not* a method for arriving at the truth of language but rather, like the other forms of translation I discuss, a method for raising questions that might not otherwise have occurred. 'Etymology never provides a law and only provides material for thinking on the condition that it allows itself to be thought as well' (Derrida, 2002, p. 71).

However, having spent much time discussing the deliberate use of translation as philosophical method, let me point out that this method cannot be contained or mastered. Even when one does not intend to use translation, one is still conditioned by it. Based on Derrida's perspectives on translation Lovisa Bergdahl calls translation a 'human condition' (Bergdahl, 2009, p. 40) and explains that 'we are all in a constant state of translation meaning that we all find ourselves *in language* just as we find ourselves *in* a country, a certain family and indeed in a religion. However, none of this (language, family, land religion) "belongs" to us in any possessive sense of the term' (p. 36). Rather than saying that we 'find' ourselves in language, I might say that we *lose* ourselves in language, that every time we wish to locate ourselves in 'our' language, we are dislocated by it. The deliberate act of translation may come to an end, but the condition of translatedness exceeds this deliberate act.

INTERDISCURSIVE TRANSLATION

The deliberate creation of distance through translation is used not only in the interlinguistic sense of translation, but also in the interdiscursive sense. Although he does not use the term translation, Jacques Rancière explains beautifully how he employs interdiscursive translation as philosophical method:

> Thinking for me is always a *rethinking*. It is an activity that displaces an object away from the site of its original appearance or attending discourse. Thinking means to submit an object of thought to a specific variation that includes a shift in its discursive register, its universe of reference, or its temporal designations . . . The elaboration of these 'moments of thinking' is for me the task of a philosophy that challenges the boundaries separating the classes of discourses. (Rancière and Panagia, 2000, p. 120)

Rancière describes translation as recasting, the exercise of seeing something *in terms of* something else, where that something else is not a linguistic system such as English or French but rather a discourse or language game. For example, in *The Nights of Labor* (1989) (*Les Nuits des Prolétaires*, 1981), Rancière takes texts produced by 19th century carpenters and other workers in France, and reads these texts in a different discursive register from the one to which these texts were assumed to belong: 'It was necessary for me to extract the workers' texts from the status that social or cultural history assigned to them—as manifestations of a particular cultural condition. I looked at these texts as inventions of forms of language similar to all others' (Rancière, in Rancière and Panagia, 2000, p. 116). Rancière displaces the workers' texts from the dominant interpretive framework, in which they were seen as representations of a class condition, by putting them into an interpretive framework in which they could be seen as literary, intellectual products. Writes Rancière: 'I extracted those worker's [*sic*] texts from their socio-economic links *so as to read them as* antiplatonic philosophical myths' (pp. 120-1, emphasis added). This translation makes possible a different view not only of the texts but also of the authors of the texts themselves. Rancière reads the texts as evidence of the authors not as workers seeking equality, but as thinkers expressing a fundamental equality they already possess. Interdiscursive translation thus supports one of the central claims of Rancière's work, that intellectual equality is not a goal to strive for, but rather ought to be a presupposition that can, through the way in which people are treated when they are assumed to be equal, be verified. 'To pose equality as a goal is to hand it over to the pedagogues of progress, who widen endlessly the distance they promise they will abolish. Equality is a presupposition, an initial axiom—or it is nothing' (Rancière, 2002, p. 223).

Much of Michel Foucault's work can also be understood as interdiscursive translation: as an effort to shift scientific discourses into other discursive registers so as to enable new questions about them. Paul Rabinow writes about this method:

> During most of the 1960s, Foucault sought, in a variety of ways to isolate and analyze the structures of the human sciences treated as discursive systems. It is important to stress that Foucault did not see himself as a *practitioner* of these human sciences. They were his objects of study. Foucault never took these discourses from the inside. That is, he never posed the question of the truth or falsity of the specific claims made in any particular discipline. (Rabinow, 1984, p. 12)

In other words, Foucault did not seek to read scientific discourse according to its accepted 'grammar' of truth and falsity; instead—as if he were reading French according to the rules of English grammar—he read scientific discourse according to the grammar of power. Foucault did not dispute whether the truths put forward by scientific discourse were truths according to the discursive rules governing the distinction between true and false claims, but by reading ostensibly 'scientific' texts 'in different terms': that is, in the discursive register of power and as 'governing' texts, he produced new insights about them.

> Certainly, as a proposition, the division between true and false is neither arbitrary, nor modifiable, nor institutional, nor violent. Putting the question *in different terms*, however—asking what has been, what still is, throughout our discourse, this will to truth which has survived so many centuries of our history; or if we ask what is, in its very general form, the kind of division governing our will to knowledge—then we may well discern something like a system of exclusion (historical, modifiable, institutionally constraining) in the process of development. (Foucault, 1972, p. 218)

The question is, again and again: what questions and understandings become possible when one sees A in terms of B, when one transports A and lets it operate in the land of B? The educative effects of such displacement, of the unfamiliarity created by translation, are perhaps close to what Stanley Cavell has in mind when he posits 'philosophy as translation' (Cavell, as cited in Saito, 2007, p. 270; see Cavell, 2006).

WHAT IS A GOOD TRANSLATION?

I have described how interdiscursive translation has been used as philosophical method, but is *any* translation possible, legitimate and philosophically useful? It appears that philosophical usefulness can only be judged in retrospect: I have described the, in my view, successful interdiscursive translations conducted by Rancière and Foucault because these were the ones that were published and that have led to productive philosophical debate. I do not know whether these authors have attempted other interdiscursive translations that were not successful, perhaps because such unsuccessful work would be less likely to be published, stir up philosophical debate, and hence reach my attention.

The question of legitimacy, however, deserves more careful attention. Can any text be displaced into any other discursive register? Might some decisions to read X in the discursive register of Y be just wrong? In order to answer this question let me consider the connection between translation, especially what I have called 'interdiscursive translation', and metaphor. This is not an arbitrary choice: metaphors (from the Greek verb *meta-pherein* or transferring, carrying over) and translations (from *trans-latus*, the past participle of the Latin verb *trans-ferre*, transferring, carrying over) are closely connected linguistic displacements. Metaphor can be considered a form of *intralinguistic* translation, or translation between terms within a language. Paul Ricoeur has argued that metaphors generate new meaning by breaking the rules of old meaning: 'a metaphor appears as a kind of riposte to a certain inconsistency in the metaphorical utterance literally interpreted. With Jean Cohen, we can call this inconsistency a "semantic impertinence"' (Ricoeur, 1976, p. 50). A metaphor is 'impertinent' because it breaks the existing rules by which language conveys and produces meaning; in a successful metaphor, however, this impertinence leads to a 'semantic innovation' (p. 52): 'It is, in effect, a calculated error, which brings together things that do not go together and by means of this apparent misunderstanding it causes a new, hitherto unnoticed, relation of meaning to spring up between terms that previous systems of classification had ignored or not allowed' (p. 51). The examples of interdiscursive translation I have given are, likewise, calculated errors or misunderstandings. 'No, no', the authors of scientific texts considered by Foucault may have protested, 'you are reading our work the wrong way. This is not research about power or language, it is research about the most efficient way to manage a prison'. Foucault deliberately committed a discursive impertinence by reading this research *as* a different kind of text.

Getting away with such impertinence is a function not just of the status of the author; it is a function also of the careful attention and intention with which the text that is about to be subjected to a displacement into another discursive register has been studied. To put it differently: only after efforts at fidelity have been made can a text be productively betrayed. Derrida writes that 'all translation implies an insolvent indebtedness and an oath of fidelity to a given original— ... an oath doomed to treason or perjury' (Derrida, 2001b, p. 183). This is not a mere translation of the Italian adage *Traduttore, traditore*! (Translator, traitor!), but rather a reflection of the belief that philosophical impertinence, whether in the form of critical interrogation or interdiscursive translation, requires that one attempt to pay one's debt to the text. Fidelity may thus be the one of the paradoxical ways of legitimating the discursive betrayal and impertinence of interdiscursive translation.

APPLICATION AND TRANSLATION

As Marianna Papastephanou points out elsewhere in this volume, education is commonly considered an 'applied field'; philosophy in and of education is often expected to consist of the application of more general philosophy to the particularities of this field (Papastephanou, 2010). In some cases, this may be a fair characterisation. For instance, Immanuel Kant developed his ethical 'categorical imperative' as a general philosophy, and we can apply this imperative to find out what we should do in particular pedagogical situations. In contemporary philosophy, however, it is much less common to find the kind of general philosophy that lends itself to such application. In fact, generalisability and the possibility of applying general theory to particular situations have themselves become objects of critique. Increasingly, philosophers and other theorists understand that the context in which a theory is developed needs to be taken into account when considering whether and how that theory may be used in another context. For this reason, 'application' is more often than not a misnomer for the way in which philosophers in and of education relate to theory and philosophy. Translation offers a better conceptual framework for understanding how theory is used.

The gestures of application and translation are fundamentally different: an application is put on or over top of the phenomenon, and the general theory that is applied to a particular instance does not change. A translation from theory to practice, by contrast, confronts theory with points of untranslatability that will challenge it. Derrida speaks of translation as 'conversion', the way one may convert one currency to another, and, just as in such monetary conversion, a price has to be paid and a difference between the before and after of the conversion is incurred (Derrida, 2001b, p. 184). There are gains, losses, changes, excesses, remainders and commissions involved in all acts of translation. Gert Biesta illustrates this elsewhere in this volume when he points out that 'philosophy of education' is not just a phrase in the English language but rather an idea that 'belongs to a . . . particular Anglo-American construction of the field of educational studies'. This means, he points out, 'that we should not assume that anything that tries to translate itself into these three words can actually be translated that simply . . . . This becomes even more of a problem when acts of "counter-translation" occur and *Bildungstheorie* becomes renamed as *Philosophie der Erziehung*—for example' (Biesta, 2010, pp. 83–4). In counter-translations, not unlike the children's game 'Telephone', the remainder of translation incurs a new remainder.[5]

The term 'translational research' is now used in educational research to indicate the reciprocal connection between theory or research and practice (for example, Lagemann, 2008). Where 'application' suggests a unidirectional move from theory or research to practice, 'translation' suggests that practice speaks back to the 'original' research and that it functions as an original text in its own right, which can and should be translated back into research and theory. Translation does not merely replace application but transforms the relationship between theory and practice itself. An interesting question raised by the conception of research as translational is what the relevance of research should be. This question has been addressed in, among other places, a recent exchange in *Educational Researcher*. Although David Labaree offers some conceptual insights there into the difficulties with demands for relevance, neither he nor any of the other authors use translation as a method of raising further philosophical questions about the concept of relevance (Labaree, 2008).

TRANSLATING 'RELEVANCE'

The question of relevance is particularly important (and not just 'relevant') to philosophers of education, as our work, among other scholarly work in the field of education, is often accused and suspected of being irrelevant. Derrida has shown that the concept of relevance offers itself up for translation, and resists translation, in several ways.

> What of this vocable 'relevant'? . . . This translative body is in the process of being imported into the French language, in the act of crossing borders and being checked at several intra-European customs points that are not only Franco-English, as one might infer from the fact that this word of Latin origin is now rather English (*relevant/irrelevant*) in its current usage, in its use-value, in its circulation or its *currency*, even though it is also in the process of Frenchification. (Derrida, 2001b, p. 177)

In other words, although the English adjective 'relevant' may sound as if it has a direct parallel in the French adjective *relevant*, what Derrida calls the 'use-value' of the adjective 'relevant'—its use-value as 'whatever feels right, whatever seems pertinent, apropos, welcome, appropriate, opportune, justified, well-suited or adjusted, coming right at the moment when you expect it—or corresponding as is necessary to the object to which the so-called relevant action relates' (p. 177)—is distinctly English. When the French *relevant* is used in this way, is it is as the Frenchified English 'relevant'.

Derrida comments on the fact that he has used the French *relève* to translate two very different words: Hegel's noun *Aufhebung* and Shakespeare's verb 'seasons' in the line 'When mercy seasons justice' (*The Merchant of Venice*). This might be no more than a curiosity if *relève*-in-the-sense-of-*Aufhebung* and *relève*-in-the-sense-of-'seasons' were mere homonyms with no conceptual connection (like the noun 'bear' and the verb 'bear'). However, the fact that the French *relève* is connected to both *Aufhebung* and 'seasons' actually helps to shed light on the concept of 'relevance'. The German noun *Aufhebung*, which means at once cancellation and elevation, was used by Hegel to designate the moment that thesis and antithesis are sublated (to use a common translation) into synthesis. In *Aufhebung*, the thesis and antithesis are both preserved and negated. Writes Derrida, 'I shall therefore translate "seasons" as "relève": "when mercy seasons justice", "quand le pardon relève la justice (ou le droit)" [*when mercy elevates and interiorizes, thereby preserving and negating, justice (or the law)*]' (Derrida, 2001b, p. 195).

I might suggest the English verb 'lift' as useful translation for *relève*: 'to lift' means both 'to elevate' ('Could you lift your feet please? I'm trying to vacuum') and 'to cancel' ('She wished the ban on smoking in pubs were lifted'). I might further point out that the French *relever* may also be translated with the English 'relieving', as in 'relieving someone of his post', *relever quelqu'un de son poste*. What new insights or questions are produced when we bring the demand for 'relevant' educational research into conversation with the relation between 'relevance', *relève*, 'lifting', and *Aufhebung*? What new insights or questions are produced when we translate 'relevant research' as *la recherche qui relève*? Would 'relevant' educational research be educational research that *hebt sich auf*, lets itself be sublated?

What else could 'relevant' educational research be expected to lift, to elevate and cancel, to preserve and to negate? Should 'relevant' educational research be research that elevates educational practice so that both the research and the old practice are sublated into a new form of research-based practice and practice-based research? Or perhaps we can ask whether 'relevant' research might relieve and lift practice in the way that 'mercy seasons justice', by raising it up and letting it rise above itself. In a time where 'relevant research' and 'data-driven policy' threaten to weigh down education, this last is an appealing possibility.

When it comes to interlinguistic translation, the best translation is the one that does not reveal itself as translation and that hides the activities of the translator under a new text that does not disrupt the reader with awkward words and sentences. As Rée has pointed out, 'Novelists are supposed to sound like novelists, each in their own manner, poets like poets, and essayists like essayists; but a translator should never sound like a translator, or have an original way with words . . . Translation, conventionally conceived, is the art that conceals the translator' (Rée, 2001, p. 223). When translation is used as philosophical method, however, it deliberately and noticeably insinuates itself between the reader and the text, in order to disrupt the apparent familiarity of that text. Translation as philosophical method, then, is improper, obnoxious translation, a translation that refuses to lift (cancel) itself and is, in that sense, intentionally irrelevant.

NOTES

1. This oft-quoted remark was made by Martin Heidegger in 1942 during a lecture on Hölderlin's hymn 'Der Ister' and the translation of the Greek *tò deinón* in Sophocles' *Antigone*. In the same context Heidegger notes that it is not only the case that all translation involves interpretation, but also that all interpretation involves (intralinguistic) translation (p. 62).

2. The distinction between knowledge/*savoir* and knowledge/*connaissance* is also important in the work of Foucault, although he uses both terms in ways that are more specific than I will use for the purposes of my discussion. In *The Archaeology of Knowledge* (*L'Archéologie du Savoir*), Foucault writes, 'By *connaissance* I mean the relation of the subject to the object and the formal rules that govern it. Savoir refers to the conditions that are necessary in a particular period for this or that type of object to be given to *connaissance* and for this or that enunciation to be formulated' (Foucault, 1972, p. 15, n. 2). Translator Alan Sheridan Smith further explains that, in *The Archaeology of Knowledge*, '*connaissance* refers . . . to a particular corpus of knowledge, a particular discipline—biology or economics, for example. *Savoir*, which is usually defined as knowledge in general, the totality of *connaissances*, is used by Foucault in an underlying, rather than an overall, way' (ibid.).

3. Significantly, the first explanation offered by the *Petit Robert* dictionary for the noun *connaissance* is '*le fait ou la manière de connaître*' (the fact or the manner (way) of knowing by acquaintance) (*Petit Robert*, 1991, p. 367).

4. Jonathan Rée comments on the multi-linguistic translational trajectory of the phrase 'always already': 'The German colloquialism *immer schon* . . . often becomes *toujours-*

déjà when translated into philosophical French; in English translations of German, it will normally and properly be translated as "always", but translators of French may feel obliged to preserve the rather pointless French translationism by rendering it as the almost-absurd "always-already"' (Rée, 2001, p. 235).

5. The name 'Telephone' is common in the United States. In the UK, this game is known more commonly as 'Chinese Whispers'. This latter name reflects racist assumptions that are context-specific and hence not literally translatable: in French the game is known as *Le Telephone Arabe*.

REFERENCES

Benjamin, W. (1969) [1923] The Task of the Translator, in: *Illuminations*, H. Zohn, trans. (New York, Schocken Books), pp. 69–82.

Bergdahl, L. (2009) Lost in Translation: On the Untranslatable and its Ethical Implications for Religious Pluralism, *Journal of Philosophy of Education*, 43.1, pp. 31–44.

Biesta, G. (2010) Witnessing Deconstruction in Education: Why Quasi-Transcendentalism Matters, in: C. Ruitenberg (ed.), *What Do Philosophers of Education Do? (And How Do They Do It?)* (Oxford, Wiley-Blackwell), pp. 73–86.

Cavell, S. (2006) *Philosophy the Day After Tomorrow* (Cambridge, MA, Harvard University Press).

Derrida, J. (1998) *Monolingualism of the Other or the Prosthesis of Origin*, P. Mensah, trans. (Stanford, CA, Stanford University Press).

Derrida, J. (2001a) I Have a Taste for the Secret, in: J. Derrida and M. Ferraris, *A Taste for the Secret*, G. Donis, trans. (Cambridge, Polity Press), pp. 1–92.

Derrida, J. (2001b) What is a 'Relevant' Translation?, *Critical Inquiry*, 27, pp. 174–200.

Derrida, J. (2002) Faith and Knowledge: The Two Sources of 'Religion' at the Limits of Reason Alone, in his *Acts of Religion*, S. Weber, trans.; G. Anidjar, ed. (New York, Routledge), pp. 42–101.

Edgerton, D. (1998) De l'innovation aux usages: Dix thèses éclectiques sur l'histoire des techniques, *Annales Histoire, Sciences Sociales*, 53.4, pp. 815–1837.

Foucault, M. (1972) The Discourse on Language, *The Archeology of Knowledge*, R. Swyer, trans. (New York, Pantheon Books), pp. 215–37.

Freire, P. (2000) [1970] *Pedagogy of the Oppressed*, 30th Anniversary Edition, M. B. Ramos, trans. (New York, Continuum).

Heidegger, M. (1996) [1942] *Hölderlin's Hymn 'The Ister'*, W. McNeill and J. Davis, trans. (Bloomington, IN, Indiana University Press).

Hirst, P. H. (1975) *Knowledge and the Curriculum: A Collection of Philosophical Papers* (London, Routledge & Kegan Paul).

Labaree, D. F. (2008) The Dysfunctional Pursuit of Relevance in Education Research, *Educational Researcher*, 37.7, pp. 421–3.

Lagemann, E. C. (2008) Education Research as a Distributed Activity across Universities, *Educational Researcher*, 37.7, pp. 424–8.

Langewand, A. (2001) Children's Rights and Education: A Hermeneutic Approach, in: F. Heyting, D. Lenzen and J. White (eds) *Methods in Philosophy of Education* (New York, Routledge), pp. 144–59.

Maia, A. A. (2009) From 'Conscientização' to 'Conscientization': An Investigation of the Uses of Translation as a Method in Philosophy of Education. Unpublished manuscript.

Papastephanou, M. (2010) Method, Philosophy of Education and the Sphere of the Practico-Inert, in: C. Ruitenberg (ed.), *What Do Philosophers of Education Do? (And How Do They Do It?)* (Oxford, Wiley-Blackwell), pp. 131–49.

Le Petit Robert (1991) *Dictionnaire Alphabétique et Analogique de la Langue Française* (Paris, Le Robert).

Pickstone, J. (1993) Ways of Knowing: Towards a Historical Sociology of Science, Technology and Medicine, *British Journal for the History of Science*, 26, pp. 433–58.

Pickstone, J. (2000) *Ways of Knowing. A New History of Science, Technology and Medicine* (Manchester, Manchester University Press).

Rabinow, P. (1984) Introduction, in: M. Foucault, *The Foucault Reader*, P. Rabinow ed. (New York, Pantheon Books), pp. 3–29.

Rancière, J. (1989) *The Nights of Labor: The Workers' Dream in Nineteenth-Century France*, J. Drury, trans. (Philadelphia, Temple University Press).

Rancière, J. and Panagia, D. (2000) Dissenting Words: A Conversation with Jacques Rancière, *Diacritics*, 30.2, pp. 113–26.

Rancière, J. (2002) Afterword, *The Philosopher and his Poor*, A. Parker, C. Oster and J. Drury, trans. (Durham, NC, Duke University Press).

Rée, J. (2001) The Translation of Philosophy, *New Literary History*, 32, pp. 223–57.

Ricoeur, P. (1976) *Interpretation Theory: Discourse and the Surplus of Meaning* (Fort Worth, TX, Texas Christian University Press).

Rigal, C. (2006) Présentation du livre de John V. Pickstone: « *Ways of Knowing: A New History of Science, Technology and Medicine* » Online at http://www.rehseis.cnrs.fr/IMG/pdf/Pickstone
modif-2.pdf (accessed 3 April 2009).

Robinson, R. (1971) The Concept of Knowledge, *Mind, New Series*, 80.317, pp. 17–28.

Ruitenberg, C. W. (2008) The Epistemological Turn: The Tropological Uses of 'Ways of Knowing', in: P. Enslin and N. Hedge (eds) *Education and Multicultural Understanding: Proceedings of the 11th Biennial Conference of the International Network of Philosophers of Education* (Kyoto, Japan, The Site Committee of the 11th Biennial Conference of the International Network of Philosophers of Education), pp. 306–17.

Saito, N. (2007) Philosophy as Translation: Democracy and Education from Dewey to Cavell, *Educational Theory*, 57.3, pp. 261–75.

9
Between the Lines: Philosophy, Text and Conversation

RICHARD SMITH

I begin with some points of interest, interesting difficulties perhaps, matters that we might dwell on when we think about what philosophy is, or what kind or kinds of philosophy should be practised. About how to philosophise. First there is the oddity of allowing these questions to take us in the direction of enquiring about philosophical *method*, as if that was a matter of supposing that we might one day reach agreement on at least the broad outlines of how to do the business properly: 'rigorously and robustly' no doubt, and deserving a special chapter in the latest *Research Methodology Handbook*. To anyone who cannot see how this is odd one can only urge wider acquaintance with the history of ideas, which shows how the search for method is local and contingent, a distinctively modernist enterprise, inaugurated largely by Bacon's dissatisfaction with the legacy of Aristotle and the Peripatetic School and his attempts to formulate a 'new induction' (Smith, 2006). Philosophers' own efforts to write coherently on the topic, such as Collingwood's in his *Philosophical Method* (2005), are often self-defeating in violating the very canons that they propose: Collingwood in writing vividly and with extensive use of metaphor and simile about how the philosopher must cultivate a plain style and avoid the figurative (Smith, 2008). In any case how strange it would be to imagine—if this is what the quest for method here amounts to—that philosophy could be done by anyone who had acquired 'the method', picked up an -ology, but was unfamiliar with the history of philosophy and its texts.

Second, and following from the above, from the beginning of Western philosophy there have been those, on the one hand, who seem to have thought of philosophy as a matter for dialogue or conversation (Socrates especially, who left no writings behind) and those, on the other hand, for whom philosophy was a matter of producing texts, both ones where what is literature and what is philosophy are hard to separate and texts written in a more austere and technical style (which is itself of course a distinctive style). The distinction between text and dialogue here is similar to, though not the same as, Richard Rorty's well-known distinction between systematic and edifying philosophy: the former being the province of philosophers who aim to solve problems so that they can move progressively on to solve more problems, thus producing a philosophical corpus or record of philosophical achievement, the latter seeing philosophy, somewhat in the manner of Socrates or the early Plato, primarily as the enterprise of continuing conversations of an educative kind; and not just educative in a general sense but educative for the particular, quasi-embodied people involved.[1] These two distinctions in turn are not unconnected with what we might today, and not altogether happily, think of as the division between philosophy as research (done largely in a library, or even the proverbial armchair) and philosophy as teaching (done mainly with undergraduate and postgraduate students in universities)—the research arm or division being of course these days more prestigious since it is bound up with the allocation of resources, though it is still allowed to 'inform' the teaching (as if edifying philosophy consisted essentially in passing on the systematic kind).

At any rate many of these points are in the minds of the participants in the following dialogue. Being a dialogue it has no readily discernible 'method': it goes where it goes, something about which George, the nominal teacher of this particular class, has mixed feelings, accepting that he has some responsibility to steer it while at the same time relishing the way it seems to have a life and a mind of its own. The distinctions between the written and spoken word, between systematic and edifying philosophy, are both what the class or seminar is about, in the sense that they are at issue in the reading set and in other texts central to the module, and they are also important questions in the way that the group works. This is all very complicated, and George often thinks how much simpler things would be if only he produced some tidy aims and outcomes for each session in the approved manner. But, as students on this module have more than once perceptively observed, if they knew where they were going there wouldn't be much point in having the seminar, or not this kind of seminar at least.

George and these students have found themselves in the play of text before (Smith, 2003). Whether 'George' reflects or inspires the author of this chapter is something this author is not best placed to judge. The students are again combined, in a sense that only they will understand. The module is, roughly, about postmodernism, and its members have been wrestling, among other things, with whether 'postmodern' thinkers continue the philosophical project, demonstrate its oddity or impossibility, or take it in new directions. Being concerned with postmodernism, the module naturally begins with Plato's *Phaedrus*, which runs through the year as a *leitmotif* and ready point of reference, and explains various remarks about plane trees, cicadas, Egyptian kings and the invention of writing. The module ends with Richard Rorty's *Contingency, Irony, and Solidarity*, of which the students are supposed to have read at least the first three chapters in preparation for this seminar.

****

George: So we got there in the end—a decent seminar room for once, since they refurbished this teaching block during the vacation. No midday sun under a plane tree by the river Ilissus, or cicadas singing, but a view of our own river at least. Perhaps the shades of Socrates and Phaedrus will look on us kindly, and help us make sense of what we've been reading.

Rachel: Some of us could do with their help, George. This Rorty stuff is hard going. I thought you said it would bring together everything we've been talking about this year, make the penny drop?

George: Did I say that? It sounds like the kind of thing that I would say. Mind you, I'm not always very reliable in these matters. As you know.

Louise: There we go again. Never once have I come away from one of these seminars with a good set of notes. Oh, I know I shouldn't want a good set of notes—a recipe for forgetting, not remembering! And if anyone mentions Egyptian kings and the invention of writing I'll throw them in the river.

Mike: Or Phaedrus's addiction to Lysias's speechifying and the scroll he had under his tunic.

Amy: What Phaedrus had under his tunic: do you have to lower the tone already? *(General mayhem for several minutes.)*

Rachel: I thought you said it would bring things together in one sense in particular; not just what we've been talking about, but how we've been talking. What kind of philosophy we've been doing, if this is philosophy.

Ben: And your view of philosophy, George. Do you think of yourself as a postmodernist, are you a Rortyan, or what? I can see a bit why you always avoid this question, because you don't see yourself as having any kind of method, as if there was a 'here's how to do it' that you could teach us and we could take it away and use it like a handbook.

Jane: Because the idea of method is at the heart of modernity—Francis Bacon and his *Novum Organum*, precisely the manual for the new inductive method, or he wanted it to be. And Descartes.

Anna: Descartes? Why Descartes?

Aisha: His *Discourse* is the *Discourse on Method*, Anna. On *method*. Full title: *Discourse on the Method of Rightly Conducting the Reason, and Seeking Truth in the Sciences*. It's got method, reason, truth and science—the whole modernist package!

Ben: Alright, George, you don't have a method. Some of us had suspected that for some time. But some of this Rorty stuff sounded a bit like you. If only the irony.

George: Ok. I'll try to give you some idea of what kind of philosophy I like, in as far as I have a clear idea myself, or could give any kind of satisfactory account of how it's different from other kinds of writing. But let's make a gentle start. Would anyone like to remind us why Richard Rorty came up with this title, *Contingency, Irony, and Solidarity*? What about the first word?

Ilse: Well, he starts with language. It's just a matter of chance—of contingency—what language you grow up learning to speak. So, the example we thought of last week, back home in Germany we say *Geisteswissenschaften*, which means, literally, understanding the human spirit, but here you say 'social science'. So you grow up with assumptions about there being a scientific method, about the necessity of measuring and quantifying things, that we don't have to the same extent.

Mike: Or if you lived in the time when they had the theory of the humours, and you took it for granted that people were either phlegmatic or choleric and so on, and they were made that way and couldn't change. Or the way they talk of *erôs* in the *Phaedrus*, it has associations of passion and madness that our word 'love' doesn't have.

George: Just staying with the contingency of language for the moment— because of course Rorty has chapters on the contingency of community and selfhood as well—what are the implications of all this for the idea of truth?

Louise: Yeah, that's what I don't really get. He doesn't believe in truth, does he?

Tom: If he's saying there's no such thing as truth then . . .

Jane: We know, we know: 'then it must be true that there's no such thing as truth. Which is self-contradictory'. Spare us the cheap analytic shot. That's a method if ever I saw one!

Sam: He doesn't say there's no such thing as truth, he says that truth is a kind of empty compliment we pay to statements, or sentences—I can't remember which—that help us get things done. Help us achieve our ends.

George: And that is because he's a . . . ? *(Silence)*

Rachel: Nutcase? Professor?

George: I detect that, not for the first time, I have phrased my question badly. I was trying to prompt the response that he is a pragmatist, and a notion of truth as what helps us get where we want to go is a pragmatist theory.

Louise: As opposed to . . . ?

George: As opposed to the idea that a true sentence is one that accurately reflects the world, holds up a mirror to nature, to echo the title of Rorty's earlier book.

Jane: So the point of the contingency of language is that there is never anywhere a perfect language that tells us how reality is. There is something in the world that we call love and the Greeks called *erôs*, but there is no way of knowing it outside of these words.

Amy: This really does my head in. Surely it's either true that Socrates fancied Phaedrus or it isn't?

Mike: What, like as a historical fact, when they are characters in a story, a dialogue?

Sam: Doesn't this example make the point perfectly? Even if the *Phaedrus* reported real events, it would make all the difference whether we said Socrates loved Phaedrus, or had *erôs* for him . . .

Ben: Or the hots . . .

Mike: Or Phaedrus turned him on.

George: Which is to say, before things deteriorate even further, that it's very hard to find language that isn't shot through with metaphor. Different metaphors, different realities. 'Turned him on', for instance, suggests a very mechanistic view of human relationships. And if language is heavily metaphorical, ineliminably metaphorical, then it can't be conceived as a nice, clear and neutral set of signs that accurately reflect reality.

Emma: Sometimes I almost think I've got it, and then I think: surely there was either a big bang at the start of the universe or there wasn't? So to say that there was is either true or not true.

Rachel: What, literally big? The way you said 'that's a big ask' when I tried to touch you for a fiver the other evening? Or the way that's a big tree outside? *That* big?

Ilse: And that's before we get on to 'bang', as opposed to whether it was more like a very loud 'pop', and how there can be a bang when there's no one to hear it.

George: On a pragmatist theory, to call that particular theory of the origin of the universe 'true' is to say it's part of a story which helps us do things: to understand the age of the earth and make sense of the fossil record, for instance. Though I have to confess I personally still have an urge to say that the creationist account just isn't *true* in the sense that what it describes didn't happen. Still more so when we come to controversial historical events. Some people think Napoleon was poisoned, for example, and one day we'll find whether that's true or not. Or in the Orwellian kind of example, either Jones was at the meeting with the other party high-ups, and they doctored the photos later when he fell out of favour to make it look as if he wasn't there, or he never was actually there in the first place.

Rachel: What I have a lot of trouble with in Rorty is that it all seems to come down to agreement. Instead of looking for the truth and knowing when we've found it we sit around having civilised conversations about our aims and purposes. So we agree that we want more human solidarity—another of the words from the title—and less cruelty, and whether this or that counts as more solidarity or a world with less cruelty is just a matter of whether we think it does. Not of whether it really does or is. OK, let's accept that there are problems with the idea of truth in just the way that Rorty says. But it can't be nothing but whether or not we agree, can it? What if we all agree but only because we are dead smug and complacent and reach a cosy consensus? And who are 'we', anyway? Well-paid academics with white hair like the picture on the back of the book? No offence, George.

George: I wish, the first part of that description. Look, what Rachel has done is turn the discussion to where I thought we might find ourselves going today. It's one of our nine themes of postmodernism, neatly bullet-pointed in the module outline: the ideal of conversation comes to replace that of knowledge.

Ben: Which is why we started with the *Phaedrus* and have ended up with Rorty.

George: Yes. And now we have to take seriously Rachel's question. When is a conversation or dialogue, one of these events that we are replacing the pursuit of knowledge with, a good or successful conversation, one that takes us somewhere, however we want to put this, and when is it a bad one? Think of those conversations you have into the small hours in your disgusting shared student houses with mysterious damp patches, or of course think of a university seminar, including this one.

Ilse: This is the difference between Rorty's systematic and edifying philosophy, isn't it? We're talking about philosophy as edification, aren't we?

Louise: Come again? I think I was away for that.

Ilse (Takes file from bag, shuffles through it and reads aloud): 'Systematic philosophy, of which Anglophone analytic philosophy is a prominent example, tries to solve problems in a way that produces a body of successful philosophical solutions. Edifying philosophy takes the gadfly path, from Socrates to Derrida. It aims at continuing a conversation rather than at discovering truth. It is educative, in the sense of *Bildung*, as a matter of forming the character of the individual. It is not concerned, or much less concerned, with the "discovery, elucidation and justification of a core of fundamental truth".'[2]

Mike: Because of course Rorty has a problem with truth.

George: Which is . . . ? Anyone?

Ilse: On the systematic view, philosophy is a kind of master-discipline that addresses the relationship between language and reality. It's very often tempted by the idea of truth as a matter of holding up a mirror to nature, in the title of Rorty's earlier book, that is to say representing it. In contrast to philosophy as edifying conversation.

Louise: Oh, representation again. Everything on this module seems to come back to presence and representation. Rorty's against it, Lyotard seems to think it leads to totalitarianism,[3] and then there's Derrida and the metaphysics of presence. So if truth and meaning aren't about—aren't about—saying 'here's reality' . . .

Aisha: Then they're about going on some endless conversational trip. Is that right, George?

George: Endless, yes, in more than one sense . . .

Aisha: Here it comes, the bloody Derridean deferral of meaning again!

George: . . . but I'd have to say a few things about the idea of it being a 'trip' . . .

Tom: I see. I get it now. We're having an edifying seminar, aren't we? The point isn't to get to the truth but to go round in circles.

Emma: But in an edifying way!

Tom: Seriously, George, is this your vision of what we're doing here, of philosophy if this is philosophy? Is this what philosophy means to you? You've often hinted at your reservations about the kind of philosophy you were taught. Which was analytic, systematic in Rorty's view?

George: Reservations, yes. There was a sense when I was studying philosophy at university that the object was to identify and get beyond certain wrong turns in philosophical thinking, such as the idea that ethics just comes down to expressions of feeling—emotivism—for instance, or to see just why some of Russell's paradoxes are seductive but flawed. At the same time the way I was actually taught was quite Socratic: one-to-one tutorials where any question you asked of your tutor was likely to be answered with another question. Which was often exasperating but one eventually and slowly began to realise that philosophy wasn't a discipline where the whole point was to learn the answers and reproduce them to order.

Tom: But there were exams, and you had to get the answers right?

George: Of course. So sometimes you wondered if the edification—not that we used that word at the time—wasn't entirely serious, or if the Socratic approach was something you could really go in for properly only if you could afford not to worry about getting the good degree that would mean a job at the end. And then of course the dons, as they were known in those days, went off in the vacations to write their books, and you thought this must be the real philosophical business, in contrast to showing undergraduate students that there were no easy answers. Because those books and articles that they wrote held answers, didn't they, even if not easy ones?

Jane: That hasn't changed, has it? Our lecturers are always telling us they need to get on with their research and write their books. For promotion, or just so they don't lose their jobs.

George: Quite. Anyway, so much for the philosophical education of George, such as it was. To be honest, I find all this hard to think about clearly; partly, I suppose, because of the autobiographical element and partly, I think, because the difference between getting the conversation, the Socratic dialogue if you like, right, and getting it wrong in various ways is very slight, a dividing line that it's easy to cross without noticing it. Often just at the point where you begin to think you're getting it just right you realise you've fallen into one trap or another. In this it's a bit like more familiar forms of therapy, where it's notorious that the patient can unconsciously use his intelligence to avoid looking at things he doesn't want to look at, or the therapist's extensive experience and knowledge of the theory of therapy can get in the way of properly listening to, attending to, the patient in front of her.

Ilse: You think philosophy is quite a lot like therapy, don't you, George?

George: Yes, both in the way I've just suggested and in that, to use a famous image from Ludwig Wittgenstein, often philosophy 'shows us the way out of the fly bottle'. We buzz around in the grip of obsessions and fantasies and fixed ways of thinking, and the philosopher's job is to show that there's a perfectly straightforward way out of the bottle—it was there all the time but it's as if we were determined not to see it.

Sam: What would be an example?

George: Think of how last year we got hung up on the question of how we could possibly know other people, particularly if they were very different from us. We hadn't had their experiences, we couldn't get inside their heads, so how could we understand them?

Aisha: The answer was that we share the same public forms, the same languages, wasn't it. That's the solution.

George: Or the dissolution, because this doesn't so much solve the problem as dissolve it, show us there never really was a problem in the first place, but we worked ourselves up, buzzing around the bottle, into thinking there was.

Ilse: So Wittgenstein is an edifying philosopher, would Rorty call him that?

George: The later Wittgenstein, the author of the *Philosophical Investigations*, I think so. Not the early Wittgenstein of the *Tractatus*.

Amy: Can we go back to ways of getting Socratic dialogue wrong? Particularly since I seem to have run away with the idea that the *Phaedrus* is some kind of model of how to get it right.

George: Rachel's complaint about smug consensus would be one. People work on the differences among them and congratulate themselves on reaching some level of agreement, and then they begin to wonder if the search for consensus was really a way of avoiding discomfort. We can go back to the *Phaedrus* for other examples, and inevitably we will, but I found a telling one in a novel by Iris Murdoch recently. It's called *Nuns and Soldiers*, and one of the main characters, Guy, is dying of cancer. His wife, Gertrude, has an old friend called Anne who is staying with them. She is in a sense the 'nun' of the title: she has been in a convent which she has recently left, and she's an unusual woman—clever, principled, sees to the heart of things, most of the time anyway. She has a conversation with the dying Guy, and he tells his wife about it. I have the novel here in my bag since I haven't quite finished it. Here we are on page 100. Guy says 'I enjoyed talking to Anne'. Gertrude says 'I'm so glad'. Guy: 'It was a foretaste of heaven'. Gertrude is puzzled, and Guy explains, 'You recall some witty Frenchman said that his idea of heaven was *discuter les idées générales avec les femmes supérieures*'.

There you are: heaven consists in talking about 'general ideas', philosophical ideas, with—hard to translate—'superior women', 'bright girls', 'gifted' perhaps. The idea that life couldn't offer anything much better than that. Edifying conversations with . . .

Sam: Classy dames.

Mike: Posh totty.

Aisha: Oh, oh, he says this to his wife. To his *wife*. So she's not one of these superior females, then? How is she supposed to feel about that?

George: Exactly. Something not quite right here. Not right at all. That reminds us perhaps of the erotic dimension in the *Phaedrus*, which seems both to capture something right and wonderful about sparkling conversation, and at the same time it's a bit disturbing: as if this particular sparkling conversation isn't as elevated as it seems.

Emma: Are you our Socrates, George, are we your bright, superior girls?

George: Leaving aside the fact that Mike and Ben and Sam and Tom might have a problem with that . . .

Rachel: No, we're not, we're just characters in his bloody dialogue, we don't even exist, not really. (*There follow several minutes of pandemonium, in which can be distinguished voices saying variously: 'Nothing outside the text!' 'She feels as if she's in a play—she is anyway!' 'If this is heaven, take me to the other place'. Order resumes as George attempts to provide one of those interim summaries that the students had said, in the interim module evaluations, would be helpful from time to time.)*

George: To pull things together a little, if possible, one of our themes has been how in postmodernism, if there is anything that can be called that ... (*cries of 'yes, yes, get on with it!'*)

George: ... sorry, the theme of how the ideal of conversation comes to replace that of knowledge.

Louise: Which is edification replacing the systematic. Just for the moment there a penny dropped.

George: More or less, in Richard Rorty's terms, and it was Rorty that this seminar or discussion was supposed to be about. And we took the *Phaedrus*— this is one of the main reasons why we read the *Phaedrus*—as a way of looking at how discussion or dialogue or conversation can have a richness and resonance that goes beyond narrowly rational ways of going about understanding the world, modernist ways. We're all familiar enough with that point, I take it? (*Various responses mention the setting of the dialogue under the plane tree by the river Ilissus, Plato's use of myth and legend, the poetic nature of the language in many places, the problematisation of means–end reasoning as exemplified by Lysias's view of personal relationships, the idea of love as a kind of madness.)*

George: Well, then. Think of the conversation between Socrates and Phaedrus, rich and resonant and so on, as the kind of thing you might recall, if you were Phaedrus, as one of the better days of your life. You might say to yourself, 'It doesn't get much better than that'. You've become an Athenian statesman, say, with all the compromises, and perhaps even bribery and brutality, that might go with that career; or you've joined the management consultancy firm you had your heart on, and discovered that you've had to sign up to corporate identity and corporate ways of doing things and relentless cost-saving and means-end rationality. You might look back on the day you spent with Socrates, or you might just look back on bits of your time at university, and feel that there was something special there that it was hard to find again, something that the new world you'd joined didn't value, or even understand.

Mike: You know, all this looks a lot like the privileging of the spoken word over writing, dialogue over text. Outright phonocentrism!

Sam: Which you'll miss when you start work for Phonocenture,[5] Mike!

George: And of course what Phaedrus himself hankers for. But are there dangers in that? What exactly is Phaedrus in love with? John Ferrari, in his study of the *Phaedrus*, it's called *Listening to the Cicadas*, writes of how philosophical discussion about how to live the good life can be part of the good life itself, which is Guy's heavenly philosophical discussions; but Ferrari has a lot to say about how that can turn into a mere getting off on intellectual talk. He sees this as exemplified in the character of Phaedrus himself, who loves fine words and all the stage-setting that goes with it. Back to Amy's worries again. You wrote about this in your essay, Emma.

Emma: Yes. Phaedrus can't see that being too fond of fine words, and sitting next to Socrates and so on, risks getting in the way of doing proper philosophy, being a proper philosopher. Ferrari calls Phaedrus an impresario: he's put the play on, designed a magical set for it.[4] There's a sense of 'look at me sitting next to Socrates, look what I've arranged!' about the whole thing.

George: And perhaps Socrates is a bit seduced by this. The name 'Phaedrus' means 'sparkling' in classical Greek—who wouldn't be flattered to have a sparkling, attentive pupil like Phaedrus at their elbow? Or *femmes supérieures* if only one was so lucky.

Rachel: How rude.

Louise: Just when I think I'm getting the hang of things here it all gets turned upside down. And if someone says 'deconstruction' and the reversal of binaries I shall scream. I thought the setting of the *Phaedrus* told us something about the dangers of scientific rationality and narrow forms of reason, the means–end thinking that is all Lysias has to offer. I thought it was about conversation being better than Enlightenment knowledge and truth. And then I thought I saw how edification and systematic philosophy mapped onto all of this. Have I got it all wrong?

George: No, nothing wrong with that at all, Louise. But the ideal of conversation in contrast with ideals based around truth and knowledge can't guarantee the quality, the worth, of any particular conversation, can it? Plato writes a lot about this ideal and its characteristic ways of going wrong. The long conversation which is the *Republic* begins when Socrates and Glaucon are stopped on their way back to Athens from Piraeus, the docks, by Polemarchus and his mob. Polemarchus's father, Cephalus, is a kind of Godfather figure, who wants Socrates to come and entertain him. We need to take seriously the idea here that Socrates is stopped in his path by force of numbers, by people who refuse to listen to his request to be allowed to pass. His talent for dialectic is pressed into the service of making an elderly *mafioso* happy by giving him an evening of high-class conversation, like some philosophical Scheherazade. And this strikes a very disturbing note: is the whole of the *Republic* just a kind of entertainment, and not a rigorous philosophical dialogue?

Ilse: Ah, we were doing that in my Politics module last week. Plato himself describes the Republic, the city-state that they are talking about, as a city of words. Perhaps the whole dialogue is mere words, verbal pyrotechnics, exactly that—the entertaining conversation that Cephalus asked for.[6]

Mike: Just a moment—aren't we doing just what Phaedrus does—concentrating on the stage scenery? When the *Republic* is about justice, and the constitution of the state, and the Theory of Forms and lots of other important stuff, we're focusing on just the introduction? A bit of banter that gets the serious business going?

George: Well, perhaps sometimes the stage-setting isn't *only* the stage-setting, or we might say that to be attentive to it, even unusually attentive to it, isn't the same as to be distracted by it, to get off on it, as Phaedrus seems to.

Anna: You mean, to mistake it for the real thing, the philosophy that it's the setting for.

George: If I'm not entirely happy with that way of putting it, it's because it leaves 'the real thing', Socratic dialectic, or Rorty's edification, privileged and unchallenged, as if we knew exactly what it was and had no doubts, no reservations, about it at all. As if bringing out the familiar tropes and techniques—*elenchus* and maieutic and so on in the Socratic case—guaranteed that real philosophy was going on. No, we were right to notice that the setting of the *Phaedrus*, and its myths and stories, make us uneasy about the superior status of dialectic or philosophy. But the answer isn't to rush to the other end of the spectrum, so to speak, and uncritically embrace myths, or erotically-charged discussion by the river, or Lyotard's *petits récits* come to that, as if they were the holy grail.

Jane: Just as the story of Theuth and Thamus and the invention of writing makes us sceptical about the written word as against the spoken word of dialectic . . .

Aisha: So does the speech of Lysias, which he probably had all written out, and which Phaedrus listened to and then went away and wrote out . . .

Mike: . . . and concealed under his tunic!

Ilse: Just like we can't miss the fact that the *Phaedrus* may be a dialogue, but it's something Plato *wrote*. It's a *text*.

Amy: But these seminars—you value these, don't you, George? I remember you saying at the beginning of the year, or maybe it was last year or the year before, how the point is for us to be really here, in the flesh, not as brains on trolleys trying to spot the exam question or take down a good set of notes.[7]

George: Rachel has doubts about this, from what she said before. Isn't that right, Rachel?

Rachel: Nothing but a pack of cards! That's what we are here!

Sam: Look out, George—the playing cards at the end of *Alice in Wonderland* turned very nasty.[8]

Aisha: Seminars or the library? Books or discussion? It's as if when we're reading and talking about Rorty, Plato or Derrida we're always wondering whether the reading or the talking is better, just which of them is the real thing, more philosophical.

Ilse: Which is why Derrida warns us against trying to find something real, something unquestionably there, to underpin meaning. Truth, *logos*. Our habit of logocentrism.

Mike: And Rorty warns us against easy assumptions about truth, as if truth was just a matter of reflecting reality, holding a mirror up to it.

Tom: So there are all sorts of ways of getting philosophical dialectic wrong. What about poor old Phaedrus? What ought he to do to get it right? I mean, should he have done?

George: Let's not be too hard on Phaedrus; there are worse things than having a crush on philosophy. But perhaps he should have been more concerned for the genuine exercise of the intellect, rather than for the appearance of it; for the wisdom that gives us half of the word 'philosophy', rather than the philosopher's badge and box of tricks;[9] concerned for truth, if you like, understood not as a matter of claims purporting to mirror reality, but as a kind of seriousness of purpose—not to be confused with solemnity, of course. Looking behind the clever words for something more than clever words, something beyond.

Aisha: So what your view of philosophy is, George, is that it consists a lot of the time in asking what philosophy is. Am I the only person here who thinks that's a bit introverted?

George: Oh dear. But yes, I do think the philosopher has to lead the way in being sceptical towards claims that this or that is the right way—especially the one right way—to do philosophy. I like writers who are hospitable, though preferably with a measure of scepticism too, to a wider range of voices and styles than analytic or systematic philosophy has generally been receptive to. Which is why I enjoy Rorty and persevere with the postmodernists, though sometimes with incomprehension and despair. My image for all this is that of listening: noticing—as Ferrari does so well with the *Phaedrus*—where there are ideas in the canonical texts that mainstream interpretation has missed. Taking the language seriously, relishing the words. Attempting a close reading, as the lit crit people call it, rather than skimming in order to extract the 'philosophical meat'. The example of the opening of the *Republic* that I gave earlier. Reading between the lines, whether it's texts on the page or each other. I hope we've done a bit of that in these seminars, read each other, attend, listen to each other—not to see if Sam understands 'contingency' or Jane's got the hang of deconstruction, but for what's being said and what might be said, if other people listen carefully enough.

Louise: Perhaps you should have told us that at the beginning of the module!

George: Perhaps I didn't know it at the beginning, or didn't see it quite the way I do now, which is still not as clearly as I would like. For remember that this text and this seminar, like George himself, have been given life by you as much as—I hope!—the other way round.

Ben: I know how this seminar ends, George: we reply (consults his translation of *Phaedrus*) 'Offer that prayer for me too, for friends should share everything'. The last words of the book. Almost.

Ilse: Except that this shows again how Phaedrus underestimates the distance between himself and Socrates, doesn't it?

George: Almost the last words—remind us what the last words are, Ben.

Ben: 'Let's go'.

Rachel: Yay! And it's spot on five to the hour. Time to get out of this text and get a life!

Various voices: 'But there's nothing—nothing outside—of the text, Rachel!' (*Seminar breaks up in moderately cheerful disarray.*)

NOTES

1. Fendt and Rozema (1998) make a good case for reading many of the Platonic dialogues in this way.
2. Gutting (1999), p. 189.
3. See the last paragraph of *The Postmodern Condition* (Lyotard, 1984).
4. Phaedrus 'cannot conceive that the values of performance might actually prove a danger to the well-being of intellectual talk; cannot conceive, in other words, that he should aim to be a philosopher first, and an impresario only second' (Ferrari, 1990, p. 9).
5. One of the less known global management consulting, technology services and outsourcing companies.
6. See Smith (2009).
7. See Smith (2003).
8. 'At this the whole pack rose up into the air, and came flying down upon her: she gave a little scream, half of fright and half of anger, and tried to beat them off, and found herself lying on the bank, with her head in the lap of her sister, who was gently brushing away some dead leaves that had fluttered down from the trees upon her face. "'Wake up, Alice dear!" said her sister; "Why, what a long sleep you've had!"' (Lewis Carroll, *Alice's Adventures in Wonderland*).
9. See Ferrari (1990), pp. 32 and 39 especially.

REFERENCES

Carroll, L. *Alice's Adventures in Wonderland* (various editions).

Collingwood, R. G. (2005) [1933] *An Essay on Philosophical Method*, rev. edn (Oxford, Clarendon Press).

Fendt, G. and Rozema, R. (1998) *Platonic Errors: Plato, a Kind of Poet* (Westport, CT, Greenwood Press).

Ferrari, G. R. F. (1990) *Listening to the Cicadas: A Study of Plato's* Phaedrus (Cambridge, Cambridge University Press).

Gutting, G. (1999) *Pragmatic Liberalism and the Critique of Modernity* (Cambridge, Cambridge University Press).

Lyotard, J.-F. (1984) [1979] *The Postmodern Condition: A Report on Knowledge*, G. Bennington and B. Massumi, trans. (Minneapolis, University of Minnesota Press).

Murdoch, I. (1980) *Nuns and Soldiers* (London, Chatto & Windus).

Rorty, R. (1979) *Philosophy and the Mirror of Nature* (Princeton, NJ, Princeton University Press).

Rorty, R. (1989) *Contingency, Irony, and Solidarity* (Cambridge, Cambridge University Press).

Smith, R. (2003) Unfinished Business: Education without Necessity, *Teaching in Higher Education*, 8.4, pp. 477–91.

Smith, R. (2006) As if by Machinery: The Levelling of Educational Research, *Philosophy, Methodology and Educational Research*, Special Issue of *Journal of Philosophy of Education* 40.2, pp. 157–68.

Smith, R. (2008) To School with the Poets: Philosophy, Method and Clarity, *Paedogogica Historica*, 44.6, pp. 635–45.

Smith, R. (2009) Half a Language: Listening in the City of Words, in: M. Depaepe and P. Smeyers (eds) *Educational Research: Proofs, Arguments and Other Reasonings* (Dordrecht, Springer), pp. 149–60.

10

Method, Philosophy of Education and the Sphere of the Practico-Inert

MARIANNA PAPASTEPHANOU

INTRODUCTION

Philosophy *of* education is one of those fields that are marked by the ambivalence of the genitive 'of' that brings philosophy and education together. In its *objective* sense the genitive 'of' constructs education as an *object* of philosophical endeavour. In so doing, it typically assigns education a subservient position and the status of a specialised region of enquiry. Here is the subject (philosophy), there the object (education). To adapt Alain Badiou, who makes a similar claim about mathematics and its philosophy, the only function of education outside its institutional one seems 'to consist in helping to perpetuate a well-defined area of philosophical *specialization*' (Badiou, 2006, p. 3).

As an area of specialisation, philosophy of education becomes the arena in which general philosophical theories compete for applicability, verifiability and vindication through the concrete. Often, the concrete is tailored to the selected theory. The issue—the question that guides research and determines the method—seems to be 'what would x (philosopher) think about y (educational topic)?' or 'how could we make x's theory relevant and fruitful for y?' For instance, the topic of cosmopolitanism and education is often approached by uncritically transferring established philosophical positions into education. The assumption is that issues of educational concern are compatible with, or adaptable to, ready-made philosophical categories; the intention is then to tease out some implications, to apply philosophy to education. I have argued in the past that, in this way, the major stakes in, and the dilemmas and debates surrounding, the particular philosophical theory are bequeathed to educational theory almost unaltered (Papastephanou, 2005, p. 499). This stops educational concerns from becoming central to assessing the philosophical sources themselves; when one tries to reflect on such concerns, one becomes embroiled too quickly in the problems that beset the philosophical theory. The above formula thus blocks the possibility of education becoming the *subject* of philosophy. It blocks also the possibility of philosophy hearkening to education as the guiding force it can sometimes be, rather than viewing it as a passive recipient, the object of philosophy's concern. In other words, it discourages the articulation of a different relation between philosophy and education.

My aim (and method) here is not to replace one formula with another. This would only reassert the very prescriptivism that needs to be questioned. It would even obscure the suggestion of this essay: that specific topics must themselves be the guiding force of our effort to answer our questions; and that this may entail the interconnection of method and *aporia*—in the sense not of the perpetual dead end, as it is sometimes construed, but rather of wonder. Philosophy of education must rehabilitate the *subjective genitive* sense of the relation between philosophy and education. Education can illuminate philosophy and have a wider relevance to existence (as both the intellectual, examined life and the life of lived experience) than the one it acquires when inscribed within a mere academic specialisation. For instance, lifelong education is a precondition for any philosophy that deserves the name, a precondition that is often forgotten even by some great philosophies that, after becoming established as hegemonic discourses, excel in the eternal repetition of the same. This is not to say that the 'objective genitive' model must now become secondary, that to quote a philosopher and to draw from a philosophical theory must be forbidden to a philosopher of education. It is not to say that the dichotomy needs to be inverted in favour of the 'subjective genitive'. By critiquing philosophies that neglect education and by analysing the reasons for such neglect, I argue for the rehabilitation of modalities associated with or developed from education's everydayness. In this way I hope to illustrate how the two genitives intersect. We should not underestimate the contribution of the 'objective genitive' model with its methodological strategies to philosophy of education and to education as everyday practice. However, we should explore the possibility that education might reclaim a more active role in philosophy, engaging philosophy's attention as an interconnected and worthy partner rather than as a strange or difficult bedfellow.[1]

For contemporary philosophy itself (unlike some of its older versions)[2] has fallen into the trap of neglecting education or of relegating it to what Jean-Paul Sartre called the sphere of the 'practico-inert' (Sartre, 2004), and philosophers of education are often considered poor relations. The implicit assumption is that education is just passive and receptive of philosophical ideas, especially those that can shake it from its supposed servility to societal systems and societal reproductive aims.[3] Education is often viewed by philosophy as part of a more general societal automatism (Arendt), where knowledge (Badiou), method and statistics play a conservative role. They stop the new, the unknown and the unexpected from emerging and revitalising reality. Against this view, I claim that philosophy of education can show that method, knowledge and statistics matter in a less technical and reified sense than is usually philosophically acknowledged. To illustrate my basic argument, I discuss the educational issue of assessment in its double connection—both to practice and to the practico-inert, embracing the whole of human life, well beyond the limits of academic specialisations.

The method that seems suitable to this task comprises the following steps:

- to critically locate one of the reasons for the philosophical objectification of education (especially in its institutional form) in the fashionable dualism between everydayness and epiphany, on which educators have so far remained silent;
- to employ Sartre's idea of the practico-inert as an illustration and, in so doing, to go against the tendency in philosophy of education to neglect Sartre because he is no longer fashionable in general philosophy;
- to take assessment as an example of an educational practice that is often regarded unfavourably, as stale, uninspiring and unavoidably emergent from a supposed immersion in practico-inert everydayness, and to undo this impression by educationally rehabilitating its centrality in redemptive politics and transcendent praxis;
- to make some connections between the practico-inert and both Arendt's and Badiou's negative treatment of issues that are central to educational research, such as knowledge, human sciences and statistics;
- and, finally, to make the suggested subjective genitive mode more explicit by making educational philosophy 'answer them back'— precisely by showing how, if approached in the appropriate manner, some inexorable statistics may reveal philosophical–political inadvertence or complicity.

My grappling with the above example of cosmopolitanism functions as a vehicle for my defence of temporary *aporia* and provisional method, whose kinetic interconnection may be a means of refreshing educational philosophy. As should be evident, I am not arguing for a disengagement of philosophy and education. On the contrary, I believe that the engagement of the two becomes strengthened when one refers, say, to Badiou or Arendt from a challenging and critical philosophical–educational perspective.

EDUCATION AND THE REALM OF THE PRACTICO-INERT

With few exceptions, education is no longer central to thinking about the human being and the world outside its own academic and institutional province. Most of the philosophers we transfer to education have said embarrassingly little about education—a passage, a critical commentary the length of a chapter at most; and what they do say usually forced, as if taking the form of an awkward lecture in response to the invitation of a department of Education. More frequently, the direct concern with education is exhausted in a line here and there, impelling us to sift their texts with the fervour of prospectors for gold. But too much reverence of this kind leads philosophy of education to scholasticism, to a typically pedagogical dependence on the Master and his narrative, and this ironically, and despite its importance, entails an anti-philosophical attitude. For philosophy presupposes, to some extent, and perhaps at the right moment, an iconoclastic revolt on the part of the disciple, an unease regarding discipline, a dose of subjectification (individuation) that undoes the side-effects of uncritical objectification (socialisation). Perhaps nowhere else is this interplay clearer than in the idea of a 'school of thought', which presupposes simultaneously the scholasticism of the follower and the founding moment of divergence—that is, the break with a previous school and the disagreement with other schools of thought.

To think philosophically the 'why' of the contemporary philosophical lack of engagement with education is a task well beyond the limits of this essay. Thus here it will be attempted only indicatively, and chiefly with reference to notions such as the practico-inert, automatism, everydayness, law, method and action. To this end, Sartre's philosophy becomes very relevant, regardless of what Sartre really thought of education or of whether contemporary philosophers have Sartre in mind when they share (or even radicalise) his suspicion of everydayness, institutions and practices. Sartre's terminology is largely marginalised by contemporary philosophical vogue. Yet, more often than not, despite their coming from very different philosophical beaten tracks, contemporary philosophers concur with Sartre in an almost unconscious incrimination of the above terms. Considered in its institutional dimension, education is marked by a confinement to the status of the *social object* and by a deep-seated suspicion that is perhaps a reaction to the populist and consumerist sides of education's democratisation—to its dispersal, its systematic academic thematisation and its popularisation in the 20th century.

Social objects signify for Sartre collective structures that, as such, 'must be the subject matter of sociology' (Sartre, 2004, p. 253). Sartre does not refer to material beings but to 'worked matter', to practical realities 'with their exigencies, to the extent that they realize in and through themselves the interpenetration of a multiplicity of unorganized individuals *within them* and that they produce every individual in them in the *indistinction* of a totality' (ibid.). Sartre makes it absolutely clear that social objects 'are, at least in their fundamental structure, beings of the practico-inert field' (ibid.), with the effect that, seen as a social object, education is inextricably linked with the practico-inert. Hence, we may approach the status attributed to education by examining the practico-inert, which denotes the frozen praxis of previous generations.

Society is dominated by the practico-inert: as the 'demographic structure, the class system and the *education system*' (Craib, 1976, p. 188, emphasis added), the practico-inert assigns each individual a function. Each individual finds herself in such an organised, alienated and alienating collective. In this way, the future of the individual 'is mapped out in the practico-inert that dominates' the collective (ibid.). Collectives as social totalities—for example, institutions or organisations—are produced by processes referred to as 'totalizations' (Sartre, 2004, p. 69). After their emergence through *praxis*, and then after their establishment as practices, totalities become petrified. Much against the current apotheosis of processes and all things procedural, for Sartre the term 'process' 'denotes that impersonal sequence of events proper to the practico-inert field' (Flynn, 2005, p. 128). What Sartre 'calls the "systems" of colonialism and capitalism, for example, are processes' (ibid.).

By contrast, action is dialectical as it operates upon the consolidated existent, and this it simultaneously incorporates and transcends. In this sense, it *is* praxis but a praxis that leads towards sedimentation. In being praxis, action is both engendered and negated by (or re-submerged in) the practico-inert. The latter affects praxis with counterfinalities (Sartre, 2004, p. 232; Flynn, 2005, p. 134), generating unintended consequences that are appropriately described, I believe, as subversively ironic.[4]

Let us explore more deeply the practico-inert. The Sartrean distinction between the in-itself (*en-soi*) and the for-itself (*pour-soi*) in *Being and Nothingness* (Sartre, 1990) theorises a segregation of inert, tautological and solidified reality from its internal negation through the dynamic, spontaneous undoing of identity. The poles of the distinction between inertia and *energeia* are associated respectively with facticity and transcendence (Sartre, 1990, p. 56). We find ourselves within given realities of facticity, within a consolidated realm of social determinations that we usually take for granted, not just as inescapable but also as ontological, essential parameters of our existence. A consequence of this essentialisation is what Sartre calls our 'bad faith' (pp. 47–67)—that is, our tendency either to misconstrue the limits of our present situation as the limits of the world and of possibility, or to exaggerate the power[5] of transcendence over facticity, resulting in the end in the (re)affirmation of facticity. By falling into the trap of bad faith, we immerse ourselves in *exis* (habit), in the facticity of a daily routine, and keep any disruption of it, any transcendence of conditioning, distant. For Sartre, the transcendence of our present situation is not only possible but also an imperative for humanity, something to which we are 'condemned'. It is a task to freedom (Sartre, 1990, p. 129) usually undertaken by intellectuals, groups and movements. When education understood as an institution is placed in the realm of facticity, of inert everydayness, it can be viewed only as an obstacle to freedom, and it loses all transcendence.

'Functional heir' to being in-itself (Flynn, 2005, p. 120), the concept of the practico-inert echoes Marx's notion of the crystallisation of social activity, the 'consolidation of what we ourselves produce into an objective power above us, growing out of control, thwarting our expectations, bringing to naught our calculations' (Stack, 1989, p. 169). Sartre's association of this with institutions owes much to Dilthey's 'objectification of spirit', meant as 'the external embodiment of the lived-experience of social agents in the socio-historical world' (ibid.).[6] Sartre treats objectification negatively as an 'anti-dialectic' activity that preserves only an inert trace of the redemptive *praxis* that initially produced it. Thus, the social reality corresponding to it reflects a sedimented practice that is described as the field of the practico-inert.[7]

To clarify the position(ing) of philosophy of education: social objects are divided into collectives such as series and institutions, on the one hand, and groups (such as movements, intelligentsia, etc.), on the other, and these constitute respectively the object and subject of History (Flynn, 2005, p. 122). It is out of this perspective of the institution of education as an object/ collective that the objective genitive model of philosophy of education falls into place. The intellectual–philosopher (when free from other priorities) critiques the educator–practitioner. Instead of being a subject of History and, potentially, a vehicle of change, education is thus seen as a conservative mechanism of control, a collective to be acted upon, but one that, in receiving such action, reacts with such recalcitrance that the counterfinalities it generates cancel out all progressive efforts.

At such a juncture, a Sartrean response might be to prioritise praxis: the incriminated, inert everydayness of the institution requires the disruptive force of relentless praxis, even if this may initiate yet further sedimentations. Many philosophers share Sartre's suspicion of the quotidian and of practices associated with automatism (e.g. law, method, statistics and knowledge). However, as they do not share much else with him, they have their own ways out of the impasse and provide their own terms, which function in the place of praxis. Whether it is 'natality' (Arendt), 'evental grace' (Badiou), the 'unconditional' (Derrida), the 'ineffable' (Levinas) or the 'new' and the 'unknown' (Lyotard), the escape route from the quotidian involves connotations of a quasi-divine interruption and leap that evoke some version of the 'impossible-yet-necessary'. In doing so, they entrench the portrayal of the quotidian and its social objects as a mire of resilient, objectified reality, momentarily suspended by the subjective glimpse of the unexpected yet, in the end, always triumphant.

Terry Eagleton argues that French thought from 'the Surrealists to Sartre, from Levinas to Lyotard, Derrida and Badiou' returns 'incessantly to the break, crisis, disruption or epiphany of otherness that will tear you free of *everyday inauthenticity*' (Eagleton, 2001, p. 155, emphasis added). Michael Gardiner's criticisms of Surrealism can be edifying here: 'The Surrealists evoked the "marvellous" as an escape from or transcendence of *everyday life*'. This prompted Henri Lefebvre, Gardiner explains, 'to argue that while the Surrealists understood that daily life was *routinized* and degraded, they failed to realize that this was for *distinct sociohistorical reasons*'. For Lefebvre, the idea of 'the "marvellous" therefore expressed a "transcendental contempt for the real"' (Gardiner, 2006, p. 27, fn 5, emphasis added). Of course, we must remember that theories differ greatly even when they converge. Often the point of convergence is accidentally reached, in the sense that theorists have come to it from very different routes. Understandably, then, contemporary French philosophers diverge on the mode of transcendence they favour. For instance, Badiou treats the ineffable as different from the order of the evental

(Badiou, 2003, pp. 52ff) and vehemently criticises Derrida and Levinas (Badiou, 2001, pp. 18ff). However, by setting the worldly against the epiphanic, he shares much with his opponents. The law in Badiou's thought 'governs a predicative, *worldly* multiplicity, granting to its part of the whole its due'. In contrast to law, '*evental grace* governs a multiplicity in *excess* of itself, one that is *indescribable*, superabundant relative to itself as well as with respect to the *fixed distribution of the law*' (Badiou, 2003, p. 78, emphasis added). Further, for the later Derrida, ethics 'is a matter of absolute decisions, which must be made outside *all given norms and forms of knowledge*; decisions which are utterly vital, yet which *completely evade conceptualization*' (Eagleton, 2001, p. 156, emphasis added). For Badiou, just as for Derrida, the realm of decision is distinguished from that of knowledge and, although not ineffable, the good is considered excessive and beyond the supposed automatism of everydayness (Hallward, 2001, p. xxv).

In another instance, for Heidegger, who influenced French thought, the everyday world is fallen as it is not attuned to the truth of Being, and authenticity is located in elements that contradict the 'mundanity and habitualized repetitiveness of the everyday' (Gardiner, 2006, p. 27, fn 5). Hannah Arendt, for her part, finds that 'action, seen from the viewpoint of the automatic processes which seem to determine the course of the world, looks like a miracle' (Arendt, 1989, p. 246). Astonishingly reminiscent of both Badiou's legality and the Surrealist notion of the marvellous, 'the *new always* happens against the *overwhelming odds of statistical laws* and their probability, which for *all practical, everyday purposes* amounts to *certainty*; the new therefore *always* appears in the guise of a *miracle*' (Arendt, 1989, p. 178, emphasis added). Against the absolute quantifiers and absolute temporal determinations that I have italicised (here and above), we may ask with Eagleton: 'are there really no contradictions in this quotidian realm? Is there no selflessness, compassion, extraordinary endurance' (Eagleton, 2001, p. 159), save in the guise of a miracle?

Education does not figure as a possible escape route, as a mundane force for transcending the mundane, as a negation of segments of facticity from within other segments of facticity rather than from outside of them. In fact, education does not figure as an escape route at all. Quite the contrary, as disciplinarian practice, as part of everydayness, as imparting of, or love for, knowledge, education is relegated to the sphere of the wholesale incriminated practico-inert. Can a 'subjective genitive' philosophy of education question, put to the *test* and *assess* the above tendency? Before turning to this question, let us briefly comment on education and assessment.

ASSESSMENT, PRAXIS, PRACTICE AND THE PRACTICO-INERT

The notion of assessment refers to a social practice since, even when it concerns the natural and not the human reality, it is directed at, and in turn redirects, human action. To Arendt, the most important dimension of human intervention in the world and interaction with nature is what she calls *vita activa*, which differentiates an all-rounded human subjectivity from that of the *homo faber* (the fabricator of the world whose ideal is stability, durability and permanence) and which raises humanity beyond the limits of the *animal laborans* (the labouring living being whose ideal is abundance) (Arendt, 1989, p. 126).

The most important dimension of human intervention in the world—that is, the life of action—is unpredictable, no matter how hard one tries to design it in advance. Precisely for this reason, action is a peculiarly human characteristic, and it cannot be left to automation. Action cannot have a predetermined and unhindered course, a smooth linearity with no reflective pauses, with no intermediate critical stops and, finally, with no test of the course of action itself and without any assessment of the situation. I argue, *contra* Arendt, that, rather than deriving from any quasi-mystical source, rather than taking the form of a miracle, the transcendence of the dangerous normalcy of daily life comes from such mundane and often uninspiring practices as examining (e.g. the collective past), testing (e.g. one's actions) and assessing (e.g. humanly created realities). When these are successfully carried out,[8] the education they effect is re-forming. To test and to assess something means to determine its quality so as to shape our present stance and our future action. This stance or further action may be one of conservation and reproduction of the given in question, of intervention or modification and of transformation or annulment of the given. The criteria of both, the assessment as well as the practical reorientation it causes, reflect ideals and aims that transcend particularity and the arbitrariness of the subjective, without this ever guaranteeing, of course, that such supra-individuality is automatically safe or steadily objective.

Thus the various criteria of forms of assessment must in turn be subjected to critical evaluation. This process has to be methodologically conclusive because perennial indecision is inimical to action and indirectly perpetuates the sovereignty of the beaten track.[9] But this process is not epistemologically conclusive in any final sense, lest the sought-for objectivity turn into dogmatism. In other words, through finalism and the suspension of a re-visiting, re-current critique, the notion of process itself justifiably acquires the negative connotations of the inert procedure. To avoid following procedures automatically and unreflectively, assessment must be a lively and constant social process qualitatively differentiating, reviving and readjusting human action by promoting a new approach to things. And because the new is *not always* or by definition superior to, or better than, the old,[10] the assessment of situations is as uncertain and open to the unexpected and to reflection as only life itself can be.

As indicated, assessment addresses human action. It opens it up so that praxis may be generalised into a practice without sliding into the practico-inert. It judges consolidated practices that render life automatic, habituate everydayness, give it a statistically measurable character and exclude from it the risky and the unexpected. These practices may thus be rescued from inertia by their being assessed. Educational routine is disrupted by an unexpected question on the part of the learner exposing the teacher to risks as a knower, as a subject who acts, makes choices, takes decisions and is responsible for an opinion. The force of inertia through which learning failures or false assumptions of achievement accumulate is held in control when students confront the possibility of success or failure in a test or in answering a question. Teachers accumulate professional experience and then can live off the spoils; the security offered by the beaten track and the facile character of pre-packaged learning materials lurk in daily practice to relieve the teacher from the effort of continuously seeking new educational strategies and methods. Such safe, well-trodden paths are put to the test during an inspection, an interview and other kinds of professional performance assessment, but they are truly questioned only when a heightened reflection informs the act of assessing.

However, assessment does not just *address* action: it *is* action. This means that, just like any other human action that deserves the name, it must be subjected to reflection. Instead of being sedimented complacently and authoritatively, it must constitute an object of study and renegotiation. But sometimes practices repay assessment with counterfinality: in trying to stop practice from sliding into automatism, from becoming automatic, assessment becomes itself a stale and inert practice. As an individual or collective project, assessment suffers the deforming influence of the practico-inert. Ironically, assessment is usually promoted as a stumbling block to the unexpected, as a security mechanism for establishing a royal route where educationists are called upon to apply the 'right' methods (which happen to transcend any context). Should they fail to convince that they are acting within such bounds, educationists are penalised. In educational systems where the assessment of students' performances becomes projected onto teachers and onto the schools themselves (e.g. school choice), the success of educational recipes is judged through performance and the conquest of knowledge. Being a complex phenomenon, however, knowledge is the absolute praxis, that is, the absolute transcendence of any simplistic prescriptivism.

Unlike its reified conception, which in education, systematically, is generally asserted and endorsed, and which in philosophy is generally asserted but dismissed, knowledge constantly reshuffles the self. Apart from ironically mobilising counterfinality, the reduction of knowledge to a quantifiable and measurable set (which, when acquired, bestows social distinction and benefits) is also contradictory. A common educational prescription for all is distributed everywhere; and, with the exception of clear cases of lack of expertise or the ability to implement it, this is steadily followed, albeit that it brings about, nevertheless, very diverse results in each case of implementation.[11] What is contradictory is that, in the end, it is those who follow the prescription (the teacher and the school) who are singled out and penalised, and not the prescription and those who issue it (Davis, 1999, pp. 29ff).

The paradoxes of standardised assessment are many. The following are only some examples.[12] When assessment is based on absolutist or under-theorised educational ideals, it does not only confront problems of effectiveness but also of legitimacy. Who or what is entitled to proclaim a teacher 'good' and a school 'outstanding' on the grounds of students' success in tests and their accumulation of proof of knowledge (or of the kind of knowledge that asserts rather than questions consolidated meanings)? Why would such a student be more valued than another who may have developed a passion for learning that will be sustained throughout life, whose life becomes an 'examined' life, something that is not always easy to test or to measure?

When assessment causes competitiveness, phobias or perhaps objective fear of the consequences of failure, when it establishes external motives for learning, and when it is translated into a pursuit of results supposedly confirming the raising of standards, then the curriculum is eventually shattered. Through 'teaching to the test' (Davis, 1999, pp. 14–18), whatever curricular purposes go against the immediate attainment of the measurable goal are marginalised by all those involved in the process of teaching and learning. In creating a tension between achievement and goal-setting, the system itself creates the conditions for non-conformity to its imperatives.

Assessment as it is carried out institutionally often involves the bad faith that naturalises facticity and the bad faith that absolutises transcendence. The former treats some children as inherently incapable of learning and ends up essentialising ability. The latter holds that if the student had wished to learn, she would have learned; that she has not learned shows that she is unwilling to learn. This kind of bad faith also ignores the factical constraints imposed on children by their existential situation and ends up essentialising motivation. Finally, when assessment is standardised, it becomes sterile and unfair at all levels. When exam questions are routinised, students learn to use knowledge only within specific contexts and become unable to turn it into knowledge for life. They spill it on paper, they cash out the social significance of that 'achievement' and thus become free at last to forget the painful experience, along with whatever knowledge they have 'acquired'.

As for the assessment of the teachers themselves, Davis remarks that 'if inspectors were honest with the schools and teachers they inspect, they would admit that what they are *really* trying to do is to discover whether teachers are using the approved methods' (p. 37). When educators are assessed, such evaluation is often open to 'customer' and other power relations that, up to now, no system has managed to control. If we could examine the kinds of rumours about unjust assessment and unfair decisions that circulate in corridors, pubs and other, semi-private spaces of confidentiality, we would have concrete data demonstrating how heavily injured the faith of the assessed in the process itself is. In all such cases, assessment is reduced to a Sartrean 'inverted praxis' (Sartre, 2004, p. 161)—that is, a practice working against its own logic.

Does this 'sociality' of assessment entail that its development into a worthy process will never be realised? Or that it is not a necessity? Should the lack of absolute objectivity lead us to surrender to the kind of automatic, unreflective daily routine, where the risk, even the educational value, of the failure that empowers and urges us to try again is avoided? This would destroy the most important dimension of assessment, which is not its function in sifting and sorting but its role in diagnosis, which is orientated towards self-awareness and to a sharpened knowledge of reality. Assessment must judge what has really been accomplished. The danger of knowledge becoming automatic[13] and blocking the dynamism of thought (a dynamism that is mobilised by the desire for truth) is perhaps transcended by a conception of education that breathes action into the search for knowledge. *Dia-gnostically*[14]—that is, through knowledge—we plunge into the depths of action, surrendering to its risks and its gifts. We assess diagnostically, we learn about and readjust the way we act, and perhaps we change course. If we stop, we grant the existent, the well-worn, an absolute priority, and we limit our role to serving it.

Yet, curiously, assessment as praxis and not as the practico-inert presupposes changes that differ from those one would recommend for assessment itself: however a method or assessment is refined, if a society operates at two levels, its schools will do the same and its citizens will be moulded accordingly. The one level comprises those who walk on a path from which all or most obstacles are removed. Protected children have a secured future prepared by the over-protective adults who run ahead to make sure that their children are not in the schools of the many or who prove that the schooling they provide (as teachers or as designers of educational policy) leaves no good customer without a successful professional course in life. The other level operates in an ongoing regression, since educational ghettos block any possibility for the osmosis of cultural capital, in a vicious circle of ever-growing disconnection of the world of the privileged and 'cultivated', on the one hand, from the world of the masses, on the other. Still, despite the hopeful anticipation of contented parents and authorities, the two levels, the two worlds, are destined to be inexorably and existentially connected in a relation of mutual counterfinalities and inverted praxes.

Before we assess performance we must assess the totality of the crystallised practices supporting and perpetuating the current, worldly situation, the particular socio-historical conditions, part of which is, however minor this may seem, educational assessment as we know it up to now. For much educational counterfinality, as an effect of the realm of the practico-inert, occurs because so much is expected from educational assessment itself, as if there were no further changes in the individual, the society and the world beyond schooling. Education concerns the whole society, not just schools. However, it seems that, especially from late modernity onwards, societies have, to an important degree, been programmed to long for maximal results through minimal effort in changing and redirecting themselves. The philosophical disruption of such automation may come from putting the blanket incrimination of the quotidian (and of laws, statistics, facticity, knowledge, assessment and methods) to the test and from restoring to education its lost transcendence.

EDUCATION, METHOD AND THE INCRIMINATION OF THE EVERYDAY

I take Sartre, Arendt and Badiou as emblematic intermediary stops in a philosophical course of suspicion of facticity, of realities related to law, knowledge and everydayness. The positive and constructive dimension of the objectification of praxis and its deposit in practico-inert forms is bypassed by Sartre, who loses sight of the fact that 'partial victories in the struggle for human dignity achieve a practico-inert status in laws and institutions' (Aronson, 1987, p. 217). Badiou and Arendt also rely on an indictment of any consolidation, even if that is of amassed evidence. For instance, knowledge is, to Badiou (1999, p. 37; 2003, p. 45), just as to Arendt (1989, p. 178), a manifestation of human automation and statistical repetition that solidifies hierarchies and perpetuates the *status quo*. Badiou wishes to rescue truth from all this habituation by grounding truth in the eruptive and subversive event, just as Arendt grounds hope in natality.

For some postmodernists, truth is unknown and therefore relative. However, for thinkers who share some postmodern ontological assumptions about humanity's predatory employment or treatment of 'knowledge' but wish at all costs to avoid their relativist conclusion, the phrase 'truth is unknown' does not merely describe a disjunction of truth and knowledge, but rather a contradiction in terms. Truth is unknown not because it escapes the order of knowledge but because it shatters it: for Badiou, who follows Lacan on this (Hewlett, 2004, p. 343), there is 'no knowledge of truth', for 'truth makes a hole in knowledge' (Badiou, 1999, p. 80). All in all, knowledge connotes automation, transmission and repetition, whereas truth is interruption, break and risky decision.

Within Badiou's framework, the human sciences (and, I suppose, the term includes the field of education) appear in tension with philosophy because they have become the home of the statistical sciences. They are:

> ... themselves caught up in the circulation of meaning and its polyvalence, because they measure rates of circulation. That *is their purpose*. At base they are in the service of polls, election predictions, demographic averages, epidemiological rates, tastes and distastes, and all that certainly makes for interesting labour. But this *statistical* and *numerical information* has *nothing to do* with what humanity, nor what each absolutely singular being, is about ... Philosophy is thus required by the world to be a philosophy of *singularity*, to be capable of pronouncing and thinking the singular, which *is precisely what the general apparatus of human sciences does not have as its vocation*. (Badiou, 2005, pp. 39–40, emphasis added)

The above converge with Arendt's arguments about the infiltration of practice and criticality with statistics and calculative reason, and about a possible overcoming of this reification through a conception of evental action as 'miraculous' and 'unexpected' (Arendt, 1989, p. 246). 'To act in the form of making, to reason in the form of "reckoning with consequences", means to leave out the unexpected, the event itself, since it would be unreasonable or irrational to expect what is no more than an "infinite improbability"' (p. 300).

Therefore,

> The laws of statistics are valid only where *large numbers* or *long periods* are involved, and acts or events can statistically appear only as deviations or fluctuations. The justification of statistics is that deeds and events are rare occurrences in everyday life and in history. Yet the meaningfulness of everyday relationships is disclosed *not in everyday life but in rare deeds*, just as the significance of a *historical period shows itself only in the few events* that *illuminate* it. The application of the *law of large numbers and long periods* to politics or history signifies nothing less than the wilful obliteration of their very subject matter. (Arendt, 1989, pp. 42–3, emphasis added)

The import of such insights is evident, but in their sweeping generality they betray an automatism, a rushed over-generalisation. Predictably, 'in reality, deeds will have less and less chance to stem the tide of behaviour, and events will more and more lose their significance, that is, their capacity to *illuminate historical time*'. We may agree with Arendt that 'statistical uniformity is by no means a harmless scientific ideal'. But the idea that statistics 'is the no longer secret political ideal of a society which, *entirely* submerged in the *routine* of *everyday* living, is at peace with the *scientific* outlook *inherent* in its very existence', ibid., p. 43, emphasis added) divests science of any political significance and relegates it automatically to the realm of the practico-inert.

Instead of conceding to statistical uniformity the whole of everydayness, we may allocate to the statistical the appropriate province and distinguish it from its harmful, yet exaggerated mediocrity. This, however, involves a prior and measured rehabilitation of everydayness. *Contra* Sartre's wholesale indictment of 'fundamental sociality' as practico-inert (Flynn, 2005, p. 135), *contra* Badiou and Arendt's epiphanic, the terrain of human *drama* (coming from the verb *dran*, to act) is the quotidian.[15] 'The content that is *tested* by a moral principle is generated not by *the philosopher* but by *real life*. The conflicts of *action* that come to be morally judged and consensually resolved grow out of *everyday life*. Reason as a *tester* of maxims' *finds* these conflicts. It does not create them (Norris, 1993, p. 77, emphasis added).

Some such test growing out of everyday life may occur, in my view, precisely through some inexorable statistics about large numbers and long periods *illuminating* historical time: '113 million children have no basic education . . . There are one billion non-literate adults, two-thirds are women and 98% live in the developing world. In the least developed countries, 45% of the children do not attend school. In countries with literacy rate [*sic*] less than 55% the annual per capita income is about $600' (Tully, 2008, p. 27).

Here is the facticity underlying some of the above data of bad educational results, which is so drastically bypassed in the sweeping automatism of the incrimination of statistics and knowledge:

> 840 million people are malnourished. 6,000,000 children under the age of 5 die each year as a consequence of malnutrition. 1.2 billion people live on less than $1 a day and half the world's population lives on less than $2 a day. 91 out of every 1,000 children in the developing world die before 5 years old. 12 million die annually from lack of water . . . 1 in 5 does not survive past 40 years of age. (Tully, 2008, p. 27)

In the mundane 'crises' just illustrated (and without any intention of romanticisation), the philosopher might find the contradictions, heroism, selflessness, compassion and extra-ordinary endurance she longs for and so rarely finds in other daily routine. She may also find their extreme opposites: *exis* (habitual adaptation) in servility, selfishness and betrayal that arouse the anxiety of the observer and a longing for a better world. For the edges of the existing world challenge the prescribed limits of possibility. And the contrasting realities:

> . . . the wealth of the richest 1% of the world is equal to that of the poorest 57%. The assets of the 200 richest people are worth more than the total income of 41% of the world's people. Three families alone have a combined wealth of $135 billion. This equals the annual income of 600 million people living in the world's poorest countries. The richest 20% of the world's population receive 150 times the wealth of the poorest 20%. (Tully, 2008, p. 27)

As for consumption, 'the richest fifth of the world's people consume 45% of the world's meat and fish; the poorest fifth consume 5%. The richest fifth consume 58% of total energy, the poorest fifth less than 4%. The richest fifth have 75% of all telephones, the poorest fifth 1.5%. The richest fifth own 87% of the world's vehicles, the poorest fifth less than 1%' (p. 28). And it was estimated, at the start of the century,

> . . . that Internet users in Africa number approximately 1.5 million. Of these, 1 million are in South Africa, leaving the remaining 500,000 among the 734 million people on the continent. This equates to one Internet user for every 1500 people compared to a world average of one user for every 38 people, and a North American average of one in every four. (Lelliott, Pendlebury and Enslin, 2000, p. 48)

Finally, in case one thinks that improvement is slow or that all that is needed is simply a more consistent yet slow pace to betterment (*encore un effort* and we shall get there), consider the following: 'In 1960, the share of the global income of the bottom 20% was 2.3%. By 1991, this had fallen to 1.4%' (Tully, 2008, p. 28).

This catalogue of statistical and numerical information could go on, as there have been many cases of dislocated, wronged and massacred populations in the small corners of the earth as well as cases of environmental destruction—frequently *because of* the Western world's conception of its geopolitical and financial interest. As these cases concern large numbers and occur over long periods of time, and as they tend to happen elsewhere, they have not, philosophically, been dignified with the status of the singular event and so have not come to function in a metonymic way. Philosophy has often sleepwalked its way through various *testing* times.

Rather than rushing to place such statistical data in the practico-inert, I suggest that we treat them as what they truly are: that is, singular voices of historical events, messages from real life. The event connotes a dramatically felt synchrony. But its being historical reminds us that the past exists not only in memory or even in the traces of monuments and documents but also as a prolonged past that determines the present.[16] To adapt Sartre's parlance, here, the event as occurrence becomes part of History 'by its happening for-others'. It is registered in the practico-inert as 'an inert universal memory' (Sartre, 1960, p. 122), and it remains, as Flynn puts it, 'thereafter to modify the situations of those who interiorize it in their own projects' (Flynn, 2005, p. 131). In simpler words, data such as the above may exert some influence and effect some modification. This influence may take 'the form of "exigency", deforming consequences, counterfinalities, and all the other types of "inertial force" we have attributed to the practico-inert' (Flynn, 2005, p. 131). Such data and the way they voice the realities of the privileged few and the underprivileged masses put our ways of forming philosophical questions about multiculturalism, cosmopolitanism and the like to the test. Bypassing that voicing bears witness to our practico-inert, 'objective' attitude to education and to the sedimentation of the methods we use for answering the questions we pose.

It is not just that, prior to their research in multiculturalism, cosmopolitanism and the like, educators must be educated by Derrida, Arendt, Badiou and others. While such philosophy of education is a task of great importance that should not be treated lightly, educators should also raise the inexorable singularity of the real context of the research question as a yardstick for judging the preferable philosophical method, perhaps prior to entrusting notions such as cosmopolitanism or multiculturalism to philosophical establishment. Educators can also be educated by those segments of (local and global) reality that have rarely or never engaged the consistent attention of philosophies and have not, therefore, been disseminated in the philosophy of education.

CONCLUSION: ROUTES, ROUTINES, METHODS AND *APORIAS*

When the question is about education, cosmopolitanism and multiculturalism or about international relations, the *routine method* is to follow relevant philosophical works. But, more often than not, this routine fails to hearken to reality, to interpret and judge, and to suggest the redirection of that reality. In its abstraction, it is exposed by the above statistics as inadequate. The voicing of daily historical events adds to our research question a facticity that demands from us, now that we know of its singularity, that we respond by critiquing rather than relying on the theories that have bypassed this facticity. More simply, it demands that we take another route and find another method.

Why would one care to know about what had once happened in a small corner of the earth? Why would one learn about the here and now of people and nature beyond one's immediate concern? How do we educate people to desire such knowledge and to turn it into decision and action? How do we assess in awareness of all this? We cannot know the answers before actual debate and research, although we may imagine many possible candidates for the position of truth in each singular case. We may know only the exigent beginning and the provisional end of our own effort to answer, to share with others and to offer suggestions. And these are given by two kinetic concepts that I see as complementary: *aporia* and method. They are kinetic because, etymologically, they both involve routes. Literally, *aporia* means not knowing the route, since *a* (without)+*poros* (path) signifies a condition in which no passage is available. Real life and everydayness present us with impasses, *aporias* in the double sense of dead end and wonder, that can move us to thought and action. Method comes from *methodos* which is composed by the preposition *meta* and the noun *odos* (route, road). Against the static, routine connotations of the well-marked, straight beaten track that accompany the word method, *meta+odos* bears connotations of chasing, going after something and of finding a route towards it. This further entails that the thing that is searched for shows the way and sets the pace. The temporal priority of the thematised quotidian makes sense, however, only along with the logical priority of *aporia* (of finding the taken-for-granted sterile and revisiting it) and of method (of interpreting, judging and suggesting action). As we saw in a previous section, assessment broadly understood also concerns the selection of a path. So long as the researched issue is different from the previous ones, it is possible that the route we must take to approach it will need to be different too, that our path may be a specific one or that we may need to pave another. This is no relativism, but a philosophy of singularity that becomes a criterion for judging the most appropriate way to knowledge. It can work against *exis* (habituation) by welcoming the displacement that education as desire to know, to go beyond the impasse, causes to sedentary philosophical endeavour.

To be true disruptions of consolidated meanings, action, praxis and the event (and the enlarged thought they require) presuppose the exigency to learn, to desire knowing and to respond to everydayness thoughtfully. Instead of setting 'epiphanic' notions as primary aims or ideals of philosophy, thus reducing education to the practico-inert, we must acknowledge instances where learning should be an end-in-itself and can effect the disruption of inert realities, philosophies and sciences. If one does not learn to wonder, reality remains unnoticed and non-thematised. If one asks too few questions, the search for truth is not set on course. In this way, method is the response to *aporia*, *aporia* is the rebirth of method, and education and philosophy are allies. The challenge to respond to the singularity that comes from real life, to find a path, is, amongst other things, an invitation to (re)education and a demand for a method somewhat unique.

NOTES

1. To paraphrase Badiou again, the confrontation with education 'is an absolutely indispensable condition for philosophy' (Badiou, 2006, p. 14).
2. In Greek antiquity, education was not just a passive object of analysis, a case that had to be explained away, interpreted or judged. It was considered a way for transforming the self and the world. We must not forget that Aristotle's *Nicomachean Ethics*, a point of reference for most ethical philosophies ever since, was written to serve educational purposes. In later times, Rousseau was an educator–philosopher, *Bildung* enjoyed centrality in German Idealism, Dewey gave philosophy of education a new impetus and Freire considered education a path to emancipation.
3. This assumption explains both the fact that education only very rarely comes up in philosophical debate and the fact that, even when it is discussed, it is approached in a condescending way, indifferent to education's own conceptual resources.
4. Ironically, such counterfinality mixed with contradiction seems to affect philosophy as such: philosophy neglects education because it understands it solely or principally in institutional terms rather than as exposition of the individual to ideas, facts or possibilities that might draw them into better ways of living and acting. But at that very moment when philosophy's attention turns to politics, it displays more faith in institutions or organisations than in the remoulding of the self. It trusts globalised public *fora*—the UN, UNESCO and so on (a supposed dispersal of communicative power transformed into institutional power, implying, therefore, the institutionalised sense of education at most)—more than any transformative human action through self-reflective and world-disclosing learning experiences.
5. For example, the idea that all you need in order to achieve something is just to wish for it.
6. The difference is that Sartre refers to worked matter whereas Dilthey refers to the inscription of the human mind on objects (Stack, 1989, p. 169).
7. The latter is seen as Sartre's concession to Louis Althusser's notion of 'structural causality' but, unlike Althusser, Sartre reserves for praxis a primacy over the practico-inert (Flynn, 2005, p. 124). This primacy has never been forgiven by adherents to the postmodern vogue and has been one of the reasons why its proponents have lost any interest in Sartre.
8. Though there is no guarantee, mundane or epiphanic, for such success.
9. Facing the exigency of decision-making, where theoretical undecidability meets the practical necessity of acting, the uncertain agent returns to the well-tried recipe.
10. *Contra* Arendt, that natality engulfs renewed energies (implicit in beginning again) in no way entails the major (let alone radical) difference of the new from the old that was outlived.
11. The reasons are well known: not all children share the same cultural capital or motivation, not all geographical areas offer comparably rich learning experiences, not

all educational achievements are uniformly measurable and not all random factors can be controlled.

12. For a more detailed account, see Andrew Davis (1999), to whose text I am indebted here.

13. True, in its narrowest sense, knowledge may denote the consolidation of a position through a selective emphasis on the amassed proof of that position. Therefore, it may bring with it greater difficulty in breaking with the certitudes we cling to and in seeking further the truth that the proof may have obscured.

14. *Gnosis* is the Greek for knowledge and the Greek preposition *dia* means, amongst other things, 'through'.

15. By everydayness, I do not refer strictly to daily life is in our contemporary world. I refer, rather, to the everyday as the complex, invaluably rich modes of actual existence, irrespective of time and space. This sense of everydayness encompassing liberating forces and suppressed potentialities that contradict habitualising tendencies characterises even the worst dystopia. Thus the way I employ the term is close to Agnes Heller's use. To her, as Gardiner explains, 'daily life cannot be understood as a "thing" or "system", or even an "attitude". Instead, she conceptualizes the everyday as an ensemble of historically constituted practices and forms of subjectivity that are complexly related to and mediated by other structures, institutions and practices'. Thus, the everyday is 'a universal human experience' and as such it exists 'in all societies, although of course the actual content of the mundane life-world and its relationship to wider sociohistorical forces is historically variable . . . Heller asserts that in pursuing the goal of "humanizing" and democratizing everyday life we must strive to nurture utopian hopes within a largely (but not inevitably) dystopian society that exists in the present day' (Gardiner, 2006, pp. 24–5).

16. For Sartre, for example, the past is, amongst other things, 'operative in the practico-inert mediation of the colonialist' and the capitalist system (Flynn, 2005, p. 131).

REFERENCES

Arendt, H. (1989) [1958] *The Human Condition* (Chicago, IL, The University of Chicago Press).
Aronson, R. (1987) *Sartre's Second Critique* (Chicago, IL, The University of Chicago Press).
Badiou, A. (1999) *Manifesto for Philosophy*, N. Madarasz, trans. (New York, State University of New York Press).
Badiou, A. (2001) *Ethics: An Essay on the Understanding of Evil*, P. Hallward, trans. (London, Verso).
Badiou, A. (2003) *Saint-Paul: The Foundation of Universalism*, R. Brassier, trans. (Stanford, CA, Stanford University Press).
Badiou, A. (2005) *Infinite Thought*, O. Feltham and J. Clemens, trans. (London, Continuum).
Badiou, A. (2006) *Theoretical Writings* (London, Continuum).
Craib, I. (1976) *Existentialism and Sociology* (Cambridge, Cambridge University Press).
Davis, A. (1999) Educational Assessment: A Critique of Current Policy, *Impact No. 1*, Philosophy of Education Society of Great Britain.
Eagleton, T. (2001) Subjects and Truths, *New Left Review*, 9, pp. 155–60.
Flynn, T. R. (2005) *Sartre, Foucault, and Historical Reason* (Chicago, IL, Chicago University Press).
Gardiner, M. E. (2006) Marxism and the Convergence of Utopia and the Everyday, *History of the Human Sciences*, 19.3, pp. 1–32.

Hallward, P. (2001) Introduction, in: A. Badiou, *Ethics: An Essay on the Understanding of Evil* (London, Verso).

Hewlett, N. (2004) Engagement and Transcendence: The Militant Philosophy of Alain Badiou, *Modern and Contemporary France*, 12.3, pp. 335–52.

Lelliott, A., Pendlebury, S. and Enslin, P. (2000) Promises of Access and Inclusion: Online Education in Africa, in: N. Blake and P. Standish (eds) *Enquiries at the Interface: Philosophical Problems of Online Education* (Oxford, Blackwell).

Norris, C. (1993) *The Truth About Postmodernism* (Oxford, Blackwell).

Papastephanou, M. (2005) Rawls' Theory of Justice and Citizenship Education, *Journal of Philosophy of Education*, 39.3, pp. 499–518.

Sartre, J.-P. (1990) [1943] *Being and Nothingness*, H. E. Barnes, trans. (London, Routledge).

Sartre, J.-P. (2004) [1960] *Critique of Dialectical Reason, vol 1*, A. Sheridan-Smith, trans. (London, Verso).

Stack, G. J. (1989) Review of J. S. Catalano's *A Commentary on J.-P. Sartre's 'Critique of Dialectical Reason'*, *Journal of the History of Philosophy*, 27.1, pp. 167–70.

Tully, J. (2008) Two Meanings of Global Citizenship: Modern and Diverse, in: M. A. Peters, A. Britton and H. Blee (eds) *Global Citizenship Education* (Rotterdam, Sense Publishers), pp. 15–41.

Index

accountability, and traditional education 87, 88
affirmative deconstruction 76
African Americans, and fair assessment 66, 67
Alice in Wonderland (Carroll) 128
Allen, Woody 73
American Philosophical Association 1–2
Anglo-American tradition, and the philosophy of education 83
anxiety, and fair assessment 62
aporia and method 146–7
application, and translation 112–13
Aquinas, Thomas 24
Arendt, Hannah 6, 43, 44–5, 81, 142–5
 and the practico-inert 132, 133, 136, 137, 138–9
argumentation, and philosophical reconstruction 11–12
Aristotle 37, 118
art education 20
Artaud, Antonin 94
artists' statements 4–5
assessment
 and deconstruction in education 79–80
 and human action 137–41
 see also fair assessment
Austin, J. L. 80
authority, and critiques of traditional education 89–90
automatism, education as 132, 134

Background Beliefs, language of 31–3
Bacon, Francis 118, 120
bad faith, and the practico-inert 135, 140
Badiou, Alain 131, 132, 133, 136–7, 142, 143, 145
banking education 87–8, 88–9, 94
Bennington, Geoffrey 74, 76
Bergdahl, Louisa 109
Beveridge, Liam 6

Biesta, Gert 7, 43–4, 45, 46–7, 48, 49, 51, 76, 113
Bourdieu, Pierre 94
Boyd, Dwight 28
Boyer, Ernst 38
Brecht, Bertolt 94
Bridges, D. 3
Bristol University 65
Burbules, Nicholas 20
Butler, Judith 43

California, University of, Baake case 66, 67, 69
Cambridge University 61
Caputo, J. D. 76–7
categorical imperative 112
Cavell, Stanley 111
Christianity, and discernment 35, 36
city, the, selfhood and education 46, 48
class, and unfairness in 11-plus selection 68–9
cognitive constructionism 20
cognitive functioning, and fair assessment 60–1
cognitive–affective experience, and moral values 29, 30, 36
Cohen, Jean 111–12
Collingwood, R. G. 1, 8, 118
communication
 and deconstruction in education 80–1
 sender–receiver model of 78–9
construct validity, and fair assessment 57
constructivism, moral 32–6
constructivism–realism debate 6, 10, 13, 14–15, 16–20
constructivist metaphysics 20
conversation, and texts 7, 118–20
cosmopolitanism and education 131, 133, 145
counter-translations 113
critical education 87–92, 93, 99
cultural capital 64, 141

Davis, A. 140
Deconstructing Harry 73
deconstruction 7, 73–84, 95
   defining 73–4
   in education 7, 77–82
   metaphysics-in-deconstruction 74–7
   and philosophy of education 82–4
Derrida, Jacques 3–4, 4–5, 6, 123, 128,
   145
   and deconstruction 7, 73–7, 80–1, 95
   and the philosophy of education
      82–3, 84
   and the practico-inert 136, 137
   on translation 108–9, 112, 113, 113–
      14
Descartes, René, *Discourse on Method*
   8, 120
Dewey, John 49, 83, 92–3, 94, 100
   Democracy and Education 80
   Experience and Education 87–8,
      89–90, 91
diagnostic assessment 141
dialectical argument 6–7, 24–39
   conceptual frameworks of 25–6, 38
   and the ethics of transcendent virtue
      8, 27–30, 36–8
   and Nash's *Real World Ethics* 27–8,
      31–8
dialogue, and philosophical reconstruction 11, 18–20
Dilthey, Wilhelm 135
disability accommodations, and fair assessments 56–62, 70
discernment, and practical wisdom 35,
   36
Dworkin, Ronald 69
dyslexic students, fair assessment of 56–
   8, 60, 62

Eagleton, Terry 136, 137
Edgerton, David 105, 106
edifying philosophy 123
Eisner, Elliot 43
emotions, knowing 106
English translations of knowing 106–7
Enlightenment
   and method 95, 97, 98, 99, 100
   and selfhood 50–1

epistemology, and critiques of traditional
   education 88–9
equality of opportunity, and fair assessment 67–8, 70
ethics
   of transcendent virtue 28–30, 36–8
   see also professional ethics teaching
ethnicity, and fair assessment 65, 66,
   67, 68
etymology, and translation 109

fair assessment 54–71
   and 11-plus selection 68–9
   disability accommodations 56–62, 70
   and motivation of candidates 63–4
   and music conservatoires 64–8
Ferrari, John, *Listening to the Cicadas*
   126–7, 129
Fisher, A. 11
Flynn, T. R. 145
Foucault, Michel 43
   and interdiscursive translation 110–
      11, 112
freedom, and deconstruction in education
   81–2
Freire, Paulo 87–8, 88–9, 90–1, 92, 93–
   4, 100
French translations
   of knowledge 105–6, 107
   of relevance 114

Gadamer, Hans-Georg 95, 97–8
Gardiner, Michael 136, 137
gender, and fair assessment 63–4, 65,
   68
German translations
   of knowledge 105, 107
   of relevance 114
Goodman, Nelson 6, 12, 13, 14, 15, 16–
   17, 18, 19

Habermas, Jürgen 75
handwriting, and fair assessment 61–2
Hardy, Thomas, *Tess of the d'Urbervilles*
   42–3, 47, 49
health issues, and fair assessment 62
Hegel, G. 75, 114
Heidegger, Martin 77, 103, 137
   Being and Time 49–50

hermeneutic method   95, 97–8
Hertzberger, Hermann   46, 48
Higher Education, fair assessment in
     58–9, 65, 66
Hirst, Paul   103–4, 105
historical reconstruction   12
Hollenbeck, K.   59–60
Honisch, Stefan   5
Houston, Barbara   106
human condition, and translation   108–9
Husserl, Edmund   49, 95

identity and selfhood   7, 43–53
immanent analysis   12
interdiscursive translation   109–12
interlinguistic translation   115
intrinsic moral values   28, 29, 30, 36
intuition pumps   67

Jactot, Joseph   96, 101, 102
Journal of Philosophy of Education   3
Jussila, Juhani   12, 15

Kant, Immanuel   4, 75, 112
Kearney, Richard   73–4
knowledge, translating 'ways of know-
     ing'   103–7
Kripke, Saul   55

Labaree, David, *Educational Researcher*
     113
Langewand, Alfred   107
Le Guin, Ursula   66–7
learning disabilities, and fair assessments
     56–62
Lefebvre, Henri   136
Levinas, Emmanuel   43, 46, 48, 136, 137
lifelong education   132
Lingis, Alphonso   45
Locke, John   42, 67
Lonergan, Bernard   24, 26, 38
Lyotard, J.-F.   123, 136

MacIntyre, Alasdair   6, 24, 25
Maia, Angélica   108
Marx, Karl   135
Matthews, Michael   20
meritocracy, and fair assessment   66–8

metaphors   121–2
     and interdiscursive translation   111–12
metaphysical realism   20
metaphysics-in-deconstruction   74–7
method
     and *aporia*   146–7
     education and the incrimination of the
          everyday   142–5
     philosophical research methods   1–8
     and presumptive tautology   95–102
     routine methods   145–6
     translation as philosophical method
          103–15
methodolatry   2, 3
methodological inheritance   8
Midgley, Mary   33
Montonen, Kaisu   12
moral bricolage   35
Moral Character, language of   33–2, 36
moral constructivism   32–3
moral values
     and the ethics of transcendent virtue
          28–30
     intrinsic   28, 29, 30, 36
Mouffe, Chantal   38
multiculturalism and education   145
multidisciplinary research, and dialogue
     18–19
Murdoch, Iris, *Nuns and Soldiers*   125
music conservatoires, and fair assessment
     64–8

Nagel, T.   68
Nash, Robert J., *Real World Ethics*   27–8,
     31–8
Nietzsche, F.   77
Nurmi, Kari E.   12

Oakeshott, Michael   43, 51
objectification, and the practico-inert
     135–6
objective genitive model   132
ontology, and selfhood   49–50
otherness, and deconstruction   75, 76

Papastephanou, Marianna   112
parega, and works of art   4–5
Peirce, C. S.   14

performative speech acts, and deconstruction 80
Peripatetic School 118
Peters, Richard 43
Phenix, Philip 103
the phenomenological self 53
phenomenological method 95
philosophical importers/exporters 8
philosophical reconstruction 11–21
  and dialogue 18–20
  and plurealism 13–15, 16, 17–18,
    19, 20
  and systematic analysis 12, 15–17
*Philosophy, Methodology and Educa-
tional Research* 3
philosophy as research 1–2
Pickstone, John, *Ways of Knowing* 105–6
Plato 6, 43, 74, 94, 119
  Phaedrus 119, 120, 121, 122, 125,
    126–7, 128–9
  Republic 127, 129
plurealism 13–15, 16, 17–18, 19, 20
postmodernism 142
  dialogue on 119–29
the practico-inert 132, 133–41
  assessment and human action 137–41
  and statistics 143, 145
pragmatism 121, 122
  Nash's ethic of pragmatic moral
    consensus 36
presence, metaphysics of 75, 76
presumptive tautology 7, 94–102
primary schools, fair assessment and Key
    Stage 2 reading tests 63–4
procedural knowledge, translation of
    103, 104–5
professional ethics teaching 6–7, 24
  and Nash's *Real World Ethics* 30,
    31–8
progressive education 43, 87, 88–92,
    92–3, 94, 99
propositional knowledge, translation of
    103, 104
Puolimatka, Tapio 13
  The Nights of Labour 110

Rabinow, Paul 110
Rancière, Jacques 7, 93–102
  Disagreement 97

and interdiscursive translation 109–
    10, 111
'The Emancipated Spectator' 94
The Future of an Image 94
The Ignorant Schoolmaster 94–5,
    100–2
Rawls, J. 68
reading tests (Key Stage 2), and fair
    assessment 63–4
realism
  constructivism–realism debate 6,
    10, 13, 14–15, 16–20
  metaphysical 20
Rée, Jonathan 108, 115
relevance, translation of 113–15
research
  evaluating research projects 10
  multidisciplinary 18–19
  philosophy as 1–2
  relevant educational research 115
  translational 113
Research Assessment Exercise 1
research methods 1–8
Ricoeur, Paul 95, 111
Rigal, Christine 105–6
Robinson, Richard 103
Romanticism, and selfhood 43
Rorty, Richard 2, 12, 19
  Contingency, Irony and Solidarity
    119, 120–1, 122–3, 126, 128,
    129
Rosenberg, Jay F. 11
routine methods 145–6
Russell, B. 124

Sagan, Françoise, *Bonjour Tristesse*
    106
Sartre, Jean-Paul 132, 133, 134, 135–6,
    142, 143, 145
  Being and Nothingness 135
Scheffler, Israel 6, 10, 12–13, 14–15,
    17–18, 19, 20
scholasticism 134
science, philosophy of 10
scientific texts, and interdiscursive trans-
    lation 110–11
Second Language Moral Brief 33–4
selection (11-plus), unfairness in 68–9
selfhood and education 7, 43–53

Shakespeare, William   107, 114
Smith, R.   3
social justice   26
social mobility, and 11-plus selection   68–9
social sciences, and philosophical research methods   2–3
Socrates   118, 119, 121, 123, 124, 125, 126, 127, 128
Sound of Silence, The   106
spectatorship, and critiques of traditional education   90–1
statistics, and the incrimination of the everyday   142–5
subjectification, and the presumptive tautology   97
subjectivity and selfhood   7, 44–6, 47–51, 53
Surrealism   136, 137
systematic analysis, and philosophical reconstruction   12, 15–17
systematic philosophy   123

tabula rasa concept   42
teachers, assessment of   140
test modification, and fair assessment   59–61, 63–4, 70
texts
    children's picture books   6
    and conversation   7, 118–20
    prefatory statements   3–4
    scientific texts and interdiscursive translation   110–11
    systematic analysis of   12, 15–17

theory–practice gap, in philosophical education research   10
theory–practice relationship, and translation   113
Third Language of Moral Principle   34
traditional education
    complicity with   92–3
    progressive and critical objections to   87–92, 94, 99
transcendent virtue, ethics of   28–30, 36–8
transcendental idealism   49
translation   7, 103–15
    and application   112–13
    counter-translations   113
    distance and defamiliarisation   107–8
    and the human condition   108–9
    interdiscursive   109–12
    interlinguistic   115
    of relevance   113–15
    'ways of knowing'   103–7
translational research   113
truth, and the ethics of transcendent virtue   28–9
Tully, J.   144

universities, and research methods   1, 2

Wales, University of   62
Wittgenstein, Ludwig   54, 55–6, 58, 67, 70, 124–5
worldmaking   15, 16, 21

Young, Iris Marion   26
Young, M.   66